BREAKING AWAY

BREAKING

Texas A&M University Press
College Station

AWAY

*How the Texas A&M System
Changed the Game*

Tim Gregg

Foreword by Henry G. Cisneros

This paper meets the requirements of ANSI/NISO Z39.48-1992 (Permanence of Paper).
Binding materials have been chosen for durability.
Manufactured in the United States of America.

Library of Congress Cataloging-in-Publication Data
LCCN 2021940917
ISBN 978-1-64843-041-1 (cloth)
ISBN 978-1-64843-042-8 (ebook)

Unless otherwise indicated, all images are courtesy Texas A&M University System.

In memory of
Charlotte Han Sharp,
First Lady of the Texas A&M University System

CONTENTS

A gallery of images follows page 128.

The Morrill Act and the Texas A&M University System

Henry G. Cisneros

The senator from Vermont stood in the well of the Senate and spoke with conviction about an idea that he had championed for a decade but that seemed barely imaginable in that moment. It was the summer of 1862, fourteen months since the start of the Civil War, and the news from the battlefront was of bloody clashes and massive casualties suffered by the Union forces, even the possibility that Washington, DC, might be captured. As Sen. Justin Morrill rose to speak, the Seven Days' Battles were underway in Virginia. It was clear to anyone who may have doubted that the war would be long and catastrophically costly in lives and treasure.

Senator Morrill understood that when the war eventually ended, whatever the outcome, the nation would have to be rebuilt. He imagined ways to bind the wounds in the embattled states, to put the damaged nation back on a trajectory of expansion to the West and recommence commercial transactions with the newly industrializing economies of Europe. He knew that would require bringing literacy to an expanding population. It would require building roads and dams to open the West. It would necessitate agricultural services and animal husbandry to feed the masses, and it would demand acceleration of scientific discoveries and engineering inventions.

Senator Morrill's case was persuasive. The Congress of the United

States passed the Morrill Act that summer, and President Lincoln signed it on July 2, 1862. The Morrill Act authorized the creation of "land grant colleges" in the states, so named because the legislation awarded federal land to the states that agreed to establish public colleges dedicated to instruction and research in the practical skills needed to build the nation. With the proceeds from selling that land or from generating revenues from it in other ways, the states would establish colleges to teach food production, road building, power generation, waterway navigation, animal science, mining, mechanics, human nutrition, military instruction, land management, and public safety.

Senator Morrill's vision was the 1860s iteration of the compelling US ideal articulated in a letter written by John Adams to his wife, Abigail, in the previous century: "I must study politics and war that my son may have liberty to study mathematics and philosophy. My son ought to study mathematics and philosophy, geography, natural history, naval architecture, navigation, commerce, and agriculture, in order to give their children a right to study painting, poetry, music, architecture, statuary, tapestry, and porcelain."

That ideal captured the essence of the young nation's secular faith. The first duty of a nation is to declare itself, establish its sovereignty, and then strengthen itself and organize to defend its existence. According to Adams's generational progression, the nation would eventually achieve the artistic, musical, architectural, and human splendors of an advanced civilization. But in the 1860s, the intermediate work of building the nation remained to be done. There was practical work to be done. The intermediate steps required that minds be infused with the most advanced scientific and engineering knowledge of the day, that hands be trained to deploy the most productive agricultural and building methods, and that public values be directed to shaping the physical environment and expanding the economic opportunities to accelerate national progress. The land grant colleges did precisely that.

Few legislative expressions of the national will have succeeded more thoroughly than the Morrill Act. Its legacy is irreversible progress and indelible enhancements of the US quality of life. Michigan State University has produced thousands of engineers who helped develop the US automotive industry and create the "arsenal of democracy" that supplied the margin of victory in World War II. Oklahoma State has pioneered the petroleum extraction techniques that made heartland oil and gas products a linchpin of US energy independence. Clemson University has improved the agricultural products needed as textile feed stocks and advanced the technology of textile manufacturing. Cornell University has introduced approaches to animal health that have steadily advanced principles of nutrition for the nation. The University of California, Davis, has applied its life sciences research to help make the Central Valley in California one of the most fertile and productive agricultural regions in the world. Purdue University's contributions to aerospace research have accelerated every aspect of US aviation from commercial flights to space exploration. Iowa State University researchers have made real the promise of plant-based fuels to power the country's vehicles. These are but a few examples of groundbreaking contributions to national progress made by the extraordinary blossoming of the land grant universities.

A leader in this honor roll of achievement is Texas A&M University, originally named the Agricultural and Mechanical College of Texas in 1876. It is neither my personal attachment to the university nor regional pride that leads me to the conclusion that the Texas A&M System has risen to the pinnacle of the land grant institutions in the United States. In the same way that a "most valuable player" in professional sports is judged not only by his or her individual performance metrics but also by his or her responsibility for a team's success, the Texas A&M System must be assessed not only on its size, rankings, research volumes, and faculty profiles but also on its undeniable impact on the progress of Texas and the nation. The Texas A&M System is composed of eleven universities and eight state agencies in its agricultural extension, engineering, and emergency management services. The flagship campus of Texas A&M University is home to more than 71,000 students, the second-largest university campus in the nation after the University of Central Florida. The system of A&M universities enrolls more than 153,000 students. The component institutions include the Texas network of county-based agricultural research and extension stations, an engineering experiment and training system, and emergency response, nutrition, and oceanographic institutions. In Texas, if an activity involves agri-life, petroleum, public works, or nutrition, it almost certainly involves Texas A&M.

It is not a coincidence that Texas has grown into the second most populous state in the nation, the top job producer in the nation, and the leading destination for companies and households relocating from across the nation. The fundamentals of Texas are solid; its undergirding systems work, from roads to seaports and airports, from water systems to power reserves, from food production to petroleum extraction and refining. This robust internal competence is the result of 145 years of designing, building, improving, and expanding. Texas A&M has been there every step of the way.

The challenge for an institution so extensive in its reach and so embedded into the foundations of a state as large as Texas is whether it can keep up with the times.

Can it adjust to economic cycles, to the obsolescence of some industry sectors, and to the advent of completely new specializations? Can it adapt its fundamental mission as social mores change, demography progresses, and teaching methods evolve?

The answer to these questions depends in large part on whether the institution's leadership understands the inevitability of change, possesses the foresight to distinguish the trendy from the essential, and attracts people who are excited to work at the cutting edge. This book chronicles the way Texas A&M has addressed change over the last decades and especially during the tenure of its present chancellor, John Sharp.

Under Sharp, Texas A&M has understood that the central core of the land grant ideal applies in perpetuity. A nation must constantly invest in the knowledge capital of its people to prepare itself for change, for growth, and for progress. If the American people are endowed with the confidence to think independently and imbued with the commitment to leave our world better than we inherited it, then Americans will shape a dynamic future. Americans will not be stagnant; we will harness change. Americans will not be herded; we will be assertive and determined. Americans will not be oblivious; we will adapt and act.

In a previous era, the land grant vision was building roads; today it also involves building data centers, spacecraft, and deep-ocean facilities. Once the mission was rural public health; today it also includes biomedical nanotechnologies, genetic computing, and urban nutrition improvement. In the early years, A&M's mission was assisting farms, ranches, and small towns; today it is supporting economic development in a state with twenty-five fast-growing metropolitan areas, four of which have core cities ranked in the ten most populous in the nation. Such has been the adaptation of the land grant culture to today's challenges at Texas A&M.

Sharp is the perfect fit for these challenges. He knows modern Texas well. As public controller of Texas, he traveled to every part of the state, urban and rural, and he audited every agency of the state government to assess how it was meeting the state's challenges. As chancellor, he has drawn on a lifetime of knowledge and experience to apply Texas A&M's prodigious capabilities to the needs of Texas. His tenure has produced for the Texas A&M System its greatest advancements in reach, relevancy, and respect. And because Texas as a state has outperformed the nation by so many metrics, it is correct to assert that Texas A&M has set the standard for what a land grant institution should be.

Based on a lifetime association with Texas A&M, I would like to offer a few personal observations. The first is a reflection on the observation of former Texas governor Ann Richards, who once told me that John Sharp was the best natural politician she had met since Pres. Lyndon Johnson. In my judgment, Governor Richards meant that Sharp is the most determined public leader of our time in envisioning public goals and the most capable in seeing them to completion. The governor was totally correct. Many people believed that Sharp was destined to one day be governor of Texas; fate determined otherwise. But it is my sincere belief that Sharp has touched as many lives in profound ways as he would have in any other public post by the way he has applied the capacities of Texas A&M in Texas and as an example to the nation.

A final personal note: I was a student at Texas A&M in the Corps of Cadets and a graduate student in urban and regional planning from 1964 to 1969. I arrived on campus with a general sense of wanting to pursue a career in service to our country, probably in the military. When I learned of A&M's origins in the Morrill Act, studied the land grant concept, and observed A&M's public role across Texas, I came to understand how public service could mean building better lives for people through every academic field, every career, and every industry. The 1960s were a challenging time in our country. The civil rights inequities, the Vietnam War discord, the political contention including assassinations and riots forced me to see that the original land grant mission must be updated for our time. The core idea of human empowerment for national progress was just as valid in 1968 as it had been in 1862. That concept deepened my respect and love for Texas A&M. It came to be the beacon for my work as a mayor, as a cabinet officer, as an investor in housing and infrastructure, as a private citizen, and as a regent and supporter of Texas A&M. Texas A&M was the best possible place to learn those values, and it remains so today. Tim Gregg has written a book that compellingly tells the story of the modern era at Texas A&M and of the successful evolution of a venerable institution of higher education firmly rooted in the highest aspirations and values of a great nation.

BREAKING AWAY

A History of Breaking Away

Go far enough back in Texas history, and you will realize that, indeed, "breaking away" is sort of what Texans do best.

The first people to settle what today is known as Texas were Indigenous tribes that would come to be known by names such as Caddo, Apache, Coahuiltecan, Neches, and Tonkawa.

Spanish explorers later "discovered" the region and adopted the name used by the Caddo people. It sounded like "taysha," so the Spanish translation became *tejas*, a word meaning "friend."

Under Spanish rule, New Spain, as Mexico was then known, had little use for Texas, in part because the Indigenous peoples were firmly entrenched and desired to maintain their homeland.

In 1820, an enterprising Connecticut Yankee by the name of Moses Austin ventured to the Spanish provincial capital of *San Antonio*—where present-day San Antonio is located—with an intriguing proposition. He wanted to colonize the territory he called "Texas" and would do so with a band of Anglo families, frontiersmen, and speculators from the North.

Persistence paid off, and Austin was awarded an *empresarial* grant for an area of land comparable in size to the state of Delaware. Within a year, though, Austin was dead and Mexico had declared its independence from Spain. But Austin's dream remained alive, thanks to his eldest son, Stephen.

While Moses Austin's life ambition was to get rich—and he tried every which way he could—the young Stephen F. Austin went in pursuit of political standing. He was elected to the legislature of the Missouri Territory at age twenty-one. At twenty-six, he ran for Congress as a representative of the newly established Arkansas Territory. When he lost that election, he moved to New Orleans, Louisiana, to study law.

Those plans were temporarily dashed with the death of his father. Stephen's mother, Mary, pleaded with her son to keep his father's pioneering dream alive. Her entreaties eventually proved successful.

In time, Stephen secured his own *empresarial* grant from the new Mexican government and brought his first group of "colonists" to Texas in 1825.

While Mexican authorities were initially supportive and mostly took a hands-off approach with the new arrivals, Austin and his fellow settlers quickly found the Indigenous tribes to be less hospitable. Then, after the rise to presidential power of the ambitious and authoritarian Mexican military leader Antonio López de Santa Anna, it became clear that the tranquil existence Austin had hoped to find in Texas was unachievable. Thus a decade after realizing his father's *empresarial* dream, Austin and a congregation of other leaders of his colony sought to break away from the tyranny of Mexican rule.

The "Texians" began their fight for independence on October 2, 1835, declared their independence on March 2, 1836, and won their independence on April 21, 1836, after the eighteen-minute Battle of San Jacinto near present-day Houston.

Fewer than ten years later, Texas relinquished its independence and was admitted into the United States of America. Change came again in 1861, when Texas broke away from the Union along with the secessionist Confederate States of America and fought with the South in the Civil War.

On the losing side after the war and again a part of the Union, Texas eventually turned its attention to higher education. While the state constitution mandated a public university, a "land grant" institution sprang forth first. Under terms of the Morrill Act, land grant schools were made possible by the sale of federal lands and were designed to "promote the liberal and practical education of the industrial classes in the several pursuits and professions in life." The act also required each school's curriculum to include mandatory military training.

Thanks primarily to the efforts of Harvey Mitchell—a Brazos County judge, clerk, treasurer, tax collector, postmaster, and superintendent of public instruction—the Agricultural and Mechanical College of Texas, known for many years as AMC, was opened on land five miles south of the city of Bryan in 1876.

The new school welcomed four dozen students to its campus. Jefferson Davis, the leader of the failed Confederacy, was initially offered the AMC presidency, but he turned down the job. Davis recommended a more qualified candidate, his friend Thomas Gathright, who served as the superintendent of public instruction for the state of Mississippi. Under Gathright, a large percentage of the school's initial faculty and staff had roots in the Deep South, many having served as Confederate officers in the Civil War.

Soon after the A&M College of Texas opened its doors, the state legislature approved a second land grant college for the education of "colored youth." That school became Prairie View A&M College.

And, in a sense, with the establishment of Prairie View, the Texas A&M University System was born.

Today, the A&M System is one of the largest networks of higher education in the nation, with a budget of $6.3 billion. Through an affiliation of eleven universities and eight state agencies, the Texas A&M System educates more than 150,000 students and makes more than 22 million additional educational contacts through service and outreach programs each year.

A third member of the A&M System was added in 1917. The John Tarleton Agricultural College was established in 1899 on the grounds of the old Stephenville College in Stephenville, Texas, near Fort Worth. Today, Tarleton State University sports an enrollment of more than 12,000 students.

In 1947, the first chancellor of the Texas A&M System was named. Gibb Gilchrist assumed that position while also serving as president of the Texas A&M flagship campus in College Station. He stepped down as A&M president in 1948 but remained in the chancellor's post until August 1953.

Another A&M president, Marion Thomas Harrington, replaced Gilchrist as chancellor and held the position for the next twelve years.

James Earl Rudder, a World War II hero and staunch military man with political experience as the Texas state land commissioner, succeeded Harrington as president of the A&M flagship in 1959, then added the duties of chancellor upon Harrington's retirement in 1965.

It was during Rudder's time as president that Texas A&M College, facing both an enrollment and identity crisis, ended its lengthy legacy as an all-white, all-male military school. Not unexpectedly, given the school's staunch and sacred traditions, both influential former students and a sizable segment of those students within the Corps of Cadets vehemently opposed the move.

Rudder, though, had an influential ally in his quest to promote change: the vice president of the United States.

A force in Texas politics for many years—and a former junior high schoolteacher before that—Vice Pres. Lyndon Johnson strongly urged Rudder to change with the times. While the move was not easy, Rudder steered his school away from the abyss of irrelevancy and set the stage for its future growth not only in student numbers but also in academic reputation and research endeavors.

In the process, Rudder and the Texas A&M System Board of Directors—as the panel was known at the time—also changed the name of the flagship to Texas A&M University.

Following Rudder's untimely death on March 23, 1970, at the age of fifty-nine, Jack Williams ultimately assumed duties as both president and chancellor. A Virginia native who came to Texas A&M from Clemson University, Williams would be the last to serve in a dual leadership capacity.

In 1989, under the guidance of Chancellor Perry Adkisson—a longtime member of the A&M Department of Entomology and an internationally renowned researcher in insect pest management and crop protection—the A&M System doubled in size, adding schools in Kingsville, Corpus Christi, and Laredo. A year later, West Texas State University in Canyon, Texas, became West Texas A&M.

Since then, four more schools have been added to the A&M System roster, with existing colleges in Commerce, Texarkana, Killeen, and San Antonio adopting the Texas A&M name. That expansion came under the leadership of Chancellor Mike McKinney, who joined the A&M System in 2006 after serving as chief operating officer at the University of Texas Health Science Center in Houston. Formerly a practicing physician, McKinney had also once worked as chief of staff to Gov. Rick Perry. Given Perry's ties to Texas A&M as a former student and his loyalty to McKinney, it was not a surprise that McKinney was named as A&M System chancellor. In time, however, McKinney became a polarizing and frequently controversial figure in Aggieland.

Seen as a champion of the system's regional schools, McKinney often bumped heads with top administrators of the flagship campus in College Station. His public disputes with Texas A&M's first female president, Elsa Murano, over her leadership priorities led to her dismissal in 2009 after less than a year and a half in office.

With Murano's forced resignation, McKinney announced the next A&M president might be considered also to serve as chancellor. This triggered a first-ever no-confidence vote of a system chancellor from the flagship's faculty senate, one in a series of disputes in which McKinney eventually found himself embroiled.

R. Bowen Loftin, vice president and CEO of Texas A&M's branch campus in Galveston, was named interim president following Murano's departure. He then assumed the role on a full-time basis in 2010.

Loftin was not destined to become chancellor, although some have suggested he often conducted himself as the ultimate authority.

After McKinney announced in May 2011 his intention to step down as chancellor, the system regents quickly narrowed their search to one man, a candidate whom the governing board had previously approached.

"When they first asked me if I was interested in becoming chancellor," John Sharp says today with the kind of candor that has become his hallmark, "I told them I was making too much money in the private sector to leave. But when they asked a second time, my stock options had vested and I had made enough money in business to follow the leadership mantra of President Sam Houston."

Paraphrasing the first president of the Republic of Texas, John Sharp sums up his own unique management style: "Do right and to hell with the consequences."

Where that mindset has taken the Texas A&M University System since Sharp's return to Aggieland is contained in the pages to follow.

1

Wildfires

As the summer of 2011 slipped into September, the state of Texas was ablaze, literally among countless acres of grasslands throughout the state, and figuratively within the sizable fan base of the Texas A&M University football program.

For years, Texas had experienced a severe absence of rain, culminating in 2011 with the worst one-year drought in state history. Beginning in February of that year and lasting until October, more than thirty-one thousand wildfires scorched more than four million acres of land and destroyed nearly three thousand homes. Investigations would reveal that more than 98 percent of the fires were "human-influenced" events.

While the wildfires dominated local, state, and national news from late winter until early fall, sports pundits from around the country—and particularly in Texas—were focused on the ongoing saga of college football realignment. Beginning in 2010, major universities in unprecedented numbers were abandoning long-standing conference affiliations in search of greater revenue-producing alliances for their football programs and athletic departments.

By far the most intriguing realignment scenario unfolded in the Big 12 Conference. Two schools, Nebraska and Colorado, had already departed, leaving the rest of the league in a state of uncertainty and concern. Much was at stake as realignment discussions among other Big 12 schools escalated during the course of the summer. The outcome of these negotiations would have nothing to do with the athletic achievements of young men and women, nor the tabulation of final scores on their fields of play. Rather, a "suit-and-tie set" of network television executives, conference administrators, university athletic directors, and school presidents were at the fulcrum of discussions that could reshape the athletic topography.

Nowhere were fan passions more extreme than in Texas, particularly for supporters of the state's two most tradition-laden football-playing schools: the University of Texas and Texas A&M University. As realignment talks escalated, ebbing first in one direction and then another, a previously unimaginable consequence began to emerge.

The long-standing football rivalry between the Longhorns and the Aggies was on the precipice of becoming a casualty in the quest for the seemingly almighty athletic dollar.

But let's put "life and death" into perspective, and do so beyond the realm of football, athletics, and conference affiliations. Instead, let us examine the experiences of an individual whose professional and personal lives were inextricably entwined with the Texas wildfire outbreak of 2011.

Rich Gray is a longtime employee of the Texas A&M Forest Service. He's called Texas home for more than twenty years, but he's by no means a product of the Lone Star State.

In fact, Gray admits, "I'm a Yankee. I grew up south of Buffalo, New York."

Family vacations to Colorado during Gray's youth made a big impression. He had grown up with a fondness for the outdoors, but his spirit soared to unsurpassed heights with time spent in the Rocky Mountains. That is why, when Gray looked at potential college destinations, he chose Colorado State University (CSU).

Gray majored in range and forest management and graduated from CSU in 1988. For the next nearly ten years, he worked for the Colorado State Forest Service. In 1997, he left to join the Texas Forest Service (TFS) at its Conroe station. A year later, he was transferred to the Bastrop field office near Austin.

Established in 1915, what is now known as the Texas A&M Forest Service was created to address a long-standing need for the development of a statewide plan for forest conservation. Originally called the Department of Forestry, the agency's mandate called for it to "assume direction of all forest interests and all matters pertaining to forestry within the jurisdiction of the state." In 1993, the Texas legislature expanded the agency's responsibility to include "coordination of the response to each major or potentially major wildland fire in the state."

The agency's affiliation with Texas A&M dates back to conception and stems from the school's land grant mission to provide service to the broad population of the state. Few Texans, however, associated the agency with the college, until John Sharp's ascendancy into the chancellor's post.

"People knew the Forest Service was putting out fires in Texas," Chancellor Sharp says forcefully of the agency's current name change, which occurred within a year of the 2011 wildfire outbreak. "But they didn't know a bunch of damn Aggies were doing it." (Chapter 10 discusses the system's "rebranding" efforts under Sharp in more detail.)

By the time of the 2011 Texas wildfires, Gray had been living in Bastrop for some fourteen years, posted to the Forest Service extension office there. The Bastrop station normally oversaw fire suppression activities for ten Central Texas counties, but in 2011, firefighters in the local command saw duty across the state.

Earlier in the year, wildfires had ravaged 90 percent of the state park surrounding Possum Kingdom Lake, west of Fort Worth. Four months after those blazes were suppressed, a new ranch fire broke out near the lake. Gray, as a task-force coordinator, was sent there to manage the Forest Service response.

It was while on that assignment, some five hours from home, that Gray received a phone call in the early evening of Saturday, September 4. The call was from his daughter.

"I had told her in the spring that after school got out, she and I would go fishing," Gray remembers. "Given that I was gone a lot that summer, I thought she had forgotten about my promise."

She had not.

Gray says his daughter's call was not to scold him for his failure of parental duty, but in conveying a larger piece of news, she did bring it up.

She said, "Daddy, have you heard about the fire here in Bastrop?"

"Yes, honey, I have," Gray told his daughter. "I'm trying to get home as soon as I can."

"Well, I know we're not going fishing anytime soon because we're being evacuated."

Gary recalls now, "And just like that, she hung up the phone without saying another word."

For Rich Gray, the Texas wildfires had suddenly gotten very personal.

With his family in danger from a monstrous conflagration like the one he was fighting in Palo Pinto County, Gray kept his wits "compart-mentalized" and quickly called a friend to expedite his family's safe removal from their home.

By the time official evacuation plans were implemented, the Gray family home was empty. But before Gray could get home himself, fire had destroyed that home.

In all, more than 1,600 homes and some 40 businesses were lost in the Bastrop County Complex wildfires. The blazes, which would take more than a month to contain fully, were and are the most destructive fires in state history.

The town of Bastrop is located less than forty miles from the Texas State Capitol in Austin. The day after Gray's family was moved to safety, Gov. Rick Perry took a tour of the devastated area. Because of what he witnessed, Perry announced the mobilization of Texas Task Force 1, the state's elite one-hundred-member search-and-rescue team that also operated under the management responsibilities of the Texas A&M University System. Task Force 1 joined first responders and other emergency workers in assisting those whose lives had been impacted by the devastation in the Bastrop area.

"The guys who make up Task Force 1 are an outstanding group," Gray says. "Knowing they were getting involved was comforting for the whole community, my family included."

Texas Task Force 1 conducted door-to-door search-and-rescue efforts during their weeklong stay in the Bastrop area. While none of the hundreds of homes they searched revealed loss of life, two people died because of the Bastrop fires.

Throughout the state of Texas, the 2011 wildfire outbreak also claimed eight other lives, including those of four firefighters.

In the aftermath, the death toll of livestock and pets was never officially tallied, but according to Gray, those numbers surely would have taken on staggering proportions if not for the work of two more Texas A&M University System agencies.

"The Veterinary Emergency Assistance Team did great fieldwork tending to domesticated and farm animals while the fires were burn-ing," says Gray. "Given the number of fires we were dealing with, particularly in the spring, their resources were stretched, but their impact preserved assets and saved lives."

"Meanwhile," Gray adds, "our AgriLife extension agents played a key role in helping ranchers get food to their herds after their grazing fields were destroyed."

Gray is quick to deflect his own personal story involving the Bastrop fires. He's grateful his family's lives were spared, but the loss of possessions, keepsakes, and family heirlooms was difficult, particularly for his two daughters.

"That had a pretty big impact on their lives for a while," he admits.

"But so many others lost a lot more than we did," Gray continues. "And we weren't the only people associated with the system to be affected. Two other firefighters lost their homes, as did three Texas Forest Service employees and several people working with the AgriLife extension office in Bastrop."

After the fire, some who lost homes rebuilt. Others moved on and moved away. Nearly a decade later, Bastrop County remains in a state of recovery.

Gray moved in 2016, promoted into a management position with the Forest Service in the Texas Panhandle. Yet another promotion, in 2018, moved him to TFS headquarters at the old A&M System administrative building located in the College Station Business Center on the south side of the city.

Gray's title now is chief regional fire coordinator.

While the Bastrop County fires were still burning, another wildfire outbreak occurred in Grimes County on September 5, ultimately consuming another eighteen thousand acres of Texas ranch land and home sites.

The next day, September 6, the Texas A&M University System Board of Regents met in a special session via conference call to officially appoint a new chancellor.

Jay Kimbrough, another former chief of staff to Governor Perry, had been serving as interim chancellor since McKinney's resignation two months before. Prior to being named to the post, Kimbrough had worked as a special advisor to the regents.

"We are fortunate to have someone of John Sharp's ability and prestige take over the A&M System," regents chair Richard Box said. "Chancellor Sharp is a dedicated public servant who has done many important and noteworthy things for Texas, as well as the nation, during his career."

Sharp called it "an honor to be selected" to head up the system and told the regents he would "work very hard to be worthy" of his new duties.

For Sharp, the appointment amounted to a homecoming of sorts. The native of Placedo, Texas, had attended Texas A&M and graduated with the Class of 1972. A member of the corps staff of the Corps of Cadets, Sharp eventually was elected student body president prior to his senior year. One of his fellow cadet classmates was a yell leader at the school.

His name was Rick Perry.

Upon assuming the A&M System chancellorship, Sharp praised Kimbrough for providing a "steady hand" as the interim head. At the same time he was named interim chancellor, Kimbrough was also given the permanent position of deputy chancellor.

One of John Sharp's stipulations for accepting the chancellor job was that he would be given authority to assemble his own staff. As former Texas state comptroller, Sharp had saved the state billions of dollars in an austerity program called the Texas Performance Review that he had rolled out in the early 1990s. Sharp hoped to pull several of his former aides in the comptroller's office to work with him at the helm of the A&M System.

Thus less than a month after taking the system's reins, Sharp dismissed Kimbrough as deputy chancellor.

"The position was no longer needed," Sharp said at the time.

As Kimbrough was being given this unexpected news by Sharp's new legal team, the former interim chancellor, a Vietnam-era Marine Corps veteran, did not take the news well. According to a Texas A&M University Police Department spokesman, Craig Dudley, Kimbrough "refused to hand over his keys and pass cards and brandished a knife in a nonthreatening manner."

Kimbrough reportedly said, "If anyone is man enough to take them"—referring to the keys and pass card—"bring it on."

Ultimately, Kimbrough left the building—with a police escort— "peacefully, if reluctantly," according to the police report.

When given the news of the incident, Governor Perry—seeking a new job himself as president of the United States—called the confrontation a "personnel matter within the Texas A&M System."

"I have the utmost respect for and confidence in both Jay and John," Perry said.

Early critics of Sharp's leadership of the Texas A&M University System often suggested he orchestrated a "scorched-earth" policy in attempting to right the perceived wrongs of how the institutions and agencies had been previously administered.

History and this book will show those critics were mostly wrong.

"You just have to put on lead pants and say, 'I know I'm right,' and keep on going," Sharp says of dealing with the naysayers who have opposed the policies, procedures, and projects that have proven to be the hallmarks in both his political and academic careers.

"It was actually very liberating coming over here," Sharp says of moving into the chancellor's office. "I spent my entire political life worrying about what my constituents thought, and whether or not I was doing the right things for them.

"Now all I have to worry about is what nine people [the board of regents] think of the job I'm doing."

John Sharp turned out to be one of the A&M regents' easiest and best decisions. But at the same time they were preparing to hand over the system's leadership responsibilities to Sharp, that same group of leaders was also dealing with a matter that would have an equally significant impact on the A&M landscape.

Remember, those Texas wildfires were not the only thing turning up the heat in Texas in the summer of 2011.

2

Greener Pastures

When Texas A&M University's move to the Southeastern Conference (SEC) finally became official on the evening of Sunday, September 25, 2011, Gene Stallings was at home with his wife, Ruth Ann, at their ranch north of Paris, Texas.

Both had been born and raised in the Paris area.

Stallings's "Hike-A-Way Ranch" honors both the sport in which he had spent most of his life and a favorite family pastime.

"'Hike,'" as Stallings reminds visitors, "is what the quarterback says to begin each play. The word also refers to something I've spent a lot of time doing with my children and grandchildren through the woods and pastures on this property."

"I think I've walked every inch of the place," he adds, "and I have the arrowhead collection to prove it."

Many call Gene Stallings the single most influential figure in steering Texas A&M toward membership in the SEC, the most prestigious sporting affiliation of universities in the country.

With close ties to both Texas A&M and the SEC, Stallings was uniquely qualified to weigh in on a matter that, for many, took on nearly life-and-death proportions.

Stallings both played and coached football for the Aggies. As a player in the 1950s, he was a "Junction Boy." As head coach, he led the A&M program from 1965 to 1971.

Stallings also spent seven years as head coach at the University of Alabama. Under his watch, the Crimson Tide won a national championship in 1992.

In between those two college coaching stints, Stallings won a Super Bowl title as an assistant coach with the National Football League's Dallas Cowboys.

If anyone knows what it takes to put together a winning football program, it is Gene Stallings.

In 1967, at the age of thirty-two and in just his third season as a head coach, Stallings guided Texas A&M to its first Southwest Conference (SWC) championship in more than a decade. In that year's season-ending Cotton Bowl Classic played in Dallas on New Year's Day, Stallings's Aggies upset an eighth-ranked Alabama team that had won the Associated Press national championship just two years before.

On that day, the student got the best of "the Bear."

Paul "Bear" Bryant won six national championships as head football coach of the Alabama Crimson Tide. But before he became a legend in the SEC, Bryant spent four years in charge of the football program at Texas A&M. It was Bryant, preparing for his first season as head coach of the Aggies, who infamously took his team into the Texas Hill Country for preseason workouts in the late summer of 1954.

There, on A&M's adjunct campus in Junction, Bryant put his charges through a ten-day stretch of torturous practices and drills. In doing so, he looked to determine which of his players were willing to pay the price he demanded to achieve success.

More left the camp than finished it.

Stallings was among those who "survived."

"Quitting never entered my mind," Stallings says of the experience, "although there were times I would have liked to have died."

The Aggies' reward for their Junction experience: a 1–9 record for that 1954 season.

In another two years, though, the "Junction Boys" were champions of the SWC, a first for A&M since the three consecutive league crowns—and a national championship—won by Coach Homer Norton from 1939 to 1941.

Following the 1957 season, in which John David Crow became A&M's first Heisman Trophy winner, Bryant resigned to become head coach at Alabama, his alma mater.

With Stallings's playing eligibility at an end, Bryant hired him to be a member of his first Alabama coaching staff.

That history made the 1968 Cotton Bowl an intriguing encounter. And as the final gun sounded ending the game and the two head coaches trotted toward the center of the field, a new chapter in the saga of their enduring football friendship was written. As Stallings approached his mentor, Bryant bypassed the traditional postgame handshake, instead lifting Stallings high into the air in what could only be described—for obvious reasons—as a "Bear" hug.

That game, it would seem fitting to suggest, and that moment of mutual respect and shared affection between two extraordinary men, marked the beginning of a nearly half-century journey that would end with Texas A&M following Bear Bryant's lead into the ranks of the SEC.

After his eventual retirement from coaching, Gene Stallings sat on the Texas A&M University System Board of Regents from 2005 until 2011. Then Texas governor Rick Perry, a fellow former student of Texas A&M, appointed Stallings as an "east-Texas" representative.

"The board of regents' main responsibility," Stallings says today, "is to hire presidents."

"We do not hire coaches," Stallings adds, emphatic in his words. "We don't run athletic departments. We hire presidents that run our schools."

Eleven schools, including the A&M flagship in College Station, make up the system's roster of institutions, thus there is a frequent need to find a new man or woman to put in charge on a system campus.

The regents do, on a regular basis, weigh in on matters important to the system as a whole or, when the need arises, its individual institutions.

As fans of college football will recall, 2010 marked a crossroads for the sport. Television-rights fees had risen to unprecedented proportions, thanks in large part to the enormous investment the ESPN cable network was making in the game. Major conferences, soon to be labeled the "Power 5," were looking to expand membership and broaden their broadcast footprints, thus increasing their financial value to television executives. More prospective viewers meant larger sums of money for exclusive rights to televised coverage of games.

Thus was born a college football game of "musical chairs."

The Big 12 Conference, of which A&M had been a member since 1994, suffered two major defections in the late spring of 2010. Perennial power Nebraska announced its move to the Big 10, while the University of Colorado made known its intentions to join the Pac-10.

As it turned out, Colorado was but a small consolation prize for the storied West Coast league. The Pac-10 had courted several Big 12 institutions, most notably Texas, Texas A&M, and Oklahoma, but those efforts fell apart when the Big 12 agreed to Texas' terms pertaining to revenue distribution that favored the Longhorns.

Texas had led the prospective westward exodus of Big 12 schools. The university's then president, Bill Powers, was himself a graduate of the Pac-10's University of California, Berkeley. Powers, in turn, had made a convincing case to A&M president Bowen Loftin that the Pac-10 was a better fit for their schools, both academically and athletically.

Where Texas went, Texas A&M would surely follow. Or so many assumed.

For more than eighty years to that point, Texas A&M had participated in intercollegiate athletics alongside the University of Texas, mostly as members of the SWC. For much of its existence, that league comprised eight Texas schools and the University of Arkansas.

A&M's intrastate football rivalry with the University of Texas (UT) goes back even further. The schools' first gridiron clash came in 1894. A&M failed to score in its first eight games with Texas. Finally, in 1902, the Aggies prevailed, beating the Longhorns by an 11–0 score.

A&M's status as an early underdog to its intrastate rival transcended the outcome of football games. Mandated by the state's original constitution, what became the University of Texas held the favor of state policy makers from the time it opened its doors in Austin. While the land grant school attracted mostly young white males from the rural regions of the state, UT's student body was seen as more diverse and more affluent.

Aggies coined the term "tea-sip" to belittle the highbrow ways of their collegiate counterparts. Still today, one of A&M's most fervent rallying cries embraces the two schools' cultural divide, beseeching that "Farmers, fight!"

In a move portending A&M's eventual exodus to the SEC, Arkansas shifted its alliance from the SWC to the SEC in 1990. Four years later, the SWC completely imploded thanks to a legion of football recruiting scandals within many of the league's elite programs. The Big Eight assimilated the four top schools from Texas—UT, A&M, Texas Tech, and Baylor—to form the Big 12 Conference.

That expanded new league assumed two divisions of play. However, despite its newcomer status, Texas assumed authority over the Big 12 as if by birthright. This eventually sent both Nebraska and Colorado out through what would eventually become the conference's revolving membership door.

A year later in 2011, the Pac-12—renamed with the addition of Colorado and Utah to the league ranks—once again pounded the drums of further expansion with a goal of adding four more schools to create a "superconference." And the Big 12 again seemed a prime target, unsettled by rumblings of a cable network devoted solely to University of Texas athletics, called the Longhorn Network.

As a new member of the Big 12, UT had originally persuaded the conference to base the division of television revenues on the number of TV appearances that each school made. In leagues like the Pac-12 and SEC, television revenues were distributed equally among all institutions.

The University of Texas—along with Oklahoma, the other perennial powerhouse in the Big 12—insisted on unbalanced revenue sharing within the conference. This ensured that Texas would get its abundant share of the financial pie and that programs like Kansas, Iowa State, and Missouri, all lesser money-making machines than Texas and Oklahoma, would find it harder to escape the bottom of the conference standings.

With the Big 12 in a state of upheaval and uncertainty in the early months of 2011, the Pac-12 again seemed like a logical departure destination for the schools at the top of the league heap. Among power brokers and influencers within the Lone Star State, it was unimaginable that Texas A&M wouldn't follow the Texas lead. Yet among the policy makers on the A&M System Board of Regents, a West Coast pilgrimage was far from preordained.

Aggieland, it turned out, had finally grown weary of playing second fiddle in the Lone Star State. The time was right to chart a new and different course.

"We had been informally discussing conference affiliation for some time," Regent Phil Adams says. "Things in the Big 12 were a mess. We weren't sure the league would last and we needed to consider other options. Before he left the board, Coach Stallings had made it clear where he thought we needed to be."

"I knew something about the Southeastern Conference," Stallings says of the role he played in steering Texas A&M toward the SEC. "I still had a good relationship with a lot of coaches there, as well as with the commissioner's office. I would think those relationships certainly didn't hurt our chances of getting into the league."

"Coach Stallings was dead-set against going to the Pac-10," says Adams, who played football at A&M under Stallings in the late 1960s and early 1970s. "He thought that was a terrible idea, and in time, most of us on the board of regents agreed with him."

Stallings's reasoning, according to Adams, was sound.

"We had nothing in common with the schools out west," Adams says. "As Coach pointed out, the idea of West Coast night games getting started at 10 o'clock back here in Texas wasn't exactly fan-friendly.

"Plus, the thought of the 'Fightin' Texas Aggie Band' playing at halftime of a game in Berkeley, California, was something we just couldn't imagine ever happening."

Following the Big 12's spring meeting in 2011, "there were rumors flying all over the place," according to former regents chair Richard Box. "Most of what we were hearing was that Texas was again going to take the lead in orchestrating a realignment scenario involving both UT and A&M, and that didn't sit well with the Board."

Box called a closed-door meeting for July 21, 2011, to make sense of the rumors and speculation swirling around their flagship's athletic program.

In his book *The 100-Year Decision: Texas A&M and the SEC*, Bowen Loftin says he made the case for the SEC at the closed-door session—a claim that Chairman Box disputes. Nonetheless, the meeting proved pivotal.

Box said he had insisted that Loftin and the athletic director attend.

"We knew our athletic director at the time, Bill Byrne, was holding meetings with his counterpart at Texas, Deloss Dodds," says Box. "I asked President Loftin, to make sure that both he and Byrne attended the executive session to bring us up to date on matters relating to conference realignment."

"No problem, we'll be there," was Loftin's reply, according to Box.

On the day of the meeting, the A&M president showed up alone.

"Where the hell is Byrne?" Box inquired, confused and concerned.

"He's going to join the meeting via conference call," Loftin responded.

"From where?" Box says he was incredulous at the apparent insubordination.

According to Box, Loftin explained that Byrne was in the middle of a previously planned fishing trip to Alaska—with Larry Scott.

Scott was commissioner of the Pac-12. The fact that Byrne was with him suggested one of two things to Box: the importance of the executive session had not been appropriately communicated to Byrne, or the university president and his athletic director had plans they were not yet sharing with others.

"I wanted to fire both of them on the spot," Box says today of his reaction to Byrne's absence from the meeting . . . and his whereabouts.

With the picture cloudier than ever before, Box says the regents decided it would be necessary for them to play a more active role in realignment discussions. In fact, Byrne's fishing trip with Scott—allegorically fitting, given the circumstances—firmed the resolve of the system board to set their sights firmly to the east rather than west.

"Southeast," to be exact.

Ten days later, Box; Loftin; Regents Jim Schwertner, Cliff Thomas, and Jim Wilson; and A&M System legal counsel Scott Kelly boarded Schwertner's private plane for a secret trip to New Orleans to meet with then SEC commissioner Mike Slive.

So secret was the mission that Schwertner piloted the plane and Box served as his copilot. Both men possessed extensive aviation experience, and neither was interested in bringing an outside party along to fly Schwertner's aircraft.

"Jim has more hours than most airline pilots," Box offers in recounting the trip.

The meeting, held at the Million Air fixed-based operations facility located at the Louis Armstrong New Orleans International Airport, determined many of the details of the eventual agreement put into place between Texas A&M and the SEC.

"The regents weren't aware of this at the time," Box says, "but Mike Slive wanted Texas A&M as much or more than we wanted to be a part of his league. The Texas television markets we brought to the table nearly doubled the SEC's number of TV households.

"In the two hours we were in New Orleans, we had a great meeting, and it was obvious that the chemistry between our two parties was perfect."

With the New Orleans meeting, the die was cast, but getting to the September 25 announcement that A&M would join the SEC was fraught with challenges, misinformation, and bad blood.

When word that the SEC courtship of A&M had turned serious, cries of doom and despair echoed from across the Lone Star State.

Baylor president Kenneth Starr—the former prosecutor in the impeachment proceedings against Pres. Bill Clinton—despaired the complete demise of the Big 12 if A&M went rogue. Starr threatened to sue the SEC commissioner's office if further action on the matter took place. Schwertner suggested the regents enter into an indemnity agreement releasing the SEC of legal responsibility. That move would effectively deter Starr's legal maneuvering.

The biggest blowback from the news of A&M's possible move to the SEC came from, not unexpectedly, the UT campus. The outcry from Austin was not only loud but also somewhat misleading. Aggie defection to the SEC, Texas administrative officials said, "would kill the Big 12," making no mention of their own previous interest in aligning with the Pac-12.

Other opposing views came from legislators in Austin. Dan Branch, a Republican member of the Texas House of Representatives from Dallas, was chair of the House Higher Education Committee at the time. Although he had no direct ties to the school, Branch was known to be a staunch UT supporter. After it became public knowledge that A&M was in talks to join the SEC, Branch announced his intent to hold a hearing on the matter. In his position, Branch's influence was sufficient that if the hearing was held, the potential public outcry to follow might force A&M to abandon its plan.

Just weeks away from becoming chancellor of the Texas A&M University System, John Sharp was technically still on the sidelines of the debate when Branch called for hearings on the matter. Sharp, though, at heart was an Aggie—one who possessed both an extensive network of contacts in Austin and persuasive political powers.

On vacation at his mountain home in Telluride, Colorado, Sharp decided to step into the fray and help the A&M cause. His only question was, How *could* he help?

"I knew Dan would rake A&M over the coals about going to the SEC," Sharp says today of the planned hearing. "I thought a good way to convince Dan to leave A&M alone might be to mobilize the vast numbers of Aggie faithful who regularly convened on the message boards of TexAgs.com."

Sharp's plan was simple—and perhaps a little devious—but as a former politician, he understood the boundaries of what would constitute a "fair" political fight.

"I gave the folks at TexAgs Dan's cell number and told them it might be a good idea for their followers to give Dan a call," Sharp says.

Remnants of several "Hey, Dan Branch!" threads are still viewable on the TexAgs website. Still vivid in Sharp's mind is Branch's white-flag response to the episode.

"Dan and I are good friends today," Sharp says, "but when I released his phone number, he was less than thrilled. His cell phone received so many calls, he had to put it into the freezer of his refrigerator at home to keep the thing from melting."

Or so the story goes.

The House Higher Education Committee hearing never took place. Faced with the wrath of the Aggie faithful, Branch canceled the hearing. No other serious threats or legal actions materialized, and on September 25, 2011, Texas A&M was welcomed into the SEC.

The league's initial announcement amounted to nothing more than a Sunday afternoon post on the SEC website. A&M held its press conference the next day.

From the beginning—perhaps as far back as that fateful day in Dallas when his Aggies shocked the Crimson Tide—Gene Stallings's gut told him the SEC was the right place for Texas A&M to be.

But in encouraging the Texas A&M University System's Board of Regents to pursue that ultimate end, Stallings offered a word of warning.

"Even though Gene was no longer on the board, he kept in close contact with some of us," Schwertner says today. "He was always whispering in our ear, 'The SEC is the right place for Texas A&M.'

"But he was a realist about the move, too. 'Your boys are going to get their butts beat for the first five or six years in the SEC,' he told us over and over. 'Going to get beat bad.

"'You need to do it, though, because you're going to be on TV every weekend, and that's going to help in recruiting, and eventually you're going to win a national championship.'"

Texas A&M's move to the SEC put an end—at least a temporary

one—to the storied series between the school's football team and its longtime intrastate rival representing the University of Texas.

It also eventually led to the departure of A&M's popular and outspoken president R. Bowen Loftin, who took much of the credit for masterminding the Aggies' move to the SEC in his book *The 100-Year Decision.*

It is telling that while the book was originally set to be published by Texas A&M University Press, the project ultimately wound up in the hands of a company called Dog Ear Publishing, located in Indianapolis, Indiana, after Loftin stepped down as president.

In announcing his resignation as president on July 12, 2013, Loftin said in his prepared statement, "I do miss the opportunity to teach and do research—activities that have characterized my long career in higher education." His stated intent at the time was to do just that at A&M.

In reality, Loftin had run afoul of the wishes of the A&M regents on multiple occasions, but it was his unauthorized behind-the-scenes maneuvering for A&M to align itself with the Pac-10 Conference that created a permanent divide with many to whom he reported. A&M's magical first season of SEC football success delayed what amounted to his inevitable departure. Within months of his A&M resignation, Loftin returned to the ranks of academic administration when he was chosen to head up the University of Missouri in Columbia, which, like Texas A&M, had chosen to leave the Big 12 for the SEC.

Texas A&M's move to the SEC began paying dividends. In 2018, *Forbes* magazine listed Texas A&M as the most lucrative program in college football. The Longhorn Network may have provided Texas with a steady revenue stream—the original deal, since amended, was worth $300 million over twenty years—but the school's fortunes in both football and basketball have waned since the ESPN agreement was signed. Some have speculated, at least in the early years of the network, that wall-to-wall coverage of Longhorn sports distracted UT coaches from the matter of fielding winning teams.

As for the state of the now defunct A&M-Texas football rivalry, some believe it will be resurrected someday.

Stallings is cautiously optimistic about the return of the rivalry. After all, he points out, both schools still sing about the game in their respective fight songs.

"I think A&M would like to play," Stallings observes. "What I'm less certain about is who will ultimately make the decision to get things going again. Will it be the presidents? The athletic directors? I don't think it's for the legislature to decide.

"Maybe someday the two school's chancellors will get together and work things out."

Coming of Age

Texas Aggies everywhere—and, in fact, the entire state of Texas—owe a debt of gratitude to Manuela Gutierrez for launching John Sharp into a lifetime of public service.

Sharp's journey to becoming the fourteenth chancellor of the Texas A&M University System began in the farming town of Placedo, Texas, a tiny unincorporated community located about a dozen miles southeast of Victoria along US Highway 87.

Placedo got its name from a local landowner, Plácido Benavides, who broke away from allegiance with his home country of Mexico to side with the "Texian" insurgents in the fight for Texas independence. In fact, Benavides is known as the Paul Revere of the Texas Revolution for his efforts to warn residents in and around the Victoria area of the Mexican army's impending approach in March 1836.

Roughly 114 years later, John Spencer Sharp's arrival into the world occurred with much less fanfare. Sharp was born July 28, 1950, to Melburn and Venus Sharp, an oilfield worker and an elementary schoolteacher whose lives significantly shaped the youngest of their three children.

"My dad was a great guy," Sharp says today. "He was like a lot of World War II vets of that time: quiet, loving, and he worked like a Trojan. He'd get up at 5 a.m. every morning, go off to work in the oilfields, then come home for supper in the evening.

"And then many times at night he would wake up with these nightmares. They were always the same bad dream about a Japanese soldier jumping into his foxhole and stabbing him."

Sharp says his father shared little else with his family about his experiences in combat, but he suspects the war years influenced his parental guidance regarding the importance of camaraderie and getting along with others in life.

"Probably the greatest lesson my dad taught me was that you can't have too many friends," Sharp says. "I was sort of shy when I was young, and I remember one day, my dad telling me that I needed to introduce myself to this new kid in town, Joe Stubbs.

"Joe's father had just opened a small grocery store in Placedo, and my dad thought I should get acquainted with the son.

"'I'll probably bump into him at school,' I told Dad.

"'No,' he said, 'Walk over there, tell him your name, and shake his hand.'

"That lesson stuck with me the rest of my life," Sharp says. "Maybe the pleasure I found in meeting new people is one of the big reasons I got interested in politics."

It was in the seventh grade that Sharp first threw his hat into the ring, prompted by the encouragement of young Manuela Gutierrez, a classmate at Bloomington Junior High School.

Bloomington is the consolidated school district where kids from Placedo went to middle and senior high school.

"Our teacher at the time decided one day we were going to have elections for class officers," Sharp says. "As I recall, it was sort of a spur-of-the-moment thing.

"Manuela, whom I didn't know all that well, nominated me for president, and I won."

Sharp uses the word "interesting" to describe the feeling of garnering the support of his seventh-grade peers. When election time rolled around the next year, he decided to run for class president again.

"I discovered I had to give a speech to my fellow eighth graders," Sharp remembers. "I was scared to death. I couldn't sleep for three or four nights leading up to that."

The terms "easygoing" and "home spun" are frequently used to describe Sharp's inviting manner before crowds today, but it turns out the pride of the Bloomington Independent School District feared public speaking for many years.

"I don't know when I got over it, but I got over it," Sharp says. "I still remember having to give that speech in eighth grade as an earth-shattering experience."

Sharp was selected eighth-grade class president, continuing a personal political winning streak that would extend another thirty-four years.

Upon his arrival at Texas A&M in 1968, Sharp held several elected positions, including that of student body president his senior year. What led him to Aggieland in the first place was a combination of his own soft heart and his mother's zeal to see her son succeed.

At the tender age of eleven, young John one day came upon an injured bird, a pigeon, that appeared to have broken its wing. Showing great compassion, Sharp fabricated a makeshift splint for the bird from a Popsicle stick in an attempt to bring the pigeon back to health. After caring for the creature for about a month, Sharp was elated when one day after removing the splint, the bird took flight.

"I thought I had healed him," Sharp says today of the winged companion he took to calling "Pidge." "But now that I'm older and wiser, I suspect the wing was never actually broken in the first place."

Still, the experience made a profound impression in the Sharp household.

"My mother was a fifth-grade teacher there in Placedo," Sharp says. "From the time I can remember, she was always asking me where I wanted to go to college.

"Her question was never 'if' or 'when' but always 'where.'"

Sharp knew his mother had attended the University of Texas to become a teacher, but college seemed a million miles away from the day-to-day experiences of an eleven-year-old curious about matters of the here and now.

"I was never indifferent about my education," Sharp says, "just noncommittal for a long time. But when I 'healed' Pidge, I thought maybe I should become a veterinarian.

"I asked my mother, 'Where do I go to school to learn to be a vet?'"

Venus Sharp quickly told her son: Texas A&M.

"Even though Mom went to UT"—as did Sharp's sister, Marsha, and his wife, Charlotte—"she didn't seem to care if I went there or not, so I thought telling her I'd go to A&M to be a vet would get her to stop pestering me about the subject."

During his senior year of high school, Sharp filled out the requisite forms for attending Texas A&M to study veterinary medicine. He first visited the campus just weeks before beginning classes there, a "summer-orientation thing," Sharp calls it. His father, he remembers, was impressed there was a Whataburger near the A&M campus.

As part of his orientation, Sharp got a close-up look at the A&M vet school.

"I met with the dean," Sharp says, "and he asked me why I wanted to become a vet. Since Pidge, I hadn't given the matter a lot of thought, and when I was asked the question, I sorta froze.

"Finally, I told the dean, 'Because I hear vets make a lot of money.'"

Sharp still recalls the dean's laughter and his friendly admonishment that money was not a good reason to become an animal doctor.

"In that moment, I realized I'd never really wanted to be a vet," Sharp says. "So before I started classes, I changed my major to political science."

By the fall semester of 1968, membership in the A&M Corps of Cadets was no longer mandatory. Still, Sharp decided to join the corps, although his decision was based on what he would later call "erroneous" information.

"As we got ready to leave College Station and head back home, we saw a young hitchhiker on the side of the road," Sharp remembers. Hitchhiking was, for many years, a popular and essential pastime for farm boys attending college at Texas A&M. The pursuit, at the time, was both a safe and necessary means of traveling long distances to and from school.

"A friend of mine from Bloomington High School, Michael Olsen, had made the trip with my dad and me," Sharp recalls. "When Michael and I saw the hitchhiker was carrying a little Aggie bag, we begged my dad to stop and pick him up.

"We thought it would be a good opportunity to ask a real student what it was like to attend Texas A&M."

Sharp admits today that his on-campus orientation failed to shed much light on what it meant to be an Aggie or why one would want to consider becoming a member of the Corps of Cadets.

"Even though the hitchhiker had almost no hair on his head," Sharp says, "we didn't really make the connection that he might be in the corps.

"After we squeezed him into the back seat of the car, Michael and I begin peppering him with questions. He said, 'I'm a "fish" in the Corps of Cadets.' After he explained to us what that meant, we thought it sounded great.

"In fact, it seemed a lot like the sorority my sister had joined at the University of Texas.

"'Yeah, it's a lot like that,'" Sharp says the hitchhiker deadpanned. "So, based on what he told us, Mike and I decided we wanted to be in the corps."

Sharp chuckles at what happened next.

"Shortly after school started and we began suffering through the lowly corps existence of a 'fish,' Mike and I went looking for that hitchhiker guy to give him a piece of our minds."

The Corps of Cadet experience, it turned out, did not closely resemble—then or now—"sorority life," as Sharp and his high school friend had been led to believe. But the Texas A&M University System chancellor says he wouldn't trade his involvement in the corps for anything, although he admits a few lifestyle adjustments had to be made.

"Yeah, I'd have to say I probably was a bit of a smartass back then," Sharp says with a twinkle in his eye. "One day I was dragging my footlocker down the hall of my barracks, and this guy started shouting, 'Hey, "fish Jones," you're scratching the floor!'"

The word "fish" in the A&M Corps of Cadets is never capitalized.

"Since my name wasn't Jones, I didn't pay any attention to what this fool was yelling, but he kept at it, calling somebody he obviously didn't like 'fish Jones.'

"So finally, when I realized what was happening, I acknowledge the guy in the most flippant manner I could think of.

"'Hey, "Fred," how are you doing?'"

To which the response was, according to Sharp, "Blankety-blank, you blanket-blank-blank! My name's not Fred!"

To which he replied, "Well, my name's not 'Jones,' either, you asshole!"

Such was the occasion of Sharp's initial encounter with the first sergeant of his outfit.

"I learned a lot in those next five minutes," Sharp says, smiling.

"The corps was the best training for life I could have ever had," Sharp adds. "The philosophy is that in order to become a leader, you have to be torn down, become a follower, and work your way up."

Which Sharp did, all the way to student body president and a member of the corps staff his senior year.

"The most complicated campaign I ever had, before or since," Sharp laughs today.

"At the time—and it's probably still the same—you had anywhere from five to ten different student groups campaigning for their candidates as student body president. Every one of those groups—less so the candidates—had their own idiosyncrasies." By then, about a half dozen years after A&M opened enrollment to students of both genders and all ethnicities, "the campus was becoming pretty diverse, and you had to take all that into account."

Sharp pauses, then adds, "Yell Leader elections were a helluva lot more important than student body president." And while Sharp held the title of student body president, one of his fellow "Flying Tigers"—as members of Squadron Six of the Corps' Air Force ROTC unit were known—served as Yell Leader representing the Class of '72.

His name was Rick Perry, as in future Texas governor Rick Perry.

"We lived down the hall from each other," Sharp says, "but contrary to the stories you sometimes hear, we were never roommates."

But as senior cadets, Sharp and Perry were two of the biggest men on campus.

"Rick and I sometimes made road trips when we had a free weekend during the school year," Sharp says. "I visited his family in Haskell, Texas, and he'd come to Placedo to visit mine.

"We knew each other well and worked on each other's student campaigns."

The two men's lives were destined to intersect again and again as both pursued political careers after fulfilling their military commitments after graduation from A&M.

Perry flew three years as a US Air Force pilot. Sharp served three months of active duty before being assigned to the US Army Reserve.

Of his short stay on the active-duty roster, Sharp says, "I was assigned to a ninety-day 'wander program' and stationed at Fort Gordon in Georgia. The Vietnam War was winding down by that time, and the last thing the army needed were more second lieutenants."

With dreams of turning his student political experiences into a steady-paying job and his US Army Reserve obligation established, Sharp left Fort Gordon and headed back to Texas. Given his sparkling student résumé, job opportunities in the shadow of the Texas state capitol in Austin were plentiful. He eventually went to work as an analyst for the Texas Legislative Budget Board.

It was there Sharp learned the ins and outs of a balance sheet, a skill set that would serve him well in future years.

In Austin, Sharp followed his father's good advice and grew both his personal and political networks. While a student at A&M, one of his favorite ways of making new friends was bumming cigarettes for ten cents a smoke. That triggered a lifelong nicotine addiction that Sharp eventually "tempered" into a smokeless tobacco habit for which he has become somewhat infamous in recent years.

Among Sharp's burgeoning network as a young politico in Austin was a group of "elder statesmen," two of whom would inspire him in 1978 to make his first run for political office. It started with a late-night phone call.

"I'll never forget the voice on the other end of the line," Sharp says of the fateful phone call that changed his life. "I instantly recognized the caller as Frank Erwin. He asked me, 'What are you doing?'

"'Sleeping,' I told him.

"'Well, get up and get over to the Quorum Club right now.'"

When the caller is Frank Erwin and the hour is late, Sharp says you do what you are told.

Erwin was a powerhouse among the contingent of Democratic conservatives who ran the state of Texas for many years. He had been a close confidant of Pres. Lyndon Johnson and Gov. John Connally and the chairman of the University of Texas Board of Regents. His friendship with Johnson landed the LBJ Library on UT's Austin campus.

At the time of Sharp's summons, the Quorum Club was Austin's "premiere political watering hole," according to a 2006 story in *Time* magazine, "[at a time] when Texas politicians still drank, smoked, and sparred in dark, smoky bars."

Upon Sharp's dictated arrival there, he found Erwin sitting alongside Joseph Wyatt. Sharp knew Wyatt, a University of Texas graduate and Texas state representative from Victoria, near where Sharp had grown up in Placedo.

According to Sharp, Erwin dispensed with the pleasantries.

"After he invited me to join him at his table," Sharp recalls, "Mr. Erwin said to me, 'I can't believe I'm doing this for a damn Aggie.'"

"Doing what?" Sharp asked.

"Joe is going to make a run for Congress, and we want to know if you'd be interested in running for his spot in the Texas House."

Sharp needed no time to consider the offer.

"Yes, sir, Mr. Erwin, I sure am."

By the next night, Sharp had packed up his belongings, put a note on his apartment manager's door, and driven to his parents' home in Placedo, arriving at about 5 a.m.

"What are you doing here?" his parents asked, yawning.

"I have to figure out what I'm going to do for a living," Sharp replied.

His mother and father looked at each other, both surprised and confused. They were under the assumption their son already had a steady job.

"I'm going to be running for the Texas State House District 40 seat," Sharp explained, "so I have to become a resident of the district to run for the office.

"That's why I need to find a new job somewhere around here."

Only then did Sharp's parents take notice that the small fishing boat hitched to the back of his car seemed to contain all his earthly possessions.

The late night meeting at the Quorum Club lead to a "domino effect" of decisions for Sharp. He obtained a real estate license and went into practice in Victoria, satisfying his residency requirements for the district. At the same time, he began putting together his campaign team and making key contacts within the district.

On top of all that, Sharp married his longtime girlfriend, Charlotte Han of Austin.

Three months later, on the first Tuesday of November 1978, Sharp comfortably won a seat in the Texas State House of Representatives at the age of twenty-eight.

Three years later, Sharp moved into the Texas Senate chamber. And in 1986, he won election to the Texas Railroad Commission.

Sharp then continued his political ascent by winning the 1990 Texas state comptroller race. He was reelected in 1994.

It was in that position, as the last Democrat to win a statewide race in Texas, that Sharp would earn a national reputation for austerity and forward thinking, all because he figured out a way to save the Lone Star State from the ignominy of instigating the wildcatter's most irritating impost: the implementation of a Texas state income tax.

Masters of Austerity

In looking for a successor to Chancellor Mike McKinney, the Texas A&M University System Board of Regents pondered all options, including, of course, a nationwide search for top candidates.

Some practical political advice narrowed the regents' thinking.

"I was at an event with Lt. Gov. David Dewhurst," former board of regents chair Richard Box says, "and he told me, 'When you get your new chancellor, you want somebody who can go to Austin and get money from the legislature. You don't want one of these academic types from way over yonder who doesn't know anybody here. You want somebody who understands how things in Texas work.'"

Dewhurst's counsel made sense to Box, and soon the choice was clear.

"John Sharp fit that mold perfectly," Box says. "The fact that we have somebody now that can go to the legislature and knows everybody there by first name . . . is a great advantage for us."

How big an impact has Sharp had on system funding?

In 2019, the Texas legislature approved a record $211 million in appropriations for the Texas A&M University System, which included the following:

- $12.8 million in new research funding for Texas A&M University
- $3.3 million in new money to the Texas A&M Health Science Center, thanks to the growth in Public Health and Nursing programs
- $4 million for West Texas A&M to establish a food-animal production initiative to serve the Panhandle
- $3.6 million for Texas A&M University–Texarkana to create

a "Better East Texas" program in response to the region's
educational, workforce, and health needs
- $3 million to support upper-level coursework at Texas A&M
  University–Central Texas
- $3 million to support the continued expansion of Texas A&M
  University–San Antonio as a four-year institution
- $2.3 million for engineering programs at Texas A&M
  University–Corpus Christi
- $2 million for the Texas Juvenile Crime Prevention Center at
  Prairie View A&M University
- $1.7 million for Texas A&M Engineering Experiment Station's
  workforce training program at the NASA Space Center in
  Houston
- $1.5 million for Texas A&M Engineering Experiment Station's
  Nuclear Power Institute
- $400,000 to restore funding for the Citrus Center at Texas
  A&M University–Kingsville

Sharp's familiarity with decision-makers and influencers in Texas
state government wasn't the only asset he brought into the chancellor's office. As former Texas comptroller of public accounts, Sharp also
brought money-managing experience to the system.

His creation of the Texas Performance Review, which rescued the
state from a near-certain implementation of a state income tax, is
legendary in both political and financial circles.

That title of "comptroller"—sometimes pronounced "controller"—
dates back to the fifteenth century. The word derives from the French
compte, meaning "account," and the Middle English term *countreroller*,
a medieval scribe charged with recording administrative or accounting
records onto a scroll.

As a rule of thumb, states west of the Rocky Mountains call the
position "controller," while states throughout the central and eastern
sections of the country still refer to their chief financial officer as
"comptroller."

The position of Texas comptroller of public accounts was mandated
by the original Texas state constitution. The first person to hold the
office was James B. Shaw, an Irishman born in Dublin who came to
Texas in 1837.

After serving as a private in the Texas army, Shaw became chief clerk of the state's treasury department in 1838 and comptroller a year later.

After spending eight years in the Texas legislature, John Sharp was elected to the Texas Railroad Commission in 1991. The principal duty for the three agency commissioners was, and remains, the regulation of the oil and gas industry within state borders. As chair of the commission, Sharp gained experience vital to him running the state comptroller's office.

Sharp knew that to do that job well, he needed a capable right-hand man.

"After being elected state comptroller, I started asking around about who I needed to pick as my deputy comptroller," Sharp says. "Everyone told me Billy Hamilton would be my best choice. 'He knows more about state government than anyone,' they kept telling me. I knew the name, but I didn't know much about him at the time."

Ultimately, Sharp and Hamilton would become "masters of austerity" in running the comptroller's office.

Billy Hamilton grew up in McGregor, Texas. His father, who also went by the name of Billy, worked as a postal worker. Billy's mother, who went by Willie, raised her two boys—Billy and JD—then went to work for Western Union.

When it came time to choose a college, Hamilton chose Texas Tech. But after two years, he transferred to the University of Texas—"that's where the scholarships were"—and majored in government and economics. He did his graduate work at UT's Lyndon Johnson School of Public Affairs, and a year after receiving his master's degree, Hamilton landed his first job at the Texas comptroller's office, working for Sharp's predecessor, Bob Bullock, who held the position for sixteen years.

"Mr. Bullock was still firing people when I came aboard in 1976," Hamilton says. "Before his arrival as comptroller, nothing was automated; everyone was still functioning in a 'green-eyeshades-and-ledger' manner.

"Within a couple years, the average age in the comptroller's office went from something like forty-five to twenty-nine. Most of us were young and in awe of Mr. Bullock."

And, at the same time, terrified of the man.

"I came into management in the comptroller's office after

Mr. Bullock had stopped drinking," Hamilton says. Bullock eventually succumbed to the ravages of both alcohol and cigarettes when he died in 1999 at the age of sixty-nine.

"He was scary to work for, and if you wanted to see him, you had to be prepared because things could go badly if you weren't," Hamilton says. "But I survived and learned a lot working for him."

Hamilton eventually rose to become deputy comptroller under Bullock. When Bullock announced plans midway through his final term as state comptroller to run for lieutenant governor, Hamilton left the department. He and his wife, Christine, then moved to Washington, DC, not in pursuit of a government job there but to enter the private sector, where he began financial consulting.

"My wife grew up in the Baltimore area, so we decided to move our family back East," Hamilton says. "I went to work for Peat Marwick and made a lot more money than I had working in state government.

"We loved living there, but I hated my job."

The Hamiltons had been in Washington for about two years when Sharp was elected state comptroller. When Sharp initially called Hamilton to see whether he would be interested in getting his old job back, Billy replied, "Yes, but no." While Hamilton was intrigued, he told Sharp his wife's roots were firmly planted among family and new friends.

"I don't think she's going to be interested in moving back to Texas," he told Sharp.

Thus ensued the "yellow-rose" offensive.

"I'm sure the chancellor's version of this story is going to be different from mine," Hamilton chuckles.

Somehow, Sharp convinced Hamilton to fly to Austin to meet with him. This "no-harm-in-having-a-friendly-chat" approach would become one of Sharp's signature calling cards during his tenure as A&M System chancellor.

Of Sharp's vision for the Texas state comptroller's office, Hamilton remembers, "He had big plans. He wanted to take the framework Mr. Bullock had created and do greater things with it."

Hamilton was enthused by what he heard, but upon his return to Washington, he got nowhere in his efforts to change his wife's mind.

About this time, the couple made a trip to California, where Billy had a speaking engagement at a financial conference.

"I had mentioned that to Sharp," Hamilton says of the trip, "so when we got to our room at the hotel, there were five dozen yellow roses waiting for us."

Christine, says her husband, was rendered speechless.

"When we opened the card, it read, 'Come home to Texas, Chris,' and it was signed, 'John Sharp.'"

"What does he think he's doing?" Billy's wife asked, flabbergasted. "This is embarrassing and an invasion of our privacy!"

Sharp's recollection of his courtship of the Hamiltons varies somewhat from his chief financial officer's account.

"I sent [Chris] flowers every day for a month," he begins. "When I found out they were going to San Francisco to think over my offer, we literally filled up their hotel room with yellow roses.

"She asked Billy, 'Is this going to go on for the rest of my life?'" Sharp recalls. "I think she just finally gave up.

"Resistance was futile."

And exceedingly fragrant.

"The smell of all those roses in that tiny hotel room was overwhelming," Hamilton reflects today in his version of the story. "It was so bad, we couldn't sleep at night and finally had to put the flowers on the fire escape outside our window.

"Chris was not amused."

In Hamilton's version of this flowery tale, he points out that he and his wife were not Sharp's first targets to gain an upper hand via "influence by flora." Hamilton says Sharp most infamously applied the gesture by sending a dozen yellow roses to Bullock.

"The legislature was meeting in an auditorium in one of the state office buildings," Hamilton says, "as the capitol was under renovation. As I recall, Bullock, as lieutenant governor, was pushing forward legislation to make the Texas Performance Review permanent. That was something at the time that Sharp and I had worked on for years.

"I was there that day, and when the sergeants at arms brought those flowers into the auditorium and up to the dais where Mr. Bullock was seated, the lieutenant governor got the weirdest look on his face."

After Bullock was handed the card that accompanied the flowers, he stood to address the murmuring assemblage.

"'As for these roses,'" Hamilton recalls Bullock saying, "'they are from the *comp*-troller of public accounts.'"

"'I'm not sure what we did,' Bullock continued, 'that I would deserve such an outpouring of appreciation from Mr. Sharp, but we must have had a good time doing it.'"

Texas' legislative body roared with laughter.

"Mr. Bullock could be pretty funny at times," Hamilton remembers fondly. "And so can Sharp."

Christine Hamilton eventually blessed a return to Texas, giving in to John Sharp's persuasive powers. The Hamiltons returned to the Lone Star State, where Billy accepted the offer to become Sharp's deputy comptroller.

Without question, their greatest success came during their first months in the comptroller's office, creating from scratch what came to be called the Texas Performance Review.

Simply put, they saved Texas from the humiliation of implementing a state income tax.

In a 1987 *New York Times* article about Texas' financial woes at the time, the newspaper cited "the state's rugged free-enterprise image" as the reason Texas politicians had long opposed implementing a state tax on its citizenry. Representative Mike Toomey of Houston, a Republican at a time when the state's political leadership was made up of conservative Democrats, told the *Times*, "Part of Texas's uniqueness is that we haven't got an income tax. It makes us stand out."

Oil has been a boon to the Texas economy since Capt. A. F. Lucas drilled the state's first gusher at Spindletop in 1901. Inevitably, though, what goes up must come down, and according to the *Houston Chronicle*, the petroleum market crash of the mid-1980s was "the downturn against which all others are measured."

A major slump in oil prices that began in 1982 and lasted for the remainder of the decade not only caused numerous companies to fail and countless wildcatters to flounder but also severely affected the Texas state economy. So bad were the times that an ever-increasing number of politicians began to call for a state income tax to help balance the budget.

Then comptroller Bob Bullock, who understood the state's balance sheet better than anyone else, appealed to legislators to implement a state income tax, a stance he retained in his successful run for the Texas lieutenant governor's job in 1990.

"By then," says Hamilton, "when the Texas state legislature began

putting together its biennial budget for the upcoming two years, politicians in Austin found themselves about $4 billion short of what they
needed. They were faced with either massive cuts in spending or
implementing a tax bill."

"I remember when Bullock held his press conference after winning
the lieutenant governor's race," Sharp says. "He was still calling for
implementation of a state income tax.

"Not long after, he called me saying, 'I think you should join me.'

"I told him, 'My whole life has been dedicated to making sure
there isn't ever an income tax in Texas. I think it's just a horrible
idea no matter how much money it raises.'"

Thus was born the Texas Performance Review.

Sharp asked Hamilton to head up the program.

"Success has many fathers, but to a large degree, the concept behind
the Texas Performance Review was Sharp's," says Hamilton. "It wasn't the
easiest of sells, but eventually the legislature passed a bill directing
the comptroller to do a comprehensive review of state government
spending and to make cost-saving recommendations based on that
review."

Hamilton believes many legislators were in favor of Sharp's plan
simply as a way to pass the blame to the comptroller's office when the
measure failed, as many assumed it was destined to do.

Instead—and to the surprise of many—the "masters of austerity" found $4 billion in cost-cutting measures that saved the day and
cemented both Hamilton's and Sharp's financial reputations.

As both men point out today, they simply figured out a way to
make government work better and cost less.

"We basically had no idea what we were going to do when we
started," says Hamilton. "We just took a step into the void with some
degree of confidence that we wouldn't fall into the abyss.

"We had just a few months to conduct this massive review of
the entire state government and formulate a plan to save money.

"It was a helluva ride."

Sharp and Hamilton did not stop there. Also during their run
in the Texas comptroller's office, they orchestrated a Texas School
Performance Review; implemented welfare reform through the Family
Pathfinders program; created the Lone Star Card to overhaul the state's
food-stamp program; launched the Texas Tomorrow Fund, establishing

a prepaid college tuition plan for tens of thousands of families; and oversaw the most successful state lottery start-up in US history.

Sharp served two terms as Texas comptroller. He left the office in 1998 to run for lieutenant governor, losing to his former Aggie classmate Rick Perry in one of the most bitterly contested political races in state history.

One that changed the courses of both men's lives.

Change Agents

Nothing much was at stake in the 1998 Texas lieutenant governor's race except the very heart and soul of the Lone Star State.

With Gov. George W. Bush a shoo-in for reelection and expected to become the next president of the United States, his second-in-command in Austin would become his successor as the state's chief executive. If Republican Rick Perry won the race for lieutenant governor, Bush could be assured of leaving Texas in capable GOP hands. If John Sharp triumphed, Democrats would regain the governor's mansion. Before Bush, Bill Clements had been the only Republican governor of Texas dating back to 1874.

Sharp versus Perry was the political equivalent of Frazier versus Ali. Both men entered the fray with undefeated records at the polls. Their title fight was a brutal one, with both men inflicting punishment on their rival.

A few blows may have been below the belt, but both political pugilists stood standing at the final bell.

Unlike Joe Frazier's victory over Muhammad Ali that March night in Madison Square Garden so many years ago, Sharp versus Perry was anything but a unanimous decision. Perry, the Texas agriculture commissioner, bested Sharp, the Texas state comptroller, by a margin of less than 2 percent of the more than 3.5 million votes cast.

"It was a bitter race and a bitter result for John," says Jere Pederson, a longtime friend and member of Sharp's transition teams in his roles as both Texas state comptroller and chancellor of the Texas A&M University System.

Pederson was a young analyst in the office of the Texas Legislative Budget Board when Sharp joined the staff there. Sharp was fresh out of college and a stint in the US Army Reserve.

"We became friends pretty quickly," Pederson says. "We both had the same sense of humor and got along great."

So much so that when Sharp's apartment, near Town Lake in downtown Austin, flooded, Pederson offered his place as a short-term respite.

"John piled all his belongings into an old boat he had and hitched it to his car and pulled it over to my apartment complex," Pederson recalls. "The week or ten days I had intended for John to stay with me turned into about a year.

"Finally, I had to tell him, 'If we're going to remain friends, you're going to have to find another place to live.' He did, and our friendship endured. When John and Charlotte got married, I was one of his groomsmen."

Pederson remembers Sharp having a very clear idea of the political future he wanted. Each time Sharp ran for office, Pederson volunteered to help his friend in whatever way he could.

While Sharp excelled at being a politician, Pederson found his niche in higher education. He became the chief financial officer at the University of Texas at Dallas, the University of Texas at San Antonio, and ultimately CFO of the University of Texas Medical Branch (UTMB) in Galveston.

When Sharp was elected Texas comptroller, he invited Pederson to serve on his transition team there.

"My bosses within the UT System allowed me to take some time off to help John," Pederson says. "John likes to work with people he knows and trusts. After he became comptroller, I worked as a volunteer heading up his transition team.

"I was one of those that recommended he hire Billy Hamilton as his deputy comptroller," Pederson goes on to say. "As Sharp brought new people in, it became my role to deliver the bad news as we moved people out."

Another of Sharp's new hires in the comptroller's office was Tom Duffy, whose relationship with Sharp also dated back to the Legislative Budget Board.

"I think I was still a student at the University of Texas when I first met John," Duffy says. "When he ran for the state house, I helped a little with his campaign. When he ran for state senate, he brought me on board to be his campaign manager. I continued to work with him through his time in the senate, his term as railroad commissioner, and his eight years as comptroller.

"In each of those jobs, he did some amazing things for the people of Texas."

Although he was hired several months after Sharp took over as Texas state comptroller, Ray Bonilla is another long-standing member of Sharp's inner circle.

Today, Bonilla is general counsel for the Texas A&M University System. He was Sharp's first system hire. "That was part of the deal," Sharp says, referring to the agreement he struck with the system's board of regents that Bonilla would be his right-hand legal advisor the moment he became chancellor.

As a young attorney, Bonilla worked for a time on staff for US Senator Lloyd Bentsen, the Mission, Texas, native who would later make an unsuccessful run for vice president against the Republican ticket of George H. W. Bush and Dan Quayle. Bentsen later became secretary of the treasury in the Clinton administration.

"It was through people I knew in Austin working for Bentsen that I learned about the job in the comptroller's office," Bonilla says. "I didn't know John at the time."

As a new hire, Bonilla did mostly legislative affairs and public policy research work. After about a year and a half, Sharp named Bonilla general counsel of the comptroller's office.

"That was a great job," Bonilla says today. "It was a very interesting mix of law, public policy, and politics."

After Sharp's loss in the Texas lieutenant governor's race, he served out his second term as comptroller and then left politics. He, along with Hamilton, Duffy, and Bonilla, all moved into the private sector. Pederson continued as CFO of the UTMB in Galveston until his retirement in 2006.

While working in the executive ranks of the Dallas-based global tax consulting firm Ryan, LLC, Sharp made another run for lieutenant governor in 2002 but lost again, this time to Republican David Dewhurst, by six percentage points. "In politics today," Dewhurst said at the time, "if you win by four, five, six points, that's a landslide."

Sharp's boss at Ryan, founder Brint Ryan, had served as a member of the Industry/Practitioner Liaison Group within the Texas comptroller's office during Sharp's time there.

Two of Sharp's successors in the comptroller's office also appointed Ryan to advisory positions. Ryan is currently chair of the state's Tax Policy Advisory Board and a member of the University of North Texas System Board of Regents.

After defeating Sharp in the 1998 lieutenant governor's race, Rick Perry indeed became governor of Texas in 2000 and served four terms. Like George W. Bush, he too made a run for president in 2016.

Sharp enjoys taking credit for Rick Perry's political success. After graduating from Texas A&M, Sharp quickly became familiar with the political landscape in Austin. Perry, meanwhile, joined the air force, flying C-130 transport planes. After Perry left the service in 1977, he returned to his hometown of Haskell, Texas, and took up cotton farming with his father.

As Sharp tells the story, he enticed Perry into politics, reaching out in the spring of 1984 to take the measure of his old barracks buddy's interest in a career change.

"The incumbent state rep from District 64, Joe Hanna, had announced he wouldn't be seeking reelection," Sharp says. "I was asked by Clyde Wells, chairman of the A&M Board of Regents at the time, if I knew any Aggies from that part of the state who might be interested in the vacant seat.

"I knew Rick was from Haskell County, a part of District 64, but I had lost track of him.

"I called his mother, whom I had met a few times in college. She told me Rick was back home again working the family farm."

"Have him call me," Sharp told Mrs. Perry. "I've got a business proposition to discuss with him."

When Perry returned Sharp's call, and after the two had caught up after a dozen years, Sharp suggested his college friend consider making a run for the Texas State House of Representatives. Both were conservative Democrats at the time. Democrats held most high-ranking state offices in those days.

Sharp says Perry's response was, "How much does it pay?"

"It pays $600 a month," Sharp told Perry on the phone.

"Really? That's good money." Perry told Sharp. "I'll think about it and get back with you."

Rick Perry is one of a number of former Texas Democrats who changed political affiliation in the 1980s and beyond. That list includes Phil Gramm and Kent Hance.

Perry changed parties to run for Texas agriculture commissioner in September 1989. His opponent was Jim Hightower, the Democratic incumbent. Hightower was a prohibitive favorite, but Perry pulled off the upset.

As a Democrat in the state legislature, Perry became known for his conservative fiscal leanings. "I intend to vote the same convictions," Perry was quoted in a *Texas Tribune* story after announcing his decision to become a Republican. "The only difference is there will be an 'R' now next to my name."

As fellow Aggies, Perry and Sharp eventually put their contentious race for lieutenant governor behind them, but it took a while. As Sharp recalls, atonement came about six years later through a chance encounter between the two men at an Austin gun shop. In 2005, Perry appointed Sharp to the Texas Tax Reform Commission, and in 2007 the two men worked together for the passage of Texas Proposition 15, an effort to beef up the state's support for cancer research.

Sharp considered runs for governor in 2006 and US senator in 2008, but by then, Texas had become a Republican stronghold. Instead, he continued working with Ryan, "making way more money than [he] was worth."

In fact, Perry contacted Sharp to gauge his interest in becoming chancellor of the Texas A&M University System as far back as 2006. Sharp told Perry that it would be difficult for him to leave Ryan.

"I had stock options with the company," Sharp says, "and if I would have left, it would have cost me an insane amount of money."

A&M System Regent Phil Adams remembers a conversation with Governor Perry after Michael McKinney announced his plans to retire as chancellor in mid-2011.

"Rick and I have long been friends," Adams says. "We were in San Diego for a Republican governor's conference, and while riding back to our hotel after a dinner meeting, Rick asked me if we'd begun our search for a new chancellor."

"I thought you wanted Sharp," Adams said to Perry.

"We've already crossed that bridge," Perry responded. "He can't take the job."

Adams told the governor, "That was three years ago. Maybe he's changed his mind. You want me to call him?"

Adams says Perry sat quietly for a moment, and then said, "No, I'll give him a call."

Three or four days later, Adams received a call from the governor. "I talked to John," Perry told Adams. "It looks good. He's available now."

The Texas A&M University System Board of Regents officially appointed Sharp as chancellor in a special "telephonic" meeting on September 6, 2011. At that same time, the regents named Ray Bonilla as the system's general counsel.

"Ray was the first person I talked to about coming over here," Sharp says today. "He's a perfect 'government-type' lawyer. He knows all the tricks of how people use government to slow things down, and he has the ability to speed it along."

"When I got the call, I was quite surprised," Bonilla says, reflecting on his reunion with Sharp. "It didn't take me long to realize he was offering me a pretty plum assignment.

"Working for him here at the system is a lot like it was at the comptroller's office. He has the same kind of zeal now that he had then. It's the same 'cut-straight-to-the-chase' experience."

Bonilla came late to the comptroller's office in 1991, but he was in the thick of the transition process at the A&M System.

As were a trio of other familiar cohorts—Billy Hamilton, Tom Duffy, and Jere Pederson.

"I stayed at the comptroller's office after John left until 2006," Hamilton says, "then I started a consulting practice in Austin. I did pretty well in that job.

"John asked me to come work for him at the system, but just as he couldn't afford to look at the chancellor's job until his stock options vested at Ryan, I was sort of in the same boat: I couldn't afford to go to work for the state again.

"But because I was a consultant, I could lend my time to helping John with the transition, and in many ways, it was a lot like conducting the Texas Performance Review."

Hamilton became a full-time system employee in 2013, serving as both deputy chancellor and chief financial officer.

Jere Pederson remembers his time volunteering with Sharp's system transition team as a very intense period.

"When John told me he expected to be named chancellor, I was a little concerned," Pederson says. "'Are you sure you have the votes?' I asked him, remembering Sharp's heartbreaking losses in his two races to become lieutenant governor."

Sharp assured his friend he did.

Retired from the University of Texas System, Pederson had more unencumbered time to help Sharp transition into his new role as A&M System chancellor.

Both men knew "transition" meant change.

"A big part of our job was evaluating key personnel," Pederson says. "Seeing who should stay and who needed to go."

"We interviewed other chancellors from all over the country," Hamilton adds. "In a way, it was the same 'no-stone-unturned' approach that we had used trying to find ways to save money through the Texas Performance Review."

"When John asked me to be a part of his transition team with the system, I was a little hesitant," Tom Duffy says. "I told him I didn't know much about higher education, but then he reminded me I hadn't known much about oil and gas when I went to work for him at the Railroad Commission.

"As we took a look around the system, and particularly in the chancellor's office, we found a lot of upheaval," Duffy says, "in part because there had been a lot of change, people coming and going.

"It wasn't really a very cohesive organization."

Surrounded by his cadre of trusted advisors, Sharp set to work on reshaping the image of Texas A&M and the Texas A&M University System.

"'I want y'all to look at everything very closely,'" Duffy says Sharp told the group. "'Tell me what y'all think makes sense. If you see something that doesn't make sense, let me know about that.'"

"He's very receptive to new ideas," Bonilla says. "He encourages his people to explore new things, vet them out, and work the due diligence. If the idea is a good one, he'll tell you. If he doesn't think it's going to work, he'll tell you that, too.

"He's definitely not one to let grass grow under his feet."

Pederson agrees.

"John said he was tired of his school taking a back seat to its cross-state rival," Pederson says. "He was intent on planting the A&M flag wherever he could.

"I admire him for how well he's managed to accomplish that."

6

Top Priority

In his formal interview in front of the Texas A&M University System Board of Regents' search committee, John Sharp told the group that if chosen to become chancellor, his first priority would be the establishment of a Texas A&M school of law.

Sharp had been pondering that possibility for a very long time.

"When I was a freshman in the House of Representatives," Sharp says of his first year in the Texas state legislature in 1979, "I discovered that many of my peers had ties to the University of Texas."

"At the time, there weren't a lot of businessmen like me serving in the legislature," Sharp says. He had become a realtor in Victoria, near his hometown of Placedo, to establish residency prior to his run for a seat in the House. "Most people couldn't afford to take time off from work during the four or five months in which the legislature was in session.

"That's why there were so many attorneys as lawmakers. If they worked for a firm, others could pick up their cases while they were in Austin.

"And a lot of those folks were University of Texas law school graduates, and that tended to favor UT when it came to such things as appropriations."

Sharp had the full support of the regents as well as then governor Rick Perry in his bid to become A&M chancellor. In fact, the matter of a law school for their alma mater had been a topic of discussion during the governor's private vetting sessions with Sharp before nominating him for the job.

Texas A&M University's quest for a law school, though, didn't begin with Sharp. In the late 1960s, the flagship made a play to merge with the South Texas College of Law. In fact, A&M has sought to affiliate or merge with the Houston legal school on at least three different occasions.

The institution, now called Texas College of Law Houston, was founded in 1923 as an educational outreach program of the local YMCA. Classes were first held in the basement of the YMCA building in downtown Houston. Since then, the South Texas College of Law has grown into a fully accredited private entity whose good standing has appealed to multiple A&M administrators as a quick way to add a law school to the Aggie realm.

About four years after its first unsuccessful courtship of South Texas College of Law, Texas A&M sought approval from the State College Coordinating Board to create a new law school on its College Station campus. On March 2, 1973—roughly four months after the request was filed—the coordinating board rejected the application.

Houston attorney Leon Jaworski, chair of the coordinating board's advisory committee, said the application was dismissed because there was "simply no need" for another law school in Texas.

In explaining the decision, Jaworski told the Associated Press that several members of his committee admitted to having difficulty keeping "personal prejudice" out of their decision-making process.

By the end of that same year, Jaworski—a product of Baylor School of Law—would be named special prosecutor in the US Department of Justice's investigation of wrongdoing within the administration of Pres. Richard Nixon, otherwise known as the Watergate scandal.

In 1998, a new generation of A&M regents again made overtures toward the South Texas College of Law. A public/private partnership agreement was reached, but the deal was undone as a result of a lawsuit filed by the Texas Higher Education Coordinating Board.

"The politics of that got all messed up," John Sharp remembers today.

The coordinating board took exception with A&M's "end-around" approach in the matter. System regents had not sought approval on the deal from the governing body of Texas higher education that, the courts ruled, was a necessary part of the process.

After winning the lawsuit, the coordinating board rejected the matter outright.

Shortly after he was officially named system chancellor on September 6, 2011—but a couple weeks before he "began getting paid in the job"—Sharp initiated his search for a law school to carry the Texas A&M name.

"The coordinating board had already ruled against us before and still seemed of a mindset that the state had enough law schools," Sharp says today. "That left only the option of us partnering with, merging with, or purchasing outright an existing school of law."

Naturally, South Texas College of Law was the first institution on Sharp's list. But like trying to reignite the affections of a once-spurned lover, the South Texas discussions didn't go very far.

"They weren't interested in our money or our name," Sharp says, "so, those talks lasted about five minutes."

Next on the list of possible candidates was St. Mary's University School of Law in San Antonio.

On the home front, local St. Mary's officials were open and interested in negotiating a merger deal. Those sentiments, however, were not shared at the St. Louis headquarters of the Marianist order of the Catholic Church that owns St. Mary's.

"We had proposed calling the school 'A&M St. Mary's,'" says Sharp. "Our meetings with local school officials had gone very well, so I was surprised when I was told their chancellor wasn't interested."

He continues, "I said, 'Let's go meet with him.'" Sharp is notorious for his "powers of persuasion" in a face-to-face setting. "But they told me that when the chancellor said 'no,' he meant no."

Having been spurned by two prospective partners, and with no interest in building a new school from the ground up, Sharp's quest to create a Texas A&M school of law was quickly narrowed to a single possibility: negotiating an agreement to partner with or purchase outright the Texas Wesleyan School of Law in downtown Fort Worth.

Fred Slaybaugh is president of Texas Wesleyan. He took over as top administrator of the private Methodist school in 2011. Before that, he was dean of the Texas Wesleyan School of Law for three years, from 2003 to 2006. He left that job to run the Harry Truman Scholarship Foundation before returning to Fort Worth in his current role.

As a point of order, Texas Wesleyan's official acronym is TXWES. Texas Women's University goes by TWU.

Slaybaugh says he first learned of Sharp's interest in the TXWES law school from a mutual friend.

"Dee Kelly was the senior partner in the largest law firm in Fort

Worth," Slaybaugh says. "He was chair of my Dean's Advisory Council when I was head of the Texas Wesleyan School of Law, and in that capacity, he and I became good friends. He called me in the spring of 2012 and asked me if I was interested in selling the law school."

Slaybaugh told Kelly the short answer was no.

"I reminded Dee that after TCU [Texas Christian University] lost interest in purchasing our law school in 2003, our board adopted a resolution stating the school was not for sale.

"Dee's response to me was, 'I really think you ought to come meet a friend of mine who's interested in talking with you about it.'"

That friend was John Sharp.

"I agreed to meet with John, and as a couple of 'recovering politicians,' we had a wonderful visit." Slaybaugh had served on the staff of former US senator John Stennis from Mississippi. Slaybaugh later was named an assistant secretary in the Department of Agriculture.

That initial get-together eventually focused on the matter at hand.

"I'll be honest with you, I was quite surprised when John made a very specific financial offer at that first meeting," Slaybaugh says. "Usually when people begin negotiations, they 'low-ball' their offer, but I could tell John was being both honest and straightforward.

"He had clearly done his homework."

In addition to Kelly, Sharp had another insider helping in his pursuit of the TXWES law school. Fort Worth congressional representative and former city mayor Kay Granger, who had attended Texas Wesleyan, was privy to the discussions that had taken place between the TXWES School of Law and TCU. She had told Sharp that TXWES had thrown out a $50 million price tag for the school.

"Kay gave me that information," Sharp says, "because she was a Texas Wesleyan graduate and she wanted to make sure the law school ultimately found a good home. When I told her and Dee we had no plans to move the school from Fort Worth, they got behind our effort."

Slaybaugh took Sharp's offer to the chairman of his board, Kenneth Jones, another Fort Worth attorney.

"I told Kenneth there were storm clouds on the horizon for legal education," Slaybaugh says. "Across the country, tort reform had driven down the number of jobs in the legal profession, and enrollment at law schools was trending down. We were fine at the time, but the national numbers were not encouraging."

Soon after Slaybaugh became TXWES president, he began an initiative called "Rosedale Renaissance." Rosedale Avenue not only borders
the Texas Wesleyan campus in the Polytechnic neighborhood of Fort
Worth, but the street also serves as the main commercial artery for
local residents.

The area, located southeast of downtown Fort Worth, gets its label
from the original name of Texas Wesleyan University: Polytechnic College. The Methodist Church had owned the school since its inception
in 1890, changing the name to Texas Wesleyan University in 1934 after
the financially strapped institution merged with the Texas Wesleyan
Academy in Austin.

Over recent decades, the Polytechnic neighborhood surrounding the TXWES campus has suffered from urban decay, and Slaybaugh saw a need to improve the "perception" of the area to maintain
his school's viability.

"That change became a 'brick-and-mortar' proposition," Slaybaugh
says. "We decided to become the catalyst for economic revitalization
beyond our campus to make the neighborhood a more welcoming
place to live and to go to school."

Potential proceeds from the sale of the law school could help that
initiative. "And they did," Slaybaugh says.

The TXWES board ultimately gave its approval to negotiate a deal
with Texas A&M. With no other options on the table, Sharp insisted
formal discussions with Texas Wesleyan be held in confidence. Just as
Texas A&M's move to the Southeastern Conference had thrown rival
Big 12 schools into a fury, Sharp feared a similar institutional slugfest
with TCU could occur if word of his proposed law school deal became
public knowledge. Thus for nearly a year, only a handful of TXWES
officials were aware of the prospective transaction.

"I've never been through anything quite like that first year when we
were negotiating in secret," Slaybaugh says. "We met surreptitiously,
often at small airports outside of Fort Worth, in our attempt to keep
everything in strictest confidence.

"Frankly, it was a lot of fun."

"John is one of those guys who never gets ruffled," Slaybaugh
continues. "Despite some difficulties in the negotiations, a deal was
finally done."

In fact, the two parties wound up orchestrating two separate deals.

Initially, a joint ownership arrangement was proposed, but when the division of responsibilities proved arduous to agree upon, an outright sale of the school was placed on the table. Complicating that discussion was the matter of framing a sovereign immunity clause protecting the state of Texas if Texas A&M, a state-owned school, was ever held in breach of contract.

Eventually, the two sides reached an agreement, and the announcement of the ownership change came on August 21, 2013.

Joe Spurlock has taught law at what is now the Texas A&M School of Law since the school first opened its doors, which predates not only Texas A&M's ownership of the institution but Texas Wesleyan University's as well. In fact, Spurlock, Texas Aggie Class of 1960, taught the very first class at the Dallas Fort Worth Law School, a nonprofit enterprise started by Texas Wesleyan grad and Fort Worth businessman Robert Harmon.

After graduating from Texas A&M—and before serving four years in the US Army, which included a tour of duty in Vietnam—Spurlock received his law degree from the University of Texas School of Law.

"Pretty much the whole time I've been a practicing attorney, I've also been a teacher of some kind," Spurlock says. "I've taught a wide range of subjects, and Bob Harmon was in one of my business law classes. When he came up with the idea to start a proprietary law school, he approached me about teaching there."

Like many private ventures of its kind, the Dallas Fort Worth School of Law had difficulty obtaining accreditation from the American Bar Association. Spurlock says that is what led to Harmon seeking to find new ownership for the school.

Texas Wesleyan was the only interested party.

For six years, from 1971 to 1977, Joe Spurlock served as a member of the Texas House of Representatives—in his spare time. During Spurlock's second term in the House, he and a group of fellow Aggie lawmakers attempted to push forward a bill to bring the study of law to the Texas A&M campus.

"Billy Clayton, who was also an Aggie, was the Speaker of the House during our 1975 legislative session," Spurlock says. "He led our effort after someone came up with the idea to create an 'LLM' [master of laws] through the oceanography school.

"We thought, if nothing else, maritime law could be taught at A&M.

"Our governor at the time, Dolph Briscoe, who was a big UT alum, was not in favor of our proposed move, so we didn't get very far.

"I decided not to run for reelection after that, and when I applied for a position on Governor Briscoe's staff, during my interview, he asked me, 'We aren't going to have another try at that A&M law school, are we?'

"'Of course not, Governor,' I assured him."

In the end, Sharp succeeded where others had failed.

"We've always drawn well from A&M," Spurlock says of his time on the TXWES law school faculty, "and we've always produced top attorneys at this school, even in the very early days."

Huyen Pham is another member of the Texas A&M School of Law with long-standing ties to the institution. Born in Vietnam, Pham received both her undergraduate and law degrees from Harvard University. She joined the TXWES law school faculty in 2006 when her husband, an economics professor, accepted a position with Baylor University.

"I had no idea A&M was in talks with Texas Wesleyan about the law school until the acquisitions was announced," Pham says. "I was excited about the opportunities that being a part of the TAMU brand offered but also a little apprehensive about how things would shake out.

"As lawyers, we like to look at precedent, but in this case, there were few precedents to consider."

According to Pham, things have worked out well, for both the school and its students.

"The Texas A&M System wants the school to succeed and has invested a lot of money and resources to make us better on all fronts. For our students, the benefits of being part of the A&M network have been enormous.

"Aggies are famously loyal to each other, so our students have been offered wonderful mentoring and employment opportunities as a result."

One of those students is Greg Franklin, a member of the Texas A&M Class of 2003.

"I tell people I took a 'victory lap' before receiving my undergraduate degree in 2004," Franklin says. He studied business at A&M and worked in the financial sector for several years.

"Although the money in that career path was good, sitting in an office manipulating spreadsheets all day was not fulfilling," Franklin says. "I loved being on the debate team in high school and had thought about law school some. Finally, I took my LSAT in 2009, but I didn't send out any applications."

Then, in 2013, things changed for Franklin.

"When I heard that A&M was going to acquire the Texas Wesleyan School of Law, I knew I wanted to be a part of that. So, I applied, got accepted, and within a month after we started classes, they were putting the A&M logo on the front of our building!"

The cutthroat nature of the law school experience served as the focal point for the 1973 movie *The Paper Chase*, based on a novel written by John Jay Osborn. Veteran actor John Houseman won an Academy Award for his role in the movie as Professor Charles Kingsfield.

Personifying that character in the seminal television ad for the investment firm of Smith-Barney, Houseman famously growled, "They make money the old-fashioned way. They earn it."

"My image of law school before I started was that everyone was in it for him- or herself," says Franklin, an African American. "That just wasn't the case in my own experience at the Texas A&M School of Law.

"I had fascinating classmates, wonderful professors, and the best administrators. TAMU Law has integrated the Aggie Core Values"— respect, excellence, loyalty, leadership, integrity, and selfless service— "in a way that makes sense for law students.

"Now that I'm a practicing attorney myself," specializing in construction litigation at the Dallas-based firm of Munsch Hardt, "I still spend time in downtown Fort Worth, encouraging the TAMU Law students there.

"For the students who came from outside Aggieland, I tell them, 'Your undergrad may have your heart, but you should know that A&M will always have your back!'"

Robert Ahdieh was named dean of the Texas A&M School of Law in 2018. He, too, has Ivy League credentials, with an undergrad degree from Princeton and a law degree from Yale. He came to Fort Worth after spending time as an attorney in the US Justice Department and as a member of the faculty at the Emory University School of Law in Atlanta.

Describing the current state of TAMU Law, Ahdieh, who hails from New York City, says the school has come a long way in a short amount of time.

"When I first took over, I told people that in three to five years, we would have students comparable in quality to those attending the law schools at Baylor, SMU [Southern Methodist University], and the University of Houston. I sort of considered those the 'next tier' from where I thought we were at the time.

"But we're already there."

"Let me give you a couple of indicators of where we're going," Ahdieh says. "We're the number one law school in the country in improvement of our reputation among lawyers and judges. And the number two school in that category has gone up by less than half of the rate we have."

TAMU Law is already considered one of the top schools in the study of intellectual property law. And according to Ahdieh, the sky is the limit.

"If the College of Geo-Sciences had invented alchemy," he said, "we would be jumping up and down at that level of achievement. If you look at our law school now, we are inventing 'alchemy' in terms of our students' quality improvements and our faculty-reputation scores.

"The trends we're seeing are almost unbelievable." ·

John Sharp is looking forward to the day—coming soon, he believes—when the Texas legislature will be filled with attorneys whose law school diplomas bear the logo of Texas A&M University.

First Impact

John Sharp's transition team within the chancellor's office of the Texas A&M University System acted very much like the one he put together after assuming the post of Texas comptroller. And for good reason: many of the advisors helping him attend to his new duties were the same trusted and capable individuals he had used in Austin nearly twenty years before.

Sharp knew reshaping the A&M System would require efforts similar to those that enabled him to modify oversight of public accounts for the state of Texas. In fact, the chancellor's transition team quickly saw the need for a "performance review" of the entire Texas A&M University System. The goals: find better ways to do things, save money, and make sure expenditures focused on the system's prime objectives of education and research.

The new chancellor made that message clear to the board of regents.

"Our main job shouldn't be cooking, or mowing the grass, or repairing buildings," Sharp said. "We're here to educate students."

Still, cooking, mowing, and fixing things were essential tasks in keeping a university running smoothly.

Add cleaning to that important mix.

Patricia Walker was born and raised in Bryan, Texas, and has remained close to home her entire life. She has provided custodial services on Texas A&M's flagship campus for more than twenty years. She takes her job seriously and tries to execute her duties with a welcoming smile on her face.

"I love what I do," Walker says. In her twenty years of service, she has gone from working as a custodian to serving as a shift leader.

"A lot of people like to make a good first impression, but I don't believe in that.

"I like to make a 'first impact.' When you come into my building in the morning, I want you to know that my team and I have been there. You're never going to have to wonder if your office is clean.

"I know you'll have a better day because it is."

Walker works in the system headquarters located just a short drive from the flagship's main campus. She has held her position as shift leader for a number of years and has served in that capacity since Sharp took over as chancellor. Like the rest of the system's employees, she made the move to the Moore-Connally Building in 2012 when Sharp relocated his staff from its previous location at the College Station Business Center on the southern outskirts of town.

Walker remembers when she first heard the rumors that the university was considering outsourcing campus services.

"I'm not going to lie. I was nervous," she says. "A lot of people were angry, but I was more fearful than mad because we just didn't know what might happen and whether or not we'd be able to keep our jobs if the move was made."

A painstaking review of operations by Sharp's transition team revealed wasteful management practices throughout campus services. As of 2012, the flagship was losing more than a million dollars a year providing meals to students and faculty. Similar waste was found in groundskeeping, maintenance, and custodial services. Sharp and his transition team believed immediate action was necessary and appropriate.

No one anywhere had attempted to outsource wholesale general services at a school the size of the A&M flagship.

With more than fifty thousand students on the main campus at that time and a budget to rival that of a major corporation, change typically came slowly in College Station. Despite an understanding that there might be a better way to do things, previous university and system administrators had shown little interest in effecting change.

"Those were tough economic times," Sharp says today of the state in which he found the system.

This reality meant tough decisions would have to be made.

When Sharp took over as Texas A&M System chancellor in the fall of 2011, aftershocks from the Great Recession of 2007–9 were still being felt across the country. By 2011, Texas A&M's College Station campus had lost 14 percent of its state appropriations. Sharp had made a commitment to the system board of regents that he would bolster A&M's academic and research standing. He knew—based on his experience administering the Texas Performance Review—that money usually could be found when inefficiencies in processes and procedures were identified.

"The chancellor is very focused on priorities," says Phillip Ray, who today serves as vice chancellor for business affairs for the Texas A&M University System. In 2012, he held the position of associate vice president over procurement and contracting for Pres. Bowen Loftin at the A&M flagship. One of Ray's most noteworthy achievements in that position was converting the main campus from Coke to Pepsi in 2010, severing a sixty-eight-year Aggie relationship with the Coca-Cola Company. The change in vendors generated millions of dollars in revenue for the university.

"I thought they were going to tar and feather me for that one," Ray says today, laughing. "But somehow I survived."

Better than anyone, Ray knew the workings of A&M's general services departments. Another of his key early tasks overseeing procurement was to bolster the university's use of historically underutilized businesses (HUBs) to ensure that small and minority- and women-owned enterprises were given opportunities to secure university contracts.

It was at one of Ray's HUB meetings that he met the system's general counsel, Ray Bonilla.

"At that point, I didn't know anyone in the chancellor's office," Ray says. "I certainly knew who John Sharp was from what he had done as both a legislator and state comptroller. As a financial guy, I sort of considered him and Billy Hamilton to be 'Texas legends.'

"A few months after I met Ray, he told me the chancellor was considering outsourcing some of the facility services at the university to try to both save and make money at the same time.

"He told me, 'We're just bleeding money in those departments, and it appears like we could be looking at another round of layoffs.'

"I told Ray, 'I'll do anything to avoid a layoff. Count me in.'"

Given permission by Loftin to assist in the effort, Ray took up part-time residence in the system's headquarters building. There, Ray began crafting the parameters that would serve as the basis for the system's official privatization proposal requests.

"We worked and we worked and we worked," Ray says, recalling the long hours of due diligence he put in to frame the system's outsourcing efforts. "On more than one occasion, I worked past midnight and found myself locked in the building. Other times, I got there before the cleaning crew.

"Finally, they just gave me a key."

For Ray, privatizing facilities management made perfect business sense, but his passion to ensure the effort was done right—and in the best interest of both the university and its employees—struck a personal chord for him as well.

"I had a son-in-law who worked in the physical plant at A&M at the time," Ray says. "Eventually, word got out that we were investigating the possibility of outsourcing nonacademic positions on campus, and that made a lot of people unhappy.

"Ray Bonilla had assured me the chancellor's number-one priority was that employees didn't get the short end of the stick, and I believed that. I guess it's one of the main reasons I worked so hard in putting together those RFPs [requests for proposal]. I was convinced we were on the right track, and I was determined to get the best deal possible for our employees."

Many evenings, Ray brought his work home—to an anxious audience.

"On a few occasions, I'd come home and find my wife, Janis, and our daughter, Crystal, in tears, telling me they heard that people were going to get laid off. Despite my assurances to the contrary, it was a tough time in our household and for a lot of people who had been a part of the A&M 'family' for many years."

Sharp's office made the announcement that the system would be seeking RFPs for dining services in a press release dated Friday, February 24, 2012. In that release, Sharp stated, "All of us within the A&M System have a responsibility to maximize revenues going to the faculty and their research. They are the reason we are here. Through the RFP process, we have an opportunity for the private sector to examine our support services and potentially generate additional revenues for our academic functions."

That morning a previously scheduled event was held in Rudder Auditorium, at which A&M officials intended to tell potentially affected staff about the upcoming announcement. Unfortunately, word had already hit the street.

"You all deserve our respect and loyalty," A&M's vice president for administration Rodney McClendon told the gathering of more than seven hundred people. "We are regretful of the way the issue was brought to light."

Neither Sharp nor Loftin attended the gathering. It was left to McClendon to deal with an unhappy audience.

"As we consider the proposals," McClendon told the gathering, "our employees, their benefits, and salaries will be kept firmly in mind."

On the following Monday, A&M's campus newspaper, the *Battalion*, ran a front-page story with the headline "Help wanted." Accompanying the piece was a photo of a group of nine custodial workers positioned on the Rudder Auditorium stage behind McClendon, holding a banner that read, "Are We Still Ambassadors?"

As employees of the university, facilities staff considered themselves "ambassadors" and a part of the A&M family.

In the *Battalion* story, written by A&M student Chase Carter—who today, according to his LinkedIn profile, works as the social media editor for the *Dallas Observer*—the unfurling of the sign brought the Rudder crowd to its feet in applause and agreement.

Blanca Pinalez was among those holding the banner. When interviewed by Carter, she asked, "Where was [Sharp] today? Why didn't he speak to us?"

"I want to personally ask Chancellor Sharp," she continued, "[to] answer our questions, hear our voice."

Sharp obliged a month later, generating another front-page *Battalion* story whose headline read, "Sharp end of the stick."

This time, student reporter Justin Mathers penned the story that follows:

John Sharp, chancellor of the Texas A&M University System, faced a hostile crowd of University employees packed into Rudder Theater . . . as he fielded questions about plans to outsource A&M's nonacademic services.

University employees have been up in arms since learning in late February that A&M submitted four separate requests for proposal for University dining, landscaping, custodial, and building-maintenance services.

Critics of the plan maintain that privatization of services will cause a loss of employee benefits and could result in large-scale layoffs. Critics also say that outsourcing jobs to a private company goes against the Aggie family spirit the University attempts to foster.

Sharp told the group, "The private companies we've interviewed as part of the [proposal] process have told us we can switch without having to fire anyone. We put a provision into our proposals which said to the companies, 'You will be judged based on equitable treatment of our employees and on your ability to match our wages and benefits, including health care benefits.'"

Tommy Reid, then an employee in Facility Services, remained skeptical after Sharp's remarks. According to the *Battalion* story, Reid drew a round of applause when he asked Sharp, "In light of the fact the Student Senate disagrees with this measure . . . and the entire Faculty Senate disagrees with this, Mr. Chancellor, how can you sleep at night?"

Ray was among those in attendance at that University Staff Council Forum.

"Even though I was working on putting together the RFPs for privatization, to that point I had not yet met the chancellor," Ray says. "Not many people in the president's office knew I was involved in the project, so I sort of slipped into Rudder Theater late and sat in the back of the room so I could watch and observe."

Ray wasn't the only clandestine witness to the proceedings.

"I remember President Loftin and one of his executive administrators sneaking in, too," Ray says. "Since they were a couple of rows in front of me and it was pretty dark in the back of the theater, I don't think they ever saw me."

"Sharp handled the crowd wonderfully," Ray says today. "The chancellor spoke of his commitment not to study the plan for too lengthy a period of time. If it didn't make sense from the get-go, he promised it wouldn't be done. He handled the dissenters in a very respectful manner. I thought it was great."

But as Ray watched the chancellor deal with the hostilities head-on, he couldn't help but notice that Loftin, sitting nearby, seemed to revel in the heat Sharp was taking.

"You could tell from his body language how he really felt," Ray says. "He was very, very negative against the initiative coming from the system. I had been in President Loftin's executive staff meetings, and I knew how he felt.

"I never really understood why some of the most powerful people on campus were so opposed to what the chancellor was trying to do. He made it clear that if it didn't make sense, that if it didn't protect the employees, he wouldn't do it.

"Why wouldn't you be in favor of that?"

Jeff Haye also attended that meeting. At the time, he was manager for building maintenance, a seven-year A&M employee, and a Texas A&M University graduate.

"I thought it was honorable for Chancellor Sharp to face the dissent and give people a chance to voice their feelings," Haye says. "Like most people, I was apprehensive about the outsourcing. I understood it could turn out for the better, but I also knew it would involve a fair amount of change.

"A number of the maintenance personnel who worked under me were scared about the changes, and a few who were eligible to retire did so."

True to his word, Sharp and his team wasted little time in combing through the outsourcing RFPs. Less than five months after his Rudder Center appearance, Sharp announced the selection of Compass Group USA to manage and operate dining, building maintenance, landscaping, and custodial services on the main campus, an arrangement that still exists today. In announcing the agreement, Sharp's office stated that over the course of the ensuing ten years, the arrangement could produce $260 million in revenue and cost savings for the A&M System, with a projected $125 million in revenue coming from food services alone.

The initial terms of the agreement called for Compass to guarantee the university $52 million in dining commissions over the life of the agreement.

Most significant, of the approximately 1,600 workers affected by the deal, all who wished to retain their positions were guaranteed employment for the length of the contract, as long as they fulfilled the responsibilities of their jobs.

"When the outsourcing took place," Haye says today, "there was a lot of learning that had to happen on both sides. As this was the largest higher education outsourcing ever, there were some unique challenges.

"Serving in a leadership capacity at the time, I witnessed firsthand how SSC [the educational services subsidiary of Compass Group USA] took ownership of their services and improved the work ethic of the associates.

"The outsourcing has been very successful for Texas A&M University and the associates that stayed on through the transition. And as evidenced by client feedback, the level of services has improved dramatically."

At the August 2012 media event that kicked off the new outsourcing agreement, Ray finally met his future boss.

"When John Sharp came off the stage that day, Ray Bonilla pulled him aside and introduced us," Ray says. "I remember the chancellor's face lit up when he realized who I was.

"'Ah, you're the guy,' he said, 'that's been working overtime over here.'

"'Yes sir,' I told him. 'Proud to do it. Thank you for the opportunity.'"

"Well, I appreciate you, too," Sharp told Ray.

Two months later, the two met again.

"His secretary called to set up the meeting," Ray remembers, "and when my wife later asked me what the meeting would be about, I realized I had no idea. So for the rest of the weekend, we were agonizing over whether he was going to give me a pat on the back, fire me, or send me off to some professional purgatory.

"When I walked into his office the next week, the chancellor was sitting with his boots up on his desk, chewing on a big cigar. At the sight, I thought, 'This is going to be really good or really bad.'"

As anyone who has spent time with Chancellor Sharp knows, he is a master at putting his audience, whether one or many, quickly at ease. Ray remembers Sharp spending "maybe ten or fifteen minutes shooting the s—" before getting to the point of the meeting.

"How would you like to come work for me?" Sharp asked, sitting upright with his cigar nestled in an ashtray on his desk. The chancellor has since given up cigars, but he still struggles with his craving for smokeless tobacco. Ray did not have to give Sharp's question a second thought. "Yes!" came his immediate reply.

That night, when he brought the good news home to his wife, Janis, she responded, "That's awesome! What are you going to be doing?"

Ray thought for a moment, then realized, "I don't know." He was shocked that his wife's obvious question had caught him completely off guard.

"We didn't really talk about that," Ray stammered.

"Well, how much are you going to make?"

Ray sat in silence, sheepish as he came to another realization.

"I don't guess I know."

"Well, where are you going to work?" More than a little frustration seeped into Janis's voice.

"In the system building . . . I think," came the unknowing reply.

Incredulous that Ray had let the chancellor sweet-talk him into accepting a new job about which he knew nothing, Janis finally stated the obvious.

"Here you are, the guy who negotiates all these important deals," she said, "and you can't even negotiate the terms of your own employment! Sheesh!"

As his wife turned and walked away, Ray meekly offered, "From what I've been told, if you trust him, and you work hard, and you do a good job, and you stay loyal, and you stay on the team, he'll take care of you."

Ray gave Loftin the obligatory two weeks' notice before starting his new position as chief business development officer for the system. Among the perks built into Ray's incentive package with the system was an opportunity to pursue a pet project from his days as an administrator on the flagship campus. There was one idea Ray felt had definite possibilities, although no one else in President Loftin's office had shown much interest in it.

"Yeah, that was what I called 'Campus Pointe,'" Ray says today. "Chancellor Sharp thought it was a great idea. It eventually became a public-private partnership we called 'Century Square.'"

That sixty-acre mixed-use development, featuring a range of dining, shopping, living, and recreational venues, has become an exciting and successful next-door neighbor to the A&M flagship campus along University Boulevard. (Chapter 12 discusses more about the system's use of public-private partnerships.)

As for Patricia Walker, she is still keeping John Sharp's office clean.

"When they moved to this building eight or nine years ago," Walker says, "they specifically requested that the cleaning crew move along with them. That's fabulous. That's family.

"When you really think about it, that's love."

Walker admits the outsourcing at first threw her for a bit of a loss.

"They promote from within, and I like that," she says. "I miss the teacher retirement program we participated in, but they now have a 401(k) plan. I have good bosses, and I still love my job.

"And every morning when he comes to work, John Sharp greets all of us with a warm 'Good morning!'

"I'm so grateful that he fought so that we could keep our jobs."

"The Mother of All Sabbaticals"

A stroll down the hallway of the Hagler Institute for Advanced Study to the office of its founder and director, Dr. John Junkins, reveals dozens of photographic portraits of distinguished academicians who have chosen to help enrich Texas A&M University's scholarly reputation.

These are the Hagler faculty fellows, and their career achievements, as outlined by Junkins, are impressive, to say the least.

"Jay Dunlap, from Dartmouth, was a member of the first class in 2012," Junkins says while pointing to the first of some seventy photos that line both sides of the hall. "That was before we were known as the Hagler Institute. Dunlap is a geneticist who worries about the biological clock that ticks in every cell of the human body."

It is Junkins's way to use the term "worries" when most would say "studies." In his semantics, to "worry" is to seek solutions, the keystone of the research efforts that the Hagler Institute fosters. Junkins, as an aerospace engineer, "worries" mostly about the challenges inherent to space exploration.

"Here is Peter Liss," Junkins continues, citing the accomplishments of another of the six inaugural faculty fellows of the institute. "He discovered the ozone hole and how to fix it, which earned him the title of Commander of the Order of the British Empire [OBE]."

For those unfamiliar with the ways of the Crown, OBE is one rank below that of a knight.

"Aleda Roth came to A&M from Clemson University," Junkins says, pointing at another of the photos before him. "She's a businessperson who worries about the food chain."

During Roth's stay at Texas A&M, she focused on quality issues in both food and pharmaceuticals imported to the United States from China and other emerging nations, research that has had a meaningful impact on global marketplaces.

Next to Roth's picture hangs the photo of Alan Needleman, a longtime Ivy League researcher whom Junkins describes as a "superstar." He uses that term a lot to describe his ever-growing "family" of prominent scholars.

At Brown University, Needleman served as dean of the engineering department and chair of the applied mechanics division. Like all Hagler fellows, Needleman mixes research prowess with a mentoring spirit.

"After his fellowship here, Alan became a full-time member of the A&M engineering faculty," Junkins says. "He helped start the Department of Material Science and Engineering. He just got a $12 million research grant, so he's more than paid for himself."

Junkins stops in front of the next photo, yet another member of the institute's inaugural class that helped ignite the program's long-term success. "This is Vernon Smith. He invented 'behavioral economics' while a young professor at Purdue University in the 1950s. He expanded his work in that field while at Cal Tech in the 1970s. And in 2002, he won the Nobel Prize."

Still looking at the portrait of Smith, Junkins muses that thanks to the Texas A&M Institute for Advanced Study—since 2016 the Hagler Institute—all the great minds pictured in the hallway to his office have come to Central Texas for the "mother of all sabbaticals."

Junkins recalls using that term to describe to the newly appointed Texas A&M System Chancellor John Sharp his vision for what an institute for advanced studies at Texas A&M could be.

"As I recall, John officially took over the system on a Tuesday in the late summer of 2011," Junkins says, "and I reached out before Friday of that same week."

For more than a decade before that, since 1999, Junkins had tried to convince A&M administrators to bring in the best and the brightest from elsewhere to elevate the university to a position of "national and international leadership in research and scholarship." Not until his meeting with Sharp did Junkins come up with the term "mother of all sabbaticals" to describe his vision.

Typically, in the realm of higher education, a sabbatical is a period of paid leave, often one year for every seven years of on-campus work. In Texas, sabbatical leave for college faculty is usually unpaid time off.

The term derives from the ancient agricultural practice of leaving fields fallow once every seven years to rejuvenate. More recently, the practice in both academia and business enables creative thinkers to recharge their batteries while being given opportunities to travel and explore the formation of new collaborative partnerships.

"Before John Sharp's arrival, I'd pitched this notion of bringing notable faculty to campus several times," Junkins says, "and I always got the same reply: 'Wow, great idea, but too much money.'"

Junkins's plan was to cover expenses as well as pay visiting fellows a salary commensurate with that which they would be leaving behind. In addition, his vision called for providing additional funding for research to be conducted during the fellows' stay on the A&M campus. Junkins insisted that the nomination-and-selection process for these fellowships would come not from the administration but from the faculty itself.

"Turning the 'asylum over to the inmates' was a deal-breaker for some," Junkins says, only half-jokingly.

The original Institute for Advanced Study was founded at Princeton University in 1932, and one of the first two appointments there was given to Albert Einstein. The famed theoretical physicist had first visited the Princeton campus from his homeland of Germany in 1921, both to discuss his world-famous general theory of relativity and to campaign for the establishment of a Jewish homeland.

Shortly after Einstein became a Princeton fellow, Adolph Hitler came to power in Germany. Einstein soon made his move to the United States permanent, becoming a full-time member of the Princeton faculty. He became a US citizen in 1940.

John Junkins's father fought to defeat Hitler's fascism as a young soldier from the Smokey Mountain region of northern Georgia. Upon his return from the war, George Junkins, with only an eighth-grade education, settled in Decatur, Georgia, taking up trade as a machinist.

George and his wife, Lenelle, had five children, and all five of their progeny obtained college degrees.

"They made investments in us that can only be repaid in heaven," John Junkins says of his parents' commitment to a better life for their children. "From our mother, my siblings and I learned how to judge where ethical 'true north' was. Our father helped us develop a strong goal-focused work ethic. Despite living below the poverty line for most of my childhood, ours was a family which enjoyed life to its fullest."

Junkins worked his way through college at Auburn University as a co-op student at NASA's Marshall Space Flight Center in Huntsville, Alabama.

"Eighteen months after graduating from high school, I shook the hand of Werner von Braun," Junkins says of meeting the famed World War II–era German rocket scientist who pioneered the US space program from Marshall.

Junkins attained both his master's and PhD degrees from UCLA while working full time at McDonnell-Douglas Astronautics. From there, he landed a spot on the University of Virginia (UVA) aerospace engineering faculty in 1970. His first research project in Charlottesville analyzed data from the laser altimeter that Apollo astronauts had placed on the surface of the moon.

It was during his time at UVA that Junkins was introduced to the concept of an institute for advanced study.

"Virginia's president at the time was an Elizabethan poet by the name of Edgar Shannon. It was his idea to create this 'advance-study institute' across a range of academic disciplines. It worked beautifully in my observation, as they paired their faculty with top people in a variety of fields. UVA really accelerated during that time frame."

Junkins joined the Texas A&M faculty in 1985 and was awarded the first endowed professorship in the school's College of Engineering. "I became the thirteenth member of the school's small, unranked aerospace department," he says. "Aero has more than tripled in size since then and is now one of the top ten programs in the country.

"Helping to build that department was my great academic passion for years," Junkins adds, "but I wanted my legacy to include doing something more to enhance the reputation of this school."

"I was shocked when he told me he had been trying for years without success to get his idea for this institute going," says John Sharp. "What he told me really resonated with something I was eager to accomplish. I had long wondered why Texas A&M had so few National Academy members on its faculty."

"I think we had maybe twelve or thirteen at the time I took over as chancellor." Sharp continues, "So when Junkins told me he could bring members of the National Academies to campus for these sabbaticals, it sounded like a pretty good idea to me. When I asked him how much money he needed, he said it would take $5 million to get the ball rolling, which seemed doable to me."

Sharp channeled auxiliary university funds under the system's control to the A&M flagship campus to bankroll Junkins's program.

A February 21, 2012, A&M System news release officially announced the new Texas A&M Institute for Advanced Study (TIAS):

The institute provides a mechanism for attracting world-class talent to the university and is driven by nominations of National Academy and Nobel-prize caliber researchers that align with existing strengths and ambitions of the university.

The institute aims to enrich the educational experience and advance research productivity by combining the resources of a major tier-one research institution with distinguished faculty, which will deepen the intellectual climate throughout the state of Texas and beyond.

Alan Needleman is one of several prominent academics whose initial exposure to Aggieland through what has become known as the Hagler Institute was sufficiently impressive for them to become permanent members of the Texas A&M faculty. Ten Hagler Fellows have made that transition.

Originally from Philadelphia and the son of a shoe repair shop owner, Needleman gained admission to the University of Pennsylvania, the Ivy League school based in his hometown, thanks to a "mayor's scholarship."

"Actually, I'm not quite sure how that came about," he says.

After four years at Penn, where he received a bachelor's degree in mechanical engineering, Needleman went on to obtain both his master's and doctoral degrees in engineering from Harvard University. Upon receiving his PhD, he joined the faculty at the Massachusetts Institute of Technology, where he spent five years before moving to Brown.

Needleman is an internationally respected leader in the fields of computational mechanics and computational materials science. For his work, he has been named to both the National Academy of

Engineering and the American Academy of Arts and Sciences. He is also the recipient of the American Society of Mechanical Engineers' Daniel C. Drucker Medal and Timoshenko Medal.

Yet the distinction for which Needleman is most proud is that of being a dutiful grandfather. It was the pull of family that led him to retire from Brown in 2009 and move to Texas with his wife, Wanda, a noted psychologist. Needleman accepted a position on the engineering faculty at the University of North Texas (UNT), where his daughter and son-in-law were both members of the English department.

It was while he was at UNT that Needleman was approached to become a part of Texas A&M's new Institute for Advanced Study.

Fellows of the institute do not apply. Members of the A&M faculty nominate them. Only after being vetted and approved by a faculty committee are future fellows then invited to participate.

"In the first couple years of the program," says Junkins, "I was both popular and unpopular because people would make nominations of individuals who were only 'routinely excellent full professors.'"

Those folks, Junkins says, got routinely rejected.

"It was important to me that we set a high standard for the institute," Junkins continues. "I told our faculty, 'We aren't bringing people here that are "good"; we're bringing people here that are at the elite level of their discipline. And they also have to care about developing people.

"'They need to be serious about their role as mentors.'"

Junkins adds, "We weren't trying to make headlines. We were trying to make a difference and boost the number of really excellent people in this zip code."

"John Junkins is a pretty persuasive individual," Needleman laughs. "Before I came to Texas A&M as a fellow, I already knew people on the faculty: Dimitris Lagoudas [senior associate dean of the College of Engineering] and Ramesh Talreja [aerospace engineering professor]. Ramesh and I had worked together in Denmark. But after I got here, I realized Texas A&M is home to a lot of interesting people."

During his initial six-month stay in College Station, Needleman collaborated on research with young A&M faculty in aerospace engineering, mechanical engineering, and electrical and computer engineering. As significantly, he enjoyed the culture and camaraderie he found at the school.

"That's really part of what lured me back when I was offered a full-time position here in 2015," Needleman says. "John Junkins and his wife, Elouise, are very special people. They do a terrific job making Hagler fellows feel welcome here."

When Needleman was offered his full-time appointment at A&M, he had his pick of departments within the College of Engineering. He chose the newly created material science and engineering department because he wanted to help shape the culture of the organization.

The success Needleman has had in that endeavor is evident in a six-foot-long panoramic photos. that hangs in the hallway a few doors down from his office in the Reed-McDonald Building on the main campus. It is a group shot of attendees at the department's 2019 annual picnic. A satisfied-looking Needleman is in the middle of a very large group of smiling faces—both young and old.

Needleman also continues to support the Hagler Institute enthusiastically. He is a major donor to the program's Legacy Society.

"There are a few of us who make it a point every semester to have dinner with the new class of Hagler fellows," Needleman says. "We ask each of the invited attendees to bring with them someone younger with whom they've interacted. Thus we've had a good number of students who have attended in the three or four years we've been doing this.

"One year, one of our attendees was David Lee, the prominent member of the A&M physics department who is a Nobel Prize winner. For a student to be able to have dinner with someone like that makes a real impression. That sort of thing not only develops a sense of community, but it spreads the 'tentacles' of the institute to individuals who are not necessarily associated with it."

The early success of the TIAS quickly led to the establishment of the Chancellor's Research Initiative (CRI). At the time of its launch in the late summer of 2012, Chancellor Sharp committed $100 million to help attract new faculty members, who were National Academy members, to both the Texas A&M flagship campus in College Station and Prairie View A&M University.

The program provided more than $30 million in funding for new faculty each of its first three years, from 2013 to 2015, and continues today.

"We have some of the best universities in the country," Sharp said of the entirety of the A&M System when he made the CRI announcement, "and we want to attract exceptional faculty members who will have a transformative impact upon the academic and research missions of Texas A&M and Prairie View A&M. I envision that these talented candidates will also attract additional research dollars for their work at our universities."

In 2011, when Sharp conceived of the CRI, Texas A&M had only thirteen National Academy members. The program has more than tripled that number, which in turn fueled an increase in research dollars.

The Texas A&M University System today has passed the $1 billion mark in research funding, thanks in large part to the CRI and the Texas Governor's University Research Initiative (GURI). The GURI program, which was modeled after the A&M System's CRI endeavor, also provides millions of dollars toward statewide university research endeavors.

A disproportionate amount of the governor's funds has wound up at A&M System schools, in part because of the system's commitment to adding elite academicians.

Another major contributor to the TIAS is Jon L. Hagler, the namesake for the Hagler Institute.

A native of La Grange, Texas, Hagler is a member of the A&M Class of '58. During his undergraduate years, he served as student commander of the Corps of Cadets and as a member of the Corps' Ross Volunteers, and he was named outstanding junior cadet. After receiving a graduate degree from Harvard in 1963, Hagler achieved business success in the financial industry. The Texas A&M Foundation's headquarters building on the A&M main campus also bears his name in recognition of his sizable contributions to the university.

In 2017, Hagler made a $20 million gift to the TIAS, thus becoming its namesake, too. He has been a member of the institute's external advisory board since that program was launched. The institute's annual report features a quote from Hagler: "I don't understand why we wouldn't demand the very best of ourselves. I mean . . . why not?"

"I've never explicitly asked anyone to write a check," Junkins says of the financial state of the organization he founded and continues to guide, "however, I suppose I've implicitly done so on occasion.

"As a member of our board, Jon came into my office one day and said, 'I want to talk about your budget.' I told him that while the institute was going great, its capital campaign was struggling. He looked at me and said, 'That's really disturbing.'

"'Why is that disturbing?' I asked him.

"'Because the $20 million I'm intending to give to you doesn't sound like it will be enough.'"

Junkins chuckles at the way Hagler informed him of his intended gift. Other sizable endowments and contributions have given the institute stability and the means to continue to attract the world's best academic minds to Texas A&M.

John Junkins is grateful for the support.

"I came here in 1985 at the age of forty-two, and my research has been fertilized by people's life savings," Junkins says. "I've held a sequence of endowed chairs, and once, when I did the math, I realized that if I gave everything I've got and everything I'll ever have, I could not repay the debt owed on the investment that others have made for me to do what I've done."

The Hagler Institute for Advanced Study is one way Junkins is helping to express his gratitude, both to Texas A&M and to those who invest in it.

"When I first met with the chancellor, I told him that I had already arranged for my estate to go to the institute after I was gone. The importance of the idea, not just to me but to the university as well, meant that much to me at the time, and it still does. I guess I've been able to spread that passion to others in the ensuing years."

"This is a great success story," Junkins adds. "I've worked hard, but so have lots of other people. In the end, though, it wouldn't be where it is today without the support of both Jon Hagler and John Sharp."

A Daughter of the Cumberland

Just four weeks after John Sharp officially became chancellor of the Texas A&M University System, another key hire was made on the flagship campus in College Station.

M. Katherine Banks was named dean of the Texas A&M College of Engineering and a vice chancellor for the A&M System. Previously, Banks had served as head of the civil engineering department at Purdue University in West Lafayette, Indiana. In that post, she had oversight of roughly one thousand students and nearly sixty faculty members. At A&M, enrollment in the College of Engineering at the time of Banks's hiring numbered nearly eleven thousand students, with more than four hundred tenured and tenure-track faculty.

In addition, as a vice chancellor of the A&M System, Banks would serve as director of the Texas A&M Engineering Experiment Station and administer two other state agencies: the Texas A&M Engineering Extension Service and the Texas A&M Transportation Institute.

Of the challenges presented by her multiple new duties at Texas A&M, Banks said at the time her hiring was announced, "My husband and I have six children, so we're used to the chaos."

Today, Banks says she was intrigued but also a little ambivalent when word reached her about the dean's job at A&M.

"I had been head of the civil engineering department at Purdue for six years, and I was ready for a change," she says. "I had a Fulbright grant lined up in Spain and was excited about that. When I saw the ad for the A&M job, I called the only person I knew there at the time, Robin Autenrieth." Today Autenrieth is head of A&M's Zachry Department of Civil and Environment Engineering and a valued colleague of Banks. "I told Robin I couldn't quite figure out if this was a dean's position or not, there were so many different components in the job description.

"She said, 'Well, it's pretty complicated.' That got my attention. 'Sounds interesting,' I told her.

"'It's a very difficult job,' she replied. 'You wear a lot of hats. I don't think you'd want it.'

"'I don't know,' I said. 'I'll take a look at it.'"

To know Banks is to understand she is always up for a challenge, as evidenced by the extraordinary list of her achievements at Texas A&M. After further discussion with Autenrieth, Banks decided to submit her application for the A&M engineering job. "My airport interview went really well," she says.

"Airport interviews" have become *de rigueur* in the selection of academic administrators from a nationwide pool of candidates. Applicants are flown into airports near the universities to which they are applying, and confidential meetings are conducted at the airport sites. Often, airport interviews are held sequentially on the same day, or on consecutive days, giving search committees an opportunity to meet multiple candidates in person.

As to what Banks thinks set her apart in that first interview, she says, "I think I was successful in helping them appreciate my fundraising skills." An inspection of the new home of A&M Engineering, the Zachry Engineering Education Complex, opened in 2018, provides tangible proof of Banks's ability to get things done—and paid for.

Ultimately, the committee seeking A&M's new engineering dean narrowed the list of candidates to four. At about the same time, a board of regents search committee was completing its courtship of John Sharp to become the system's new chancellor. Ultimately, the regents would have the final vote on the hiring of the flagship's new engineering dean, but a faculty committee would have a significant say in that selection.

Rival camps for candidates pursuing the engineering position emerged. One group supported Banks, who had spent her entire career as an academic. Another, which included prominent former students and a cadre of regents, favored Stephen Holditch, then head of A&M's petroleum engineering department.

Holditch, who died in the summer of 2019, was a lifelong Aggie. A member of the Class of '69, he went to work in the oil business after graduation. He eventually took a leave of absence from a job in Houston with Shell Oil to pursue his PhD at Texas A&M. Upon obtaining his doctorate, Holditch left Shell and joined the engineering faculty at A&M. At the same time, he established his own consulting firm in the Bryan / College Station area.

He became successful in both pursuits.

As an academic, Holditch was elected to the National Academy of Engineering in 1995. Two years later, his company was purchased by oil-industry giant Schlumberger and was transformed into Holditch Reservoir Technologies, with the founder retained as an advisor.

The A&M engineering dean's job opened when G. Kemble Bennett, a popular and personable administrator known to all as "Kem," stepped down after nine years in the position. Upon his departure in the summer of 2011, Bennett admitted, "Resources are not at the level we've had in the past, and there's no question cuts are going to have an impact. But I think the overall trajectory of the college remains up."

With the aftereffects of the Great Recession still being felt, tenured faculty members across the Texas A&M campus were in revolt over measures handed down by the system board of regents to "modernize" and economize how the university conducted its academic business.

Managing the state through lean financial times, Gov. Rick Perry had become a strong proponent of reforms recommended by the Texas Public Policy Foundation called the "seven breakthrough solutions," which, in essence, sought to hold institutions of higher learning—and their faculty—to the same standards of financial accountability as those imposed by the free enterprise system. Included in the reforms was a recommended cost-benefit analysis of instructors.

Then A&M System chancellor Mike McKinney, Rick Perry's former chief of staff, ultimately lost favor among the flagship faculty for his support of the measures, which generated a "no-confidence" vote in his performance from the A&M faculty senate.

McKinney's struggles to manage the system through the global economic downturn played a significant part in his resignation as chancellor in mid-2011.

The question of Banks versus Holditch ultimately boiled down to which candidate to replace Bennett as dean could most effectively improve the Engineering College's economic well-being.

Regent Phil Adams was a staunch Holditch supporter.

"There were several of us on the board of regents then who supported Steve," Adams says today. "When I moved my office to the Metro Center in the early 1980s, Holditch's consulting firm took up half the second floor. He had fifty or sixty employees. Many of them were petroleum engineers and geologists, highly paid professionals who were doing a lot of important research. He had tremendous ties to the energy industry, and I thought that would be a real financial plus for A&M. Steve Holditch and George Mitchell were the Godfathers of fracking and secondary recovery."

"I had a very high regard for him," Adams adds. "My mind was made up. I didn't give Kathy Banks a chance."

Adams was also a strong supporter of John Sharp as A&M System chancellor, but when Sharp took over, the new chancellor quickly chose to back Banks.

"She was the first major hire I was involved in as chancellor," Sharp says. "I wasn't a part of the search committee, but the first time I met her, I knew she was the kind of person that I like to deal with. She has big ideas. I would much rather work with people who I have to pull the reigns back on than ones I have to spur."

Banks remembers her first meeting with Sharp as well.

"After we spent a little time getting acquainted, he told me, simply, 'Do great things.' He took a big risk on me," Banks says.

On her first meeting with Sharp after she was hired, the new chancellor presented her two dozen yellow roses in his office.

It's what he does.

"I remember thinking," Banks says, "'This is going to be a different type of job because I can already tell this is a different kind of place.'"

With the support of Sharp and the flagship's top two administrators at the time, Pres. Bowen Loftin and Provost Karen Watson, Banks got the job. Her first task as she assumed the engineering helm in early 2012 was to win over those in a position of influence who had opposed her hiring.

Regent Adams was at the top of that list.

"Phil is the consummate Texas gentleman," Banks says, "and he's passionate about what he believes in. Even though he may have been disappointed that I got the job, he did finally agree to meet with me.

"He didn't really know me at the time, and so I sought to find common ground between us. That turned out to be my grandfather, who in his time shared the same staunchly conservative political leanings as Phil.

"I told Phil, 'After my grandmother died when I was a teenager living in the small coal-mining town of Whitesburg, Kentucky, I would regularly clean house for my grandfather. I spent a lot of time with my grandparents growing up, so I felt it my duty to help take care of him.

"'At the end of the tiny living room in his home was a chair, and above that chair he had two pictures hung side by side. One picture was a depiction of Jesus Christ. The other was a photograph of then California governor Ronald Reagan.

"'I asked my grandfather, "Papaw, don't you think that Jesus should be higher than Reagan?"

"'"They're fine the way they are," came my grandfather's reply.'

"Phil loved that story," Banks says.

"I give her a lot of credit for trying to meet with me after she got the job," Adams says today. "If I'd been in her position, I don't think I would have been as understanding and patient in attempting to bring me around to her side.

"I try not to be mean, or stubborn, or anything like that, but her office had contacted me two or three times, and I didn't return the calls. I just didn't think she was the right choice as our engineering dean.

"The calls kept coming, so finally I agreed to meet with her."

That meeting took place in a small private room in the Clayton Williams Alumni Center. Sharp had repeatedly assured Adams, "This woman thinks like we do."

"I had marked off thirty minutes on my calendar for the meeting and had other places I was going to be after that," Adams recalls. "But after spending just five minutes with Kathy, I didn't want to let her go. She was extraordinary. She had the same concept of value creation that I did.

"I knew right then and there that she'd be good in business. She could run a company if she so desired. And I knew she was going to make a helluva dean for our school."

In fact, it was the entrepreneurial savvy Banks picked up from her grandparents that not only helped her win Adams over but also served her well in steering a new course for the A&M College of Engineering.

Her accomplishments, both before and after her arrival at Texas A&M, are made even more remarkable considering she is a product of one of America's most economically challenged areas:

> The Cumberland Plateau region of Kentucky is a serrated upland in the eastern and southeastern part of the state. The plateau's half million inhabitants are among the earth's most interesting folk. Their European ancestry and American adventures constitute a remarkable page in the history of mankind.
>
> Much of the region's story is the story of coal. Coal has always cursed the land in which it lies. When men begin to wrest it from the earth it leaves a legacy of foul streams, hideous slag heaps and polluted air. It peoples this transformed land with blind and crippled men and with widows and orphans.
>
> But the tragedy of the Kentucky mountains transcends the tragedy of coal. It is compounded of Indian wars, civil war and intestine feuds, of layered hatreds and of violent death.

Harry Caudill was a Whitesburg, Kentucky, attorney and state legislator when he wrote the words above in the introduction to his book *Night Comes to the Cumberland*, published in 1963. The book gained national attention and prompted Pres. John Kennedy to create a commission to study conditions in the Appalachian and Cumberland regions. Ultimately, billions of dollars in aid poured into the area over the next twenty-five years.

Margaret Katherine Banks was a three-year-old living in Whitesburg when Caudill's book took the country by storm. Kathy was daughter to Estill and Peggy Banks, sister to Estill II and Darrin, and granddaughter to Lucky and Kathryn Banks.

Kathy Banks remembers, too, her great-grandmother—Lucky's mother—Celia Ann Adams Banks, whom everyone called "Ma." The woman's "rebel spirit," as Banks calls it, served to inspire and shape the future A&M engineering dean.

"Ma chewed tobacco, wore a sun bonnet, and took no nonsense from anyone," Banks says fondly. "She was awesome!

"My grandfather was third or fourth among a brood of ten or twelve of Ma's kids."

In those days in a place like Whitesburg, there were few doctors or hospitals, and only an informal way of adding children to the local census. Thus there was no real rush in naming a child.

"As I recall," Banks says, "my grandfather was two or three years old before his mother finally named him. She just called him 'Baby' until the next baby came along.

"The story my great-grandmother told me was that she had a dream one night. Like almost everyone else in that part of Appalachia, she was very much into 'folklore,' and in her dream, a bird came to her and whispered in her ear, 'If you name your child "Lucky," he always will be.'"

The good fortune implicit in her grandfather's eventual given name followed her own father's fortunes, which, she says, proved pivotal in her own life.

"My grandparents wound up having just one child," Banks says, "and later in my own father's life, being an only child of two hardworking individuals gave him an edge."

Lucky sent his son to college, a rare occurrence in a place like Whitesburg. Estill Banks graduated from Eastern Kentucky University in Richmond. Afterward, he met and married Kathy's mother, Peggy, who was a graduate of a two-year nursing school. The young couple settled in Whitesburg.

"The pull of that place is strong," Kathy Banks says today.

Her grandfather, Lucky, had quit school after just the third grade to work and support his family. He was a true entrepreneur from a very early age with a "never-give-up" mentality. Lucky began selling fruit from the roadside and then sold coal mined by hand. He eventually grew that little enterprise into a small but successful mining business of his own. Kathy's grandmother, whose schooling ended after the sixth grade, also possessed an entrepreneurial knack and eventually launched a small general store.

Her grandparents' work ethic and business savvy influenced young Kathy's own life. Banks loved spending time with her grandparents at the mouth of the hollow—or "holler," as she still calls it—where her grandmother's store was located.

As for what differentiates a "holler" from a hollow, one needs go no further in an online search for explanation than Whitesburg's own weekly newspaper, the *Mountain Eagle*.

According to *Eagle* staffer Jim Cornett, a hollow is a depression between two mountains, not big enough to be called a "valley." A "holler," on the other hand, symbolizes a way of life.

"A holler has a head and a mouth," Cornett writes. "The head is as far as you can go, and the mouth is where the creek runs into a larger stream of water. A holler [has] houses spaced out on both sides of the road. You can 'holler' from one house to the other to tell the latest news.

"A holler may have a small grocery store at its mouth"—like the one Banks's grandparents owned—"and if you see someone walking to the store, give them some money and your list and they will bring your groceries back with them."

"The further up the holler you lived, the poorer you were," says Banks today. "I began working at my grandmother's store when I was about six years old, stocking shelves, running the register, and when I was old enough to understand the basics of accounting, I also kept the books.

"When the poorest of our customers didn't have enough money to pay their bills, my grandmother would give me a discreet nod indicating for me not to write down their bread-and-milk purchases in the credit ledger we kept."

Generosity and compassion of that kind were the accepted way of life in the holler that helped shape Banks's future.

"It was that sense of community I experienced growing up that had a profound impact on me," Banks says. "I've never lost my passion for helping those who have not had the advantages of others."

As for her own formal schooling growing up in Whitesburg, Banks admits it was substandard and adhered to the cultural norms of the region.

"I took a chemistry class in which the teacher never actually taught us any chemistry," she says. "My high school physics class was mostly boys. Girls were expected to take home economics, but I was determined to know and understand physics."

"From a young age, I've been stubborn and persistent," Banks reveals. "I don't quit."

After high school, Banks says she "floated" for a time, not really knowing what she wanted to do. She enrolled at nearby Berea College but realized that staying close to home as her grandparents and parents had done wasn't going to lead to the life she wanted for herself.

"I had a friend in Gainesville, Florida, so on a whim, I decided to move there. I didn't tell many people that I was going because I knew most folks would try to talk me out of leaving Whitesburg."

Once she reached and settled into her new surroundings—Gainesville is home to the University of Florida—Banks went to work at a drug store stocking shelves. New friends advised her she could take classes, if she wanted, at the college without enrolling full time.

"I didn't have any type of academic background that would get me into that school now," says Banks, who was named to the National Academy of Engineering in 2014. "The University of Florida accepted almost everyone when I started taking classes there because it was a land grant school.

"Thank the Lord we have schools like that, places for people like I was, where an education is accessible."

Banks eventually earned a bachelor of science degree in engineering from Florida. As for why she chose that field of study, Banks says she was influenced by what she learned in an exercise class in Gainesville.

"A friend of mine told me she was in engineering," Banks says. "I asked her, 'So, what do engineers do?' When she told me, I remember thinking, 'That sounds cool.' I liked physics in high school, so I decided to enroll in a second-level engineering physics class. They told me I needed the first-level engineering class before I could take the second, but I ignored that and took both classes at the same time and did well in both.

"I guess that's when I knew I was in the right place."

Banks received her engineering master's degree from the University of North Carolina and her PhD in civil and environmental engineering from Duke University. Since then, she has been a member of the engineering faculty at three land grant schools: Kansas State, Purdue, and, since 2011, Texas A&M University.

When she arrived in College Station to lead the A&M College of Engineering, Banks was struck by the number of qualified applicants—more than three thousand—being turned away from the school each year. When she learned of the college's historic "cap" on enrollment, Banks felt that was a pathway to failure. Her commitment to A&M's land grant mission motivated Banks to find a way to provide engineering education to as many qualified students as possible. She came up with a radical plan to do so, which eventually became known as the 25-by-25 initiative, which established a target of twenty-five thousand engineering students at Texas A&M by the year 2025.

To achieve that objective, Banks committed to three guiding principles: to transform A&M's educational experience, to increase access to an engineering education, and to deliver an affordable engineering education to all.

Nobody thought diluting the college's limited physical resources to accommodate her proposed influx of students was a good idea. Banks says the thinking at the time was, "You need money to enhance infrastructure, then you can go after more students."

Instead, Banks took a *Field of Dreams* approach: "If you build it, they will come."

Her college did not have the money to build "it" at the time, but she knew where she could come up with the funding. Thinking more like a businessperson than an academic does, Banks realized the formula for success was both simple and straightforward.

More students meant more tuition dollars. She also believed that big ideas generated more alumni donations.

When Banks shared her vision with Chancellor Sharp, he was pleased. From his days as Texas state comptroller, Sharp knew all about creative ways of finding money.

"Can you do it?" he asked.

"I think I can," she replied.

As of 2020, A&M's engineering enrollment has nearly doubled under Banks's leadership. Of the more than twenty-one thousand students pursuing engineering degrees, about one in four at the flagship, are the first in their families to attend college. Some of those students, doubters continue to say, lack adequate preparation to compete either academically or professionally.

And that's okay with Banks. She has been down that road herself.

In 2019, Banks received the prestigious Pinnacle Award, presented by Schlumberger Limited for her dedication to future engineers. That passion has not only spurred a growth in engineering enrollment at A&M but also fueled her other notable accomplishments.

Under her watch, A&M has entrenched itself among the top-ten public engineering schools in the country. Her faculty has grown commensurately in both size and reputation. She has added top-flight academics and created "professors of practice," faculty members who have come to A&M directly from the private sector with valuable perspectives from outside academia.

Banks in 2016 created the EnMed program, as in Engineering Medicine, and located it in Houston adjacent to the world-famous Texas Medical Center. An engineering-based medical school, EnMed requires all students to have completed their undergraduate degree in engineering or computer sciences. Students will begin their dual-degree program to obtain both an MD degree and an MS in engineering. The future of medicine, the reasoning goes, is in developing technology for medical purposes.

Banks did not rest on her laurels. In 2018, she led the A&M System's successful bid to manage the Los Alamos National Laboratory, home to the US nuclear arsenal. She also spearheaded a joint $200 million initiative between the system, the state of Texas, and the US Army to create the George H. W. Bush Combat Development Complex at the system's RELLIS Campus in Bryan. Work done there on behalf of the Army Futures Command will help modernize the nation's military capabilities.

Under Banks's leadership, A&M engineering also has a new home: the Zachry Engineering Education Complex located on the north side of campus at the corner of University and Bizzell. The building contains unprecedented use of design and technology to support student learning. It also houses one of the most impressive art installations on any college campus in the country.

"Some of our students have never had the opportunity to experience real art," Banks says. "They came to engineering because it's a way to land a job.

"I feel like it's my responsibility to ensure that those students have a quality education, and that means helping them become well-rounded people. They're not well-rounded people if they don't have a chance to experience all parts of the university environment.

"And they won't be good engineers if they don't understand the creative process. Artists go through the same creative steps as engineers do. One of the best examples of how art is important to engineering design is something students use constantly: their iPhone."

The Zachry building's art collection features technology-based installations by artists from around the globe. Each piece reflects "the interdisciplinary fields of engineering," according to the Zachry Complex website.

One of Banks's favorite pieces sits on opposite ends of the lawn adjacent to the Zachry Complex. It's called *How to Build a Sphere Out of Cubes* and was created by German sculptor Olafur Eliasson. The work includes both a human-sized cube of brushed stainless steel and a larger sphere comprising dozens of the cubes.

Banks sees a little of herself and a great deal of her mission as an educator in that work.

"The individual cube symbolizes each of the new students who arrives on our campus," she says. "Our job as educators is to help them coalesce into becoming a part of something larger than themselves."

There is another way to look at the piece that reflects Banks's commitment to first-generation students whose families have entrusted Texas A&M to guide their sons and daughters to productive lives: the physical separation between the individual and the collective.

"I have to work on my disdain for those who like to isolate themselves because they feel superior to others due to perceived intellect or past experiences not available to most," Banks says. "I have no patience for that.

"I think people here would tell you that my interest in mentoring students as they move through our engineering curricula is to first and foremost make sure that everyone feels welcome. My desire to ensure that we have programs that will support those who may not have had the 'advantages' enjoyed by others comes from the sense of community that I experienced growing up in Kentucky.

"I want everyone who studies engineering at Texas A&M to feel welcome—no matter where they come from, no matter if they grew up in a small town in West Texas or in the middle of Houston. It doesn't matter. Everyone deserves to have the same level of respect, the same opportunity, the same empathy. If you give people that, they will be successful on their own.

"And this is the ethos of Texas A&M. Aggieland is a special place not only because of great engineering and academics but because of our unique culture and traditions that translate into caring for fellow Aggies. It is hard to describe but important to keep."

A "daughter of the Cumberland," Kathy Banks has come a long, long way thanks in large part to the heritage she holds so dear.

She became the 26th president of Texas A&M University on June 1, 2021.

Rebranding

Even before John Sharp officially took over as chancellor of the Texas A&M University System in the late summer of 2011, he noticed a few things that needed to be changed.

Near the top of that list was to ensure that an Aggie's good deed was recognized.

Like most Texans, Sharp kept close tabs on the wildfires that consumed millions of acres of Texas grasslands during the spring and summer of 2011. He read newspaper accounts about how the Texas Forest Service was engaged in containment efforts all across the state. He watched televised coverage of the search-and-rescue efforts by Texas Task Force 1. He followed online reporting of the work that the Texas AgriLife Extension Service was conducting to manage the well-being of livestock on ranches consumed by flames.

"I saw all the press reports on how the agencies embedded within the A&M System were doing all this good work," says Sharp today, "and nobody knew, except us, that it was a bunch of Aggies who were leading all these life- and property-saving efforts."

To Sharp, that made no sense.

"It's Politics 101," says the man who spent more than twenty years in Texas state politics. "If you want somebody to vote for you, you get your name out there with everything good that you do. The system needed to be doing the same thing. We were doing all this great work, putting out fires and rescuing people, but nobody knew it was the work of the Texas A&M University System's state agencies."

"The goodwill that comes from service to our state and its residents translates into good feelings within the Texas state legislature, where people appropriate money," Sharp adds. "We're here to serve the public. We'd like people to know what we're doing with their tax dollars, particularly when we're doing so much good."

Sharp had another reason to put the A&M brand on the universities in the A&M System: peer rankings. "If your peers haven't heard of you, that's a problem."

The rebranding began in August 2012, nearly a year after Sharp assumed the helm of the A&M System, and began paying dividends quickly. "Our Google hits increased dramatically overnight," Sharp says. By the time Sharp was done, almost every institution included "A&M" in its name:

Prairie View A&M University

Texas A&M AgriLife Extension Service

Texas A&M AgriLife Research

Texas A&M College of Dentistry (formerly Baylor College of Dentistry)

Texas A&M Engineering Experiment Station (TEES)

Texas A&M Engineering Extension Service (TEEX)

Texas A&M Forest Service

Texas A&M International University

Texas A&M Transportation Institute (TTI)

Texas A&M University–Central Texas

Texas A&M University–Commerce

Texas A&M University–Corpus Christi

Texas A&M University–Kingsville

Texas A&M University–San Antonio

Texas A&M Veterinary Medical Diagnostic Laboratory

West Texas A&M University

Texas Task Force 1, which had acquitted itself to presidential acclaim in its service at Ground Zero following the 9/11 attacks, was left unaffected by the name changes at that time, but in 2019, the agency became known as Texas A&M Task Force 1.

The only institutions to escape the A&M brand—at least so far—are

Tarleton State University in Stephenville and the Texas Division of Emergency Management, which the legislature transferred in 2019 to the A&M System, after Hurricane Harvey.

Even though RELLIS, the 2,100-acre campus and home to the Army Futures Command research hub, does not include "A&M" in its name, Sharp added the A&M logo to the brand when the Bryan facility opened in 2016.

In 2012, the rebranding of the core state agencies—TEEX, TEES, and TTI—was reasonably straightforward. Since much of the work of all three agencies took place on the site of the Texas A&M Riverside campus, as it was known at the time, the agencies' affiliation with A&M was already understood. Such was not the case at the Texas Forest Service, nor at the Texas AgriLife Research and AgriLife Extension agencies under the management of the Texas A&M College of Agriculture and Life Sciences.

In fact, just prior to Sharp's rebranding initiative, the Texas A&M College of Agriculture had undergone name changes of its own, which "complicated" things for at least one agency administrator.

"I was the director of what was then called Texas AgriLife Extension Service when Chancellor Sharp proposed to add 'A&M' to our brand," says Edward Smith, who earned three degrees in agricultural economics from Texas A&M University and began working for the Extension Service in 1975.

"When I got word of what the chancellor wanted to do, I couldn't help but go, 'Aw, shucks!' Unquestionably, the move made sense to me, but we'd just been through a name change of our own, and the thought of pitching another name change to the 254 Texas counties in which we had offices was more than a little daunting.

"I pushed back against the rebranding idea big time."

In fact, so adamant was Smith initially against the idea of rebranding his agency, he paid Chancellor Sharp a visit—to Sharp's summer home in Telluride, Colorado—to plead his opposition.

Before we explore that fateful journey, let's step back in time to gain a better understanding of the Texas A&M College of Agriculture's historical branding efforts.

Of course, Texas A&M's original charter through the Texas state legislature was as the Agricultural and Mechanical College of Texas. However, from the get-go, many referenced the school as Texas A&M, a name that has stood the test of time.

Ironically, and despite its name, A&M taught no classes in agriculture during its first few years. Instead, the school focused on classical studies, languages, literature, and mathematics. Texas farmers complained at the gross omission in the college's curriculum, and in November 1879, just three years after opening the institution, the school's president and faculty were dismissed. The state legislature then mandated that the school include bountiful offerings in the sciences of both agriculture and engineering.

More than a century later, in early 1989, the Texas A&M College of Agriculture became the College of Agriculture and Life Sciences, a rebranding exercise to keep up with the times.

"The idea of just a 'college of agriculture' did not represent what our college is," Executive Associate Dean Jim Wild told the *Battalion* student newspaper in a story on March 28, 1989. "Changing the name doesn't denote a change in the college, but a more appropriate representation of where we've been for a long time."

A key component of Texas A&M's mission as a land grant institution is to provide free and accessible information to the communities it serves. In 1915, the Texas Agricultural Extension Service was created to formalize that initiative. Eventually, the agency charged with that mission became the Texas Cooperative Extension, adopting a long-familiar label, "cooperative," which is a term describing how farmers generally pooled resources to maximize collective spending power.

The name of the Texas Agriculture Experiment Station, the research arm of A&M's agricultural extension efforts, remained unchanged—until 2007.

That's when vice chancellor and dean of the A&M College of Agriculture and Life Sciences, Elsa Murano, stirred up a tempest in Aggieland.

When Murano was named the sole finalist to become president of Texas A&M University in 2008, the A&M regents praised her ability to make difficult decisions, specifically citing her stewardship in taking "agriculture" out of the Texas A&M name.

Well, not quite . . . but almost.

Upon accepting the role of head of A&M's College of Agriculture and Life Sciences in 2005, Murano was faced with declining enrollment and an image problem. She determined that the study of agriculture was rooted in the classic notion of "cows, sows, and plows" and not in the more modern scientific aspects of study offered by the university, including chronic disease prevention, agro-terrorism, and climate change.

A consulting firm was hired, focus-group studies held, and a conclusion reached. "People harken back to what they learned in grade school," Murano said. "Being in first grade and seeing in your classroom a picture of a barn with a cow next to it. That's what agriculture is going to be forever until somebody tells you otherwise."

The consultants told Murano and her administrative team that they had two options: change the perception of the word "agriculture" or create and define a new word that wasn't yet burdened by preconceived notions.

Thus was born the term "AgriLife," based on Murano's oft-implored mantra that "agriculture is life."

Murano opted not to change the name of her college but mandated a name change for the two state agencies she oversaw. The Texas Agriculture Experiment Station became Texas AgriLife Research, while the Texas Cooperative Extension was rebranded as Texas AgriLife Extension.

The move was not eagerly accepted. Vitriol ran high among students, former students, and even members of the board of regents. Regent Gene Stallings said the term "AgriLife" reminded him of Viagra, the well-known erectile dysfunction medication. Making the name changes would also incur a cost of nearly $1 million.

The rebranding took almost two years to complete.

"I supported Dr. Murano in making the name change," Edward Smith says today. "'AgriLife' speaks to our full range of extension services and health programs. The biggest problem I had was that 254 county government entities fund our offices and travel expenses, so they have a big financial stake in a name change. Every county judge and commissioner's court has partial ownership in who we are.

"And John Sharp adding 'Texas A&M' to our name was going to force me to go back to those same people with yet another name change. I just didn't think that was a good idea."

Smith offers, somewhat shockingly for some, "Not everyone wants to be an Aggie."

That point was driven home in a letter to the editor of the *Dallas Morning News* in April 2012. In addition to rebranding the A&M

System–controlled state agencies, Chancellor Sharp wanted to change the name of the Baylor College of Dentistry in Dallas, which Texas A&M had owned since 1996.

In his letter to the *Morning News*, Phillip McMillen of Duncanville took to task Sharp's rebranding initiative:

> Not all of A&M's rebranding has been well received. Both my wife and I are graduates of West Texas State University, not West Texas A&M. We have numerous friends who are also WTSU alumni, and no one I know is happy with the name change. We were told "just be happy that they didn't change it to Texas A&M at Canyon." My retort was, "If I wanted to be an Aggie, I would have gone to A&M."
>
> So I will support John Sharp's plan to change the name of the dental school as soon as he gives me my school back. WTSU forever!

Another reader, Jim Herrera of Dallas, offered his view in limerick form:

> *John Sharp has focused his aim,*
> *To remove Baylor from the A&M name.*
> *"Let's fix what ain't broke"*
> *Is an old Aggie joke.*
> *That's why alumni want Baylor to remain.*

Smith's ire wasn't quite as keen or artistically expressed as the contributions to the *Dallas Morning News* editorial page, but he was sufficiently opposed to the rebranding of the Texas AgriLife Extension Service that he asked to speak with Sharp personally as soon as possible. It was the summer of 2012, and Sharp and his wife, Charlotte, were vacationing at their summer home in Telluride, Colorado.

Smith remembers the phone call he placed to Sharp asking whether he could drive up and spend some time with him. He was clear on the topic of his intended conversation but less clear about his intended destination.

"Before I left, I spoke to the director of AgriLife Research and the dean of the college," Smith says, "and neither were in favor of the name change. I told them, 'I'm going up there to talk him out of this.'"

"Unfortunately, I was a little confused about where I was going."

Smith remembers Sharp being a bit surprised, too, when Smith spoke of his desire to "drive up and see him." Telluride is in the Rocky Mountains, seventeen hours by car from the Texas A&M University campus.

"For some reason," Smith laughs today, "I thought Telluride was Trinidad, Colorado. My plan was to drive up to my hometown of Tahoka, Texas, then make the five-and-a-half-hour drive to Trinidad. After I got to Tahoka, I realized my mistake, but couldn't back down from the commitment I'd made to meet with Sharp in person."

Tacking on another six-hour drive to reach Telluride, Smith and his wife, Elaine, eventually found their way to the Sharps' summer home. Sharp laughed when Smith told him about miscalculating the length of the trip. "That's okay," Sharp said. "You're here. You're welcome to stay a couple days, rest up, enjoy the scenery, and we can talk."

Smith realized that he had given Sharp an immense "home-field" advantage in which they would discuss rebranding the Texas AgriLife Extension Service.

Over a few drinks their first evening together, Smith put forward his case. Sharp listened and gave Smith's argument some thought. Finally, he replied, "Nah, I want you to do this."

Smith was overwhelmed and overmatched. He did appreciate having a chance to state his case.

"All right, John, you win," Smith said. "But dammit, you go over and meet with the County Judges and Commissioners Association. I'm certain they're going to raise all kinds of hell. They chewed my butt out before, and the same thing is going to happen again."

"Sure," Sharp replied, "I'll be glad to do that."

"I found out John Sharp is a helluva lot better politician than I am," Smith says today. "He got it done. The only thing I heard from the association director was, 'You mean you're going to change the signs *again*?'"

"That's right," Smith replied before adding, "To be honest, I'm not sure we've got all the signs up from the last name change."

The word "brand" comes from the Old High German *brinnan*, which means "to burn." The practice of "branding," to burn a distinguishing mark onto livestock or property as a means of preventing theft, goes as far back as the Egyptians, 2,500 years before the birth of Christ.

Texas ranchers and cattle barons have long branded their herds as a means of indicating ownership. The wrought-iron gate outside the Kelsey Reading room of A&M's Cushing Memorial Library contains dozens of examples of Texas ranching brands.

When one thinks of "brand" today, one is much more likely to conjure up visions of McDonald's "golden arches," Nike's "swoosh," and the stylized "bitten fruit" symbolic of the Apple Computer Company. All of these serve to differentiate companies from their competition.

But in marketing terms, "brand identity" is less about a company's intent than consumers' actual marketplace perceptions of products, services, and corporate visions.

The most well-known brands today usually cost enormous sums of money to create and reinforce.

When one thinks of the Texas A&M brand, one first pictures the "block logo," the large capital "T" nestled between the smaller pairing of an "A" and an "M." There is one other element to the Texas A&M logo: the minuscule "circle R," which indicates the logo is a registered trademark of the university. Actually, the trademark is controlled by the Texas A&M University System, thus the importance of the logo's presence in identifying both institutions and agencies under the system's control.

"Texas A&M" is a brand with great recognition and great value.

Among the system agencies and regional institutions, Tarleton State University is the lone outlier to the A&M brand style guide. When the school was founded in 1899, thanks to a grant of $50,000 by local rancher John Tarleton, the original charter stipulated that the institution would always be identified by its benefactor's name. The John Tarleton Agricultural College became part of the Texas A&M System in 1917 and was renamed Tarleton State College, then later University.

East Texas State University became part of the A&M System in 1996. Bill Mahomes, a legendary Texas Aggie and current member of the Texas A&M University System Board of Regents, sat on the East Texas State board from 1989 to 1991. Mahomes is a native of East Texas, having grown up in the tiny town of Lindale.

In his role on the East Texas board, he was a strong proponent of the school becoming a part of the A&M System.

"I used to joke with the East Texas State president, Jerry Morris, and tell him that his school was good enough to be a part of the A&M

System," Mahomes says. "'We'll never be damn Aggies,' he'd reply, only half joking, I think."

East Texas (ET) chose to separate itself from the State Teachers College System in 1969. For a time, enrollment and funding at the school grew, but with the collapse of oil prices in the mid-1980s, the school foundered, and in 1986, ET was on a short list of state colleges facing possible closure.

The school survived but failed to thrive. Thus was Mahomes's recommendation to President Moore eventually looked at more seriously.

The Texas A&M University–Commerce website describes what happened next:

> For fiscal reasons, political impact, and marketing desirability, plans were put in place to seek a merger with an existing system in 1994. The question remained—which one? There were five systems in the state of Texas at the time, including our former system, the State Teachers College System, now known as the Texas State System. University administration quickly identified the A&M System as our only option for affiliation. A similar mission statement coupled with an understanding of the unique needs of a rural university made the A&M System the logical choice. As a member of the A&M System, President Morris, like all other system presidents, would report directly to the Chancellor of the System. At the time of the merger, the chancellor was Barry Thompson, an ET alumnus and former university VP. Thompson was an advocate for the merger and promised to personally recommend the merger to the A&M Board of Regents. By the end of the 1995 legislative session, the merger was approved by the ET and A&M Board of Regents as well as the state legislature.

As for what that move has meant to the old teachers college in Commerce, Mahomes says, "Being a part of the A&M System has meant a lot. We have a chancellor now who pushes the brand more than most. Students in Commerce, or Corpus Christi, or anywhere throughout the system can now say, 'I go to Texas A&M.' Those students are a part of something bigger and better than before. That means a lot, and the addition of schools like A&M-Commerce means a lot to the system, too."

Mahomes himself has been part of a "rebranding" within his own family. When he attended Texas A&M in the late 1960s, Bill became the first African American to successfully matriculate through the Corps of Cadets. The journey, as anyone knows who is familiar with the rigors of hazing that existed within the corps at the time, was not an easy one for a young Black man from the so-called backwoods of East Texas.

Mahomes also stuttered, making him an easy target for ridicule and degradation.

"It was hard, no doubt," Mahomes says today of his undergraduate experience at Texas A&M, "but my parents instilled three things in me before they sent me off to college, principles that I have never forgotten and have used throughout my adult life.

"They said, 'Always live by the golden rule. To make a friend, be a friend. And don't judge other people too quickly.'

"In the face of all the abuse I took throughout my years at A&M—abuse which never got physical, I might add—I worked hard to see the best in others, and hopefully they saw the same in me."

During Mahomes's college years and throughout much of his professional life as an attorney, he accepted the pronunciation of his last name as "*May*-homes."

That's changed.

"I wouldn't go so far as to say we've officially 'rebranded' the family name." Mahomes laughs when discussing the success of his grand-nephew, Super Bowl MVP quarterback Patrick Mahomes of the Kansas City Chiefs. "Back in East Texas, we always said 'ma-*Homes*,' but in places like College Station and in the Dallas area where I have worked most of my life, they've usually pronounced it '*May*-homes.'

"To my classmates at A&M, I'll always be 'Bill *May*-homes,' but to the rest of the world, I'm known now as the very proud great uncle to Patrick.

"I think 'ma-*Homes*' is going to persist from this point forward."

An Extreme Makeover

The "redevelopment" of Kyle Field stands as one of the most unique and significant construction projects in the history of American sports. In less than two years, an aging and mostly outdated venue was transformed into a gleaming showcase and one of college football's most breathtaking home fields, while at the same time preserving the tradition and gravitas associated with the site.

Upon completion of the project in 2015, it was infamously suggested by a member of the Texas A&M System Board of Regents that Kyle Field be rededicated as "The House That Johnny Built." And make no mistake: regardless of the foibles and personal transgressions of one Johnny Manziel, his epic 2012 Heisman Trophy–winning season as a nineteen-year-old Aggie quarterback unquestionably lit the fuse that helped spark the remarkable half-billion-dollar transformation of the storied structure.

Other significant factors also played into the ultimate success of the redevelopment of Kyle Field—which was much more than a "restoration" or mere expansion. However, in the end, as many have since said, the project was an enterprise that could have only been orchestrated by Aggies, with a former student, John Sharp, confidently at the helm.

So, yes, call it "The House That Johnny Built," but give credit where credit is due.

One thing is certain, though: it stands as an achievement worthy of its namesake.

Upon joining the faculty of the Agricultural and Mechanical College of Texas (AMC), young Edwin J. Kyle's perspective on the significance of intercollegiate athletics likely had been shaped by his time as a graduate student at Cornell University in the first years of the twentieth century.

Consider that in his final year as an undergrad on the AMC campus five miles south of Bryan, Texas, just six games composed the schedule of the school's fledgling football team, and two of those games were against Houston High School.

That was football at the "college station" circa 1898.

AMC began playing football in 1894. Its first game came against the University of Texas, and "Varsity," as UT was known in contrast to its land grant rival, prevailed 38–0. The AMC team—they were yet to be called "Farmers," and the term "Aggie" would not be associated with the school for another twenty years—then knocked off Galveston Ball High School 14–6 to complete their inaugural 1–1 season.

Meanwhile, back east, Cornell University was putting together a football powerhouse. In 1900, as Kyle began pursuit of his master's degree in agriculture at the New York–based land grant school, the "Carnelian and White"—as Cornell athletic teams were known until 1907 when they became the "Big Red"—went 10–2, with nine of their victories coming at home on Percy Field, located just south of the Cornell campus.

After completing his education at Cornell in 1902, Kyle returned to AMC to become an instructor at the college. By 1905, at just twenty-eight years of age, Kyle was named both head of the school's horticulture department and director of the General Athletics Association. It was in the latter position that Kyle campaigned for the college to create an athletic venue, similar to Cornell's Percy Field, for use by the AMC football and baseball teams.

School administrators were unwilling to invest resources into such a proposition, so Kyle marked off a portion of land under his academic control and created the first official on-campus home for the school's football team. During the ensuing 1905 season, the team posted a 7–2 record with a 5–1 mark at Kyle's field. By the 1906 season, a grateful Corps of Cadets—of which Kyle had briefly served as interim commandant while still a student himself—began informally calling the location Kyle Field, a name that stuck but would not be made official until 1956.

The first "redevelopment" of Kyle Field came prior to the 1906 season. Looking to provide seating accommodations for the ever-growing crowds attending AMC football games on Kyle's plot of land, the site's founder spent $600 of his own money to purchase the grandstands from the financially strapped Bryan Fairgrounds about three miles north of campus. That structure was disassembled and moved to campus to provide shaded seating for fans. By 1915, the on-campus gridiron accommodated nearly seven thousand spectators, many of whom still chose to stand around the perimeter of the playing field.

The AMC Farmers of 1919 went undefeated and, in fact, were unscored upon in ten games. The feat earned the school a share of that season's "national championship," with the more noted squads from Harvard and Notre Dame. With AMC's success, current and former students of the school clamored for the creation of a new stadium. A capital campaign—of sorts—was held, but only $2,500 was raised in support of the cause.

Another seven years passed before the school finally committed to the construction of a modern all-concrete facility. The cost for such a venue was expected to run somewhere in the neighborhood of $350,000.

The money was found, and construction began in 1927. Two years later, that stadium—still informally called Kyle Field and located on the same site as the present home of Texas A&M football—was opened in time for the school's end-of-year showdown against Texas. More than thirty thousand people witnessed the game that resulted in a 13–0 Aggie victory.

Since then, the venue has undergone five different renovations, including the 2013 redevelopment that also took two years but through which A&M played both the 2013 and 2014 seasons.

As for Kyle the man, despite the influential role he played in the athletic annals of Texas A&M, he is best known for his pioneering work as an educator, researcher, and proponent for the modernization of agricultural practices. Kyle became the first dean of the A&M School of Agriculture in 1911 and served in that post for more than thirty years. Upon his retirement from the university in 1944, Kyle became the US ambassador to Guatemala, appointed by Pres. Franklin Roosevelt, and then serving from 1945 to 1948 under the administration of Roosevelt's successor, Harry Truman.

By the summer of 2008, the Texas state fire marshal's office was clamoring for A&M officials to make much-needed life-safety updates to Kyle Field. Despite a north-end expansion to the stadium in 2000—called "The Zone"—and the creation of the Bright Football

Complex beyond the south end of the stadium in 2003, Kyle Field's east and west superstructures, which provided most of the stadium's seating, were showing signs of age.

Most important, much of the stadium failed to meet the construction and safety codes of the time. For four years the school had tried, unsuccessfully, to find funding to make the needed updates.

A placard posted in the press box atop Kyle Field's west grandstands suggested the venue's precarious circumstances. It alerted members of the media that "the press box would move during the Aggie War Hymn." In fact, as fans on game day linked arms and swayed in unison to culminate the school's revered fight song, the west-side upper deck swayed to a notable degree, no doubt an alarming experience for members of the media visiting Aggieland for the first time.

School officials insisted the aging Kyle Field of the late 2000s was structurally sound. Still, other issues existed that were acknowledged to be sources of concern.

In a 2004 Life Safety Code Compliance Survey of Kyle Field, an outside engineering firm deemed exit capacity at the stadium deficient. Fire detection and alarm systems also were found to be in need of major upgrades.

Perhaps the most alarming part of the safety survey was the acknowledgment that a thousand-gallon diesel storage tank was located directly under a ramp to the east stands, the side on which students stood for each game.

In a letter to Deputy State Fire Marshal Christopher Beasley, dated July 30, 2008, A&M Athletic Director Bill Byrne and Assistant Vice President for Safety and Security Christopher Meyer presented a conditional course of action.

"As you may remember," the letter read, "TAMU submitted a plan for fire and life-safety upgrades to your office in 2004 outlining a timeline for the correction of [these] deficiencies at Kyle Field. This plan was based on the anticipation of substantial gifts that would allow for a major renovation of the west side of the stadium. However, the major gift did not come to fruition."

In their letter, Byrne and Meyer pointed out that installation of an updated west-side sprinkler system had been completed in August 2006 and that other "interim measures" had also been put in place.

"At this time the athletic department is considering a construction package for the stadium that would include the creation of a south-end facility, including suites and a club level, and a major renovation of the west-side first deck. During this project . . . options would also be reviewed to improve egress from the east and west sides and address existing code deficiencies throughout the stadium."

By 2008, the hard truth of the matter was that Texas A&M's athletic department was operating in the red, with no extra money to make Kyle Field a safer place.

Following A&M's upset win over then top-ranked Kansas State to capture the 1998 Big 12 football championship, the university began construction of "The Zone" at Kyle Field, the first major renovation project in more than thirty years. The addition made for a dramatic visual upgrade to the north end of Kyle Field and increased the stadium's seating capacity to 82,600. When the Bright Complex was completed beyond the south end zone in the fall of 2003—an upgrade that coincided with the arrival of new head football coach Dennis Franchione from Alabama—A&M seemed poised to become one of college football's elite programs.

Instead, the Aggies posted a 4–8 record in Franchione's first year. Among those eight losses: a historic 77–0 setback at Oklahoma, the worst football defeat in Texas A&M history.

As far back as 2004, Athletic Director Bill Byrne had approached then university president Robert Gates with proverbial hat in hand. Byrne told Gates he anticipated major budget shortfalls for at least the next four years, and Gates agreed to provide a $16 million "loan" to help cover costs.

Continuing financial struggles, unknown to most fans at the time, were one of the reasons the massive shared revenues available to members of the Southeastern Conference (SEC) appealed to A&M officials when conference realignment discussions first took place in 2010.

Franchione lasted five tumultuous years at A&M before being unseated by the revelation of a "secret coach's newsletter," sales of which had personally benefited the Aggie football boss and were deemed to violate NCAA regulations. Franchione was replaced by Mike Sherman, who held the reigns of the Aggie football program for the next four seasons, long enough to see A&M play its last Big 12 football game before joining the SEC at the end of the 2011 campaign.

Fortunately, the cupboard Sherman left for his replacement, Kevin

Sumlin, was anything but bare. Among the stable of talented players Sherman had recruited to A&M was Johnny Manziel from Kerrville, Texas. Sherman had chosen to redshirt Manziel during his freshman year due in large part to the young man's lack of emotional maturity.

The next season, Sherman's successor, Kevin Sumlin, overlooked Manziel's tempestuous manner and made immediate use of "Johnny Football's" prodigious athletic ability.

Former A&M and Alabama head football coach Gene Stallings had warned that the Aggies could suffer through a string of lean years once they became members of the power-laden SEC. The 2012 season, though, proved anything but lean, as A&M won eleven of thirteen games, including a shocking upset at Alabama during the regular season and a victory over Oklahoma in the Cotton Bowl. By year's end, Aggie athletic coffers were overflowing, thanks in part to more than $20 million the school received as part of the SEC's revenue-sharing setup.

Following the triumphs of the 2012 A&M football campaign, Athletic Director Eric Hyman's calls to Aggie donors were eagerly accepted. Hyman had taken over for Bill Byrne when the latter announced his immediate retirement from the university on May 8, 2012. That move came less than three weeks after Pres. Bowen Loftin had assured the university community that Byrne would serve out his contract into 2013.

Hyman had particular success raising money among Aggie boosters in the oil and gas industry. With the price of oil skyrocketing to nearly $100 a barrel and A&M's future football fortunes looking bright indeed, there was plenty of money to be had.

And it didn't hurt that Hyman had something specific to sell to the well-heeled Aggie faithful: a bigger and better Kyle Field.

While Edwin Kyle studied at what would become Texas A&M on his way to a teaching career at the school, Phillip Ray came to Aggieland via a much more circuitous route. The two men do share a common denominator: the important roles their fathers played in molding their sons' adult lives.

Fergus Kyle grew up in Hayes County, south of Austin. He fought with Terry's Texas Rangers on the Confederate side of the Civil War. Afterward, Kyle returned home to earn his livelihood off the land. He prospered and was eventually elected to the Texas House of

Representatives. Kyle deeded land to the International–Great Northern Railroad where the town of Kyle, named in his honor, took root.

William Ray was a man of more modest means. An ironworker like his father before him, William called Hunt County in East Texas home. William's son, Phillip, was born in Campbell, just south of Commerce, where Phillip eventually attended what was then called East Texas State University.

Both Phillip's father and grandfather worked on building Texas Stadium, the old home of the Dallas Cowboys. As a member of the president's staff at Texas A&M University, Ray played a key role in the conception of a redeveloped Kyle Field, the one Hyman pitched to Aggie boosters.

Under Texas A&M University System Chancellor John Sharp, Ray then oversaw the construction efforts at Kyle Field, which, from 2013 to 2015, reimagined and revitalized the Home of the 12th Man.

"My father taught me there's nothing wrong with a little hard work," Ray says today. "I had my own hammer and crowbar when I was nine years old. Over many summers, Dad would take me to his job sites. He'd let me break down crates, and I got a nickel a board for pulling all the nails out.

"I still think of myself as an old construction guy, even though I have to wear a suit and tie when I go to work today."

After college, Ray took a job with E Systems, a US Department of Defense contractor that later became Raytheon. Eventually, Ray sold weapon systems for the company.

A call from his old boss at East Texas State, where Ray worked as a student, resulted in him moving into a procurement position at his alma mater. From there, Ray's career continued to follow an academic track. After his time working at East Texas, Ray became a financial administrator within the Katy Independent School District. Then in 2001, he accepted the position of associate vice president at Texas Tech University. For the next five years, and on a weekly basis, Ray made the seven-and-a-half-hour drive—one way—from the Katy area west of Houston to Lubbock in the Texas Panhandle.

"My dad took a lot of out-of-town jobs when I was a kid, so we moved around a bunch. I promised my wife and kids that I wouldn't do the same thing to them."

It was that kind of ethic, both professionally and personally, that appealed to Texas A&M Athletic Director Bill Byrne. In the fall of 2006, Byrne hired Ray as an associate athletic director, primarily to oversee operations at Reed Arena, the home of A&M's men's and women's basketball teams.

"That was an around-the-clock job," Ray chuckles. "You got tired. But, man, when they turned those lights on for games, it was something special."

Given Ray's financial background—he received his MBA from SMU—he was a good fit for a procurement job that came open on the A&M president's staff in 2008. One of Ray's most notable accomplishments in that position was ending the Coca-Cola Company's sixty-eight-year beverage agreement with Texas A&M in 2010. The cola switch was worth millions to the university, and Pepsi remains the soft drink of choice in Aggieland today.

From the moment Ray arrived in College Station, he heard talk about plans to renovate Kyle Field.

"We had some real issues over there," Ray says today. "It was in 2010 that President Loftin decided to put together a committee to study proposed stadium improvements, and I was selected to chair that committee."

The group's primary task was to conduct a feasibility study for a proposed stadium redevelopment. Key to that effort was the creation of a design concept, which required the selection of an architectural firm. Several firms were asked to present proposals. One company stood far above the competition: Populous.

No surprise there.

Beginning in 1987, virtually every new Major League Baseball stadium built in America was designed by Populous or its predecessor, HOK Sport Venue Event. The original HOK Group, headquartered in St. Louis, designed Houston's Galleria mall in the late 1960s, and then, nearly thirty years later, created the plans for the George H. W. Bush Presidential Library, which opened on the Texas A&M University campus in 1997.

"There was one guy on the Populous team that we met with who really intrigued me," Ray says of the Kyle Field feasibility committee's meetings with outside firms in 2011. "His name was Earl Santee, and he was and is one of the principals of the company. He didn't say a whole lot, but when he did speak, you listened, and inevitably, I liked what he had to say."

"One of our biggest concerns when we determined that Populous would be our top choice was that they were also bidding to do the design for the new stadium at Baylor. I asked Earl, 'Can you commit to me that you'll be devoted to our project?'"

Ray says Santee thought about how to answer the question for a long while. "That concerned me," Ray admits. "Finally, Earl replied, 'Anytime you need me here, I will drop what I'm doing and come to College Station.'"

"Earl struck me as a man of his word," Ray says, "so when he offered that assurance, it sealed the deal for me."

Ray began 2012 still on President Loftin's staff, but by the end of that year, Sharp had recruited Ray to come to work at the A&M System headquarters office. Sharp had been impressed with Ray's involvement in the system's outsourcing initiative, so when it came time to oversee the massive Kyle Field endeavor—because the system is in charge of all major construction projects on its campuses—Ray was the person for the job.

And as Sharp told Ray, failure was not an option.

The Texas A&M flagship and the 12th Man Foundation, which took the lead in fundraising for the project, announced Populous as the choice to put together the initial design study early in 2012. "We feel the Kyle Field stadium redevelopment is wholly unique," Santee said in the Populous media release announcing the project. "Together we have the opportunity to help define a new path for Texas A&M's future in what could become one of the most significant redevelopment projects in all of American sport.

"Our plan will be innovative, comprehensive, and full of passion. We will seek to define the meaningful moments of Aggie Football: the traditions, the fans, and the environment that create the best authentic sporting experience."

According to the Populous web page, which today summarizes the Kyle Field redevelopment endeavor, the project was the first of its kind "to be designed in response to demographic and market research." Through the 12th Man Foundation, more than twenty-four thousand Aggie fans provided input that "directly shaped the design and outcome of the premium amenities." Sales of those premium amenities, which included suites throughout the stadium and club-level seating on the west side, sold out just two weeks after they were announced.

A debate about the stadium's seating capacity became a significant source of friction between Athletic Director Hyman and Chancellor Sharp.

Sharp had a particularly grand vision for the stadium. He nixed the initial design that the athletic department had brought to him. He called the look "a glorified high school stadium," with uneven sides and lights mounted on poles. He wanted—and ultimately got—a true stadium bowl.

Sharp also wanted Kyle Field to become one of the biggest venues in all of college football. In the initial plans, seating capacity hovered around ninety-two thousand fans. Under that configuration, a renovated Kyle Field would have still been smaller than the Royal-Memorial stadium at the University of Texas.

"Eric Hyman was against expanding the seating capacity of the stadium," Sharp says today. "I asked him, 'We're going to spend that much money and we're not going to get any more seats? That's bullshit! We're going to have the biggest stadium in Texas. Period.'"

Hyman believed the Aggies would likely be unable to sustain their surprising first-year football success in the SEC. He felt it an imprudent move to risk too many empty seats in the new stadium in the potentially leaner years to come.

At the time, Hyman felt he had the support of a majority of the A&M System Board of Regents to keep capacity at a "more reasonable" level. Problem was, the governor was about to name three new regents.

"Eric went on to remind me that while he was new to Texas A&M, he'd been an athletic administrator for a long time. I said, 'Well, let me tell you what I've been doing for a long time. I've been counting votes, and you ain't got 'em.'"

The chancellor and the regents, who set the agenda for meetings of the board of regents, simply chose to wait for the three new regents to join the board before putting the stadium design to a vote.

In the end, Sharp won, and the new seating capacity was eventually set at 102,733, making the redeveloped Kyle Field the fourth-largest college football stadium in America. When tickets were put on sale for the 2015 season, they proved a white-hot commodity. "They sold out in eighteen minutes and fourteen seconds," Sharp says today with a laugh. "And to Hyman's credit, he called me that same night and said, 'You were right. I underestimated the Aggies.'"

"I told him thanks for his call."

Ray's first task in marshaling Texas A&M's stadium redevelopment project was the selection of a construction contractor. Ultimately, the joint venture of Vaughn and the Manhattan Construction Company was chosen, in part because the two had collaborated in building NFL stadiums in both Dallas and Houston.

Still, individual deals had to be struck with both firms, and that was left to Ray, who negotiated, as it turned out, with a pair of Aggies.

Manhattan's Greg McClure and Bill Vaughn, son to the founder of Vaughn Construction, earned degrees from the Texas A&M College of Architecture a year apart. McClure grew up in Midlothian, Texas, a University of Texas football fan. That changed when he witnessed firsthand a senior member of the Corps of Cadets brandish his sword in response to the on-field intrusions of a group of SMU cheerleaders during a game at Kyle Field on October 31, 1981.

"I remember thinking, 'Wow! Those guys take this pretty seriously!'" McClure says today. "By the time my brother and I got home from the game, I was asking my parents for an A&M jersey. I became a die-hard Aggie that day!"

McClure was named a Distinguished Alumni of the A&M College of Architecture in 2016. In 2013, it was his job to coordinate Manhattan's involvement in the Kyle Field redevelopment project, which, it turned out, required him to find a construction partner.

"We had worked with Populous on previous projects," McClure says, "but when they engaged us to assist in budgeting and scheduling for their design study, I came to the realization that what was being suggested might be impossible. The plan was to complete the project in less than two years.

"To meet that client-imposed deadline, we helped Populous put together their proposal but thought the overwhelming cost would scuttle the project. Once we knew the project was real, we knew we needed a local partner. Bill Vaughn and I had gone to school together, and I knew his company was our only viable option."

Although Vaughn Construction is based in Houston, where Joe Vaughn started the company in 1988, son Bill Vaughn calls College Station his home. The Vaughn's Bryan / College Station branch is kept busy with numerous builds on the Texas A&M flagship campus.

"We have worked continuously for the Texas A&M System since 1996," Bill says. "All of our stockholders are A&M grads.

"We had just finished work on the Memorial Student Center when the Kyle Field project was launched, so the timing was perfect for us. We had done some enabling work on Kyle Field for the 12th Man Foundation, so we knew the site but lacked the stadium experience Manhattan had."

Thus was the ideal team assembled.

As for the "aggressive" project timeline, if anyone deserves the blame—or acclaim—for setting the two-year construction deadline, it's John Sharp.

"Discussions about the stadium had been going on for a long time," Sharp says. "Over at the 12th Man Foundation, they were trying to figure out where to build it. There was some talk about moving it, but tradition prevailed.

"And I was intent on seeing that the job got done."

Coming down on the side of tradition, the A&M System Board of Regents mandated that Kyle Field be rebuilt where it stood—and to complete the project in less than two years.

That monumental task was divided into two parts. Phase I would be orchestrated between the end of the 2013 home football season and the beginning of the 2014 campaign. It would see an implosion and complete rebuild of the east stands and the creation of a multideck structure in the south end zone, filling in, as Sharp desired, the entire stadium bowl.

Phase II would begin following the last home game of the 2014 season and would involve the implosion of the west stands and a complete rebuild of that structure. Most of the proposed "premium amenities" would be located there.

"We had plenty of subcontractors who backed off from the project because of the aggressive timeframe," McClure says. "Phase I was by far the most difficult because we began work before we had the final design. It was difficult, but we all repeated the chancellor's mantra that 'failure would not be an option.'"

"For two years, crews worked 24/7/365," Sharp explains. "They took two days off: Christmas Day in 2013 and again in 2014. Otherwise, people worked around the clock until kickoff of the 2014 season. During the season, they stopped while they played games there, and then went back to work after the games were over."

The new east stands offered three decks of seating, dwarfing what had been there before. Ultimately, the new west stands of the redeveloped Kyle Field seated fewer people than the three-deck structure it replaced. Thus during the 2014 season, with work yet to begin on the west side, the stadium's capacity far exceeded its present number. In fact, for a game against Ole Miss on October 11, 2014, the attendance figure totaled 110,633, a stadium, state, and SEC conference record likely to remain unsurpassed.

"If John Sharp wasn't in the equation, we would have never taken the risk of trying to finish the project so quickly," Ray says.

A&M athletic department officials had arranged for the Aggies to play home games at Reliant Stadium in Houston during construction, but the decision was made not to pursue that course. Home games are a vital part of Texas A&M tradition and a major source of revenue for the local Bryan / College Station economy.

In 2011, a study determined the economic impact of a season's worth of A&M home football games exceeded $100 million for the local area. Both the city of Bryan and the city of College Station made significant monetary investments into the redevelopment of Kyle Field to keep home games at home during the construction period.

Sam Torn, Class of '70 and former chair of the 12th Man Foundation, led the private fundraising efforts for the redevelopment of Kyle Field. In a video he recorded in 2013, Torn told Aggieland that the new facility would be an "amplification of all our traditions."

He declared, "You're going to see a much more intimidating environment when we lower the field, bring the stands closer, enclose the south [end zone], and put canopies over the east and west [grandstands]. Our goal, by the way, is when an opposing team walks out on this field, it is going to be so loud, it is going to be so intense, that literally someone is going to wet their pants."

To ensure that ambitious goal could be realized and the project kept on time and on budget, Ray had cameras installed at the build site so that he could monitor the progress of construction.

Really?

"That is a true statement," Ray laughs today, making no apologies for becoming a literal watchdog to the project. "The chancellor entrusted me with this task, and there was no way I was going to let him down. He's a 'make-it-happen' sort of guy.

"He's got a lot of great virtues, but patience is not one of them."

Ray told the construction superintendents that he was having time-lapse cameras installed to record progress for the historical record. In doing so, he also had several real-time cameras placed inside and outside the stadium so that he could keep an eye on things remotely. If he saw crews "standing around," he let the stadium contractors know.

"I was right there with him!" Greg McClure says. "Phillip eventually gave me his feed, and I watched those cameras like a hawk, so much so that I had our senior superintendent on the project screaming at me for doing so."

The pressures generated by the project were enormous for all involved. Sharp's insistence that the stadium bowl be uniform in height on all sides created early delays, as did a decision to move the press box from its old home on the west side to the east side of the stadium. Ultimately, those adjustments, as well as Sharp's request to add the canopies atop both the east and west stands, were implemented into the final design. The canopies were designed to focus the roar of the Aggie faithful onto the field.

Thanks to the commitment and dedication of so many people, the Kyle Field redevelopment project was completed on time and on budget.

When asked whether he would have done anything differently on the project, Bill Vaughn says simply, "The fatality we had on-site still bothers me."

That came less than a month into work on Phase I, which included the implosion of the east-side grandstand structure. On December 3, 2013, a twenty-eight-year-old employee for Lindamood Demolition of Irving, Texas, Angel Garcia, was knocked off the fourth level of the north end zone complex when a section of loose concrete fell onto the piece of equipment he was operating. In February 2016, a Houston jury awarded his family $53 million in damages, citing the Manhattan-Vaughn joint-venture partnership and Lindamood for negligence. Neither Texas A&M University nor the Texas A&M University System was named in the suit.

Attorneys for Garcia's family argued that Manhattan-Vaughn "failed to take proper safety procedures because of the pressure it felt to finish the project on time."

While Garcia's death still mars the redevelopment of Kyle Field, those involved in the project look back in awe.

"That first game after we finished the job, I remember there was a young couple in our suite who had been to a Miami Dolphins game the week before," says Vaughn. "After getting a brief tour of the place, they told me, 'I don't know why any of these players would want to turn pro. This stadium is so much better than anything we've seen in the NFL.'"

Just three days before the "new" Kyle Field was officially opened to start the 2015 season—a September 12 contest against Ball State—McClure watched from the east stands as the final concrete was poured into place to complete the west stands reconstruction.

"I took a picture and sent it to my wife with a message that said, 'Sweet Mother of God, we are going to be finished.'

"My wife, who is also an Aggie, sent me back a selfie of her with tears in her eyes. She reminded me that this was the first time I had admitted that the project would be completed on time."

McClure's own tears came watching the Aggies run onto the new field prior to the Ball State game.

"I cried like a baby just taking it all in," he said, "and feeling like the weight of the world was finally being lifted from my shoulders."

Today, on both the east and west sides of the Home of the 12th Man, the stadium's name is proclaimed in signage with letters more than ten feet tall: "KYLE FIELD."

But on May 12, 2014, in a press event assuring Aggies everywhere that the stadium project was not overly ambitious and that the first phase of the facility's remarkable transition would be ready in time for the upcoming football season, A&M System Regent Jim Schwertner offered credit where he thought credit was due.

After praising Chancellor Sharp, A&M students and former students, and construction crews, Schwertner added, "The last person that we all need to thank, and I'm very serious about this, is Johnny Manziel. We talked about this project for a long, long time, but none of us were sure how quick we could pay for this."

The final price tag was $485 million, with $152 million coming from donations. The remainder was financed with bonds to be repaid with student fees, ticket sales, seat licenses, and other revenues.

Although the A&M System borrowed much of the money to rebuild

Kyle Field, Schwertner credits the excitement that Manziel brought to Aggie football with helping raise the $152 million in donations.

"My vision is someday," Schwertner said in 2014, "Aggie nation can all come together and decide that we can revise the name of Kyle Field to 'Kyle Field: The House That Johnny Built.'"

Years later, Schwertner says of his remarks, "Ten seconds after I uttered those words, my phone lit up. My own daughter called me and said, 'Dad, what the hell were you thinking?'

"Well, my mother taught me always to thank people who make a difference, and we caught lightning in a bottle with Johnny Manziel . . . and $80-a-barrel oil. I talked about that, too, that day, but nobody reported that.

"For years people gave me hell about proclaiming it to be 'The House That Johnny Built,' but I don't care because I was right, and I knew I was right, and maybe someday, maybe not in my lifetime, but someday, they're going to have a statue of Johnny Manziel somewhere around that stadium."

Many people—off and on the football field—deserve to share credit in a true team effort.

Building Boom

Building the largest college football stadium in Texas—with amenities worthy of any professional facility—may have dominated the attention of Aggie Nation, but it is hardly the whole story behind the largest construction boom in the history of the Texas A&M University System.

John Sharp and the board of regents oversaw $7.6 billion in construction projects during his first nine years as chancellor, as compared to expenditures of less than $2.7 billion in completed projects during the nine years before Sharp's arrival.

At the height of the building boom, as many as eight construction cranes dotted the College Station campus as the system erected new facilities for engineering, agriculture, veterinary medicine, and the music department, to name a few. The beehive of activity on campus did not include the new campus, RELLIS, just a few miles away in Bryan, where the several A&M system agencies and facilities for the Army Futures Command would eventually locate.

While the flagship's new construction is hard to miss, the chancellor and the board of regents spent about half of the construction funds across the A&M System's other ten universities and eight state agencies.

The construction was financed primarily with proceeds from the Permanent University Fund—fueled by rising stock and oil prices—as well as the state legislature's approval in 2015 of so-called tuition revenue bonds for many of the projects. However, Sharp employed another tactic: "One of the advantages of being a land grant university is you have a lot of land."

Chancellor Sharp, perhaps more than any other university official, has used public-private partnerships (commonly called P3s) and ground leases to finance projects that could not have been constructed with traditional financing. Of the \$7.6 billion in total projects, more than \$2.2 billion are P3s that added necessary amenities without spending taxpayer dollars or tying up the system's bonding capabilities.

The term "P3" is thrown around frequently within the confines of the chancellor's wing of the seventh floor of the Moore-Connally Building in College Station, where the system's headquarters are located.

Looking out the windows, there are P3s as far as the eye can see—Century Square, the U Centre at Northgate, Park West, the Doug Pitcock '49 Texas A&M Hotel and Conference Center—and, if you look closely to the far western reaches of the flagship campus, you will spot the Giesecke Engineering Research Building. On a map of Texas, P3s can be found on many of the system's regional campuses, in places like Prairie View, San Antonio, Galveston, Texarkana, Commerce, Canyon, and Corpus Christi.

Just what is a public-private partnership? The *Encyclopedia Britannica* website describes the term as a "partnership between an agency of the government and the private sector in the delivery of goods or services to the public."

Britannica goes on to say that a P3 "is—or should be—a mutually beneficial agreement directed toward serving a social purpose."

According to Wikipedia, "Much of the early infrastructure of the United States was built by what can be considered public-private partnerships," including turnpike roads in Pennsylvania, the country's first railroad line in New Jersey, and much of the nation's electrical grid.

"P3s certainly predate what we've done," says Phillip Ray, vice chancellor of business affairs for the Texas A&M University System. "We've had the good fortune to have had the support of the chancellor and the regents to take the good from several different models and put our own take on it."

Just as the chancellor used outsourcing as a way to economize and streamline certain campus services by putting them into the hands of private-sector experts, P3s are, according to Ray, a faster and more economical way to accomplish construction projects. This is achieved by engaging outside financiers, developers, and contractors to do what they do best: build buildings and then, when needed, manage them on behalf of the system.

As previously reported, Ray came to the chancellor's office from the A&M flagship after his work to help the system roll out its outsourcing plan for support services—such as dining, maintenance, and custodial work—proved critical to the success of the endeavor. After Ray had settled into his new job as head of real estate development for the system, Sharp asked him whether he had any "good ideas" that he wanted to explore. Ray spoke of his interest in pursuing a pair of potential P3s: what are now the Century Square mixed-use development project and the student housing complex U Centre at Northgate.

In a 2017 *Texas Monthly* article about John Sharp, entitled "Country Revival: How the Straight-Talking, Coyote-Shooting, Tobacco-Chewing John Sharp Has Led a Bonanza at Texas A&M," contributor Michael Hardy wrote of the birth of the A&M System's P3s.

"Everybody wants to be liked," Ray told Hardy of Sharp's management style, "but you have to make the right decision, and let things work out.

"John doesn't worry about popularity."

Of the system's initial P3 endeavors, Ray says, "We did the best we knew how to do at the time." Both the U Centre at Northgate, which opened in 2014, and Century Square, which launched with a rollout of student "luxury apartments" in 2016, have been successful revenue-generating uses of system-owned land. In addition, the plethora of commercial ventures operating within the Century Square complex have added sizable sums of money to the city, county, and public school tax rolls, an important "value-add" in the mind of Chancellor Sharp.

"I've certainly made a few mistakes along the way, but we've tried to learn from those mistakes as we've moved forward," Ray adds. "The one thing I know is that when I'm out on the speaking circuit talking about our P3s, everyone wants to know how we negotiate, develop, and pull them together."

Public-private partnerships, the A&M System way, are not a "one-size-fits-all" proposition. In fact, the system's first P3 project began long before Sharp or Ray arrived on the scene. In a move designed to reinvigorate the student experience at Prairie View A&M, campus leaders entered into a public-private partnership with a fledgling company, American Campus Communities (ACC), to construct a new dormitory complex. Phase I of the school's University Village project opened in 1996, just three years after owner Bill Bayless launched his company.

And that partnership has continued.

Groundbreaking for ACC's Phase IX student housing development took place in the summer of 2019. The University Village concept has expanded through the years to include University College, University View, and University Square communities, all developed and managed by ACC. In total, Prairie View's P3 endeavors have added more than one million square feet of living space for Panther students, providing nearly five thousand beds. ACC's total construction expenditures at Prairie View now stand at more than $145 million.

Today, ACC is recognized as the nation's largest developer, owner, and manager of high-quality student housing communities, with more than two hundred locations on ninety-six campuses nationwide. Those numbers include five projects in College Station, including the U Centre at Northgate as well as Esperanza Hall on the Texas A&M–San Antonio campus and Momentum Village I and II at Texas A&M–Corpus Christi.

All ACC projects with the Texas A&M System are ground-lease agreements in which the system receives both lease payments and a portion of the revenues generated through occupancy. P3s, in essence, take the system out of the development, construction, and management of construction projects, with ownership eventually returning to the system when project bonds are ultimately paid off, which can take as long as thirty to forty years.

Is the P3 concept a surefire, slam-dunk, win-win guarantee of success for all parties involved? No. As with any investment venture, risks are always a possibility.

With its collection of fifteen buildings containing more than 3,400 beds, the Park West apartment village dominates the College Station skyline. It is thought to be the nation's largest single-phase student housing project. The complex resides on a fifty-five-acre tract of land just south of A&M's collection of sports venues on the West Campus. When the P3 project was announced on July 30, 2015, system officials projected that the endeavor could generate revenue to the university of up to $600 million over the thirty-year period of the Park West lease agreement.

"We weren't necessarily looking at turning that horse pasture into a student housing project," Ray says today. "We didn't ask for that. In fact, we considered a number of proposals from various developers. All we wanted was to try to create a revenue stream for Texas A&M, and the P3 route made the most sense in our efforts to do that."

"They could have built a hotel there, a hospital, a Costco's, a

Buc-ee's, a Home Depot, anything," Ray adds, "but the best proposal we saw, as far as potential revenue for the system, was the student housing concept."

At the time, with an ongoing enrollment boom on the flagship campus, a massive residential complex for Aggie students seemed like a smart bet. The leaseholder, National Campus and Community Development (NCCD), a 501(c)(3) entity based in Austin, sweetened the initial deal by making an $18.5 million upfront payment to the system. That initial lump-sum remittance went to cover the cost of building A&M's new softball stadium, Davis Diamond, just a few blocks away from the Park West site.

NCCD served as the financier and leaseholder for three major P3 projects on the A&M flagship campus: Park West, the Texas A&M Hotel and Conference Center, and the Cain Parking Garage, which is adjacent to both the hotel and the Texas A&M Memorial Student Center.

Greg Eden is founder and president of NCCD. In his thirty-five years at the helm of the company, Eden has overseen projects serving K–12 institutions, higher education entities, and state and local government customers. In those efforts, Eden has served as an advisor, consultant, and developer, earning a national reputation as an expert on the subject of tax-exempt financing.

"In the case of Texas A&M's P3 agreements," Eden says, "tax-exempt leasing provides benefits to both the public and private partners involved in the deals. On the 'private' side—the developers, architects, and contractors—the arrangement increases their likely profit margins by lowering the cost of the projects. For public entities like the Texas A&M University System, leasing land to facilitate P3 construction initiatives frees up administrators like Chancellor Sharp to make decisions far more quickly than they could do otherwise, which ultimately enables them to realize their construction goals faster and cheaper, and without tapping into existing resources."

Many of the system's P3s are set up in this manner.

Despite the early optimism for the revenue-generating potential of the Park West project, a glut of additional student housing projects were built in the Bryan / College Station area at about the same time, all trying to take advantage of Texas A&M's growth in enrollment numbers. This glut of properties negatively impacted Park West's ability to deliver on its initial business model.

"The feasibility consultants failed to forecast this would become a saturated environment," Eden explains. But thanks to how the Park West P3 agreement was structured, the A&M System's financial exposure has been kept to a minimum. A&M pocketed its $18.5 million upfront, and its revenue sharing has been delayed until the glut disappears. Eventually, the property is returned to the A&M System's possession.

"That's one of the reasons why P3s make sense for us," Ray says of transferring the risk to the private sector.

The P3 ground lease that became the Doug Pitcock '49 Texas A&M Hotel and Conference Center was structured initially as "Cain Hall Redevelopment II," named for the former athletic dormitory originally built in 1974 just north of Kyle Field.

Cain Hall was converted to administrative offices in 2004 and then razed for the Cain Parking Garage project in 2015.

Both system and flagship administrators—as well as prominent former students—had informally discussed the need for a campus conference center for many years. Not until Chancellor Sharp's arrival were wheels set into motion on how to pay for it.

Sharp's concept was for the Cain Parking Garage and the hotel to pay for the badly needed conference center.

In a November 2017 *Wall Street Journal* story about the A&M hotel—under the headline "Coming Soon to Campus: The $100,000 Hotel Room"—Aggie alum Jack Lafield took some credit for planting the hotel bee in the chancellor's bonnet: "The Dallas oilman, a 1972 A&M graduate and current chairman of Caiman Energy, said he complained to . . . Sharp on a hunting trip several years ago how difficult it was to find hotel rooms on football game days, especially since kickoff times often fluctuate based on television schedules. That makes it difficult to plan trips in advance. Lafield told Sharp he'd be willing to pay good money to solve that hassle."

Lafield, a classmate of Sharp's at A&M, wasn't alone among deep-pocketed alums willing to foot at least a part of the bill for an on-campus hotel, but the concept failed to generate any significant traction until Sharp's random encounter with a member from an enemy camp at a Southeastern Conference (SEC) gathering. "He was a Louisiana State University [LSU] regent," Sharp says, shaky on the individual's true identity. "I asked him, 'What are you most proud of at LSU other than the football team?' And he said, 'I just love our hotel conference center.'"

Upon securing this bit of information, Sharp immediately put Ray on the task of learning more about the Cook Hotel and Conference Center on the LSU campus in Baton Rouge.

The Cook Hotel opened in 2001. The LSU Alumni Association website calls it "the gold standard among on-campus facilities across the country."

Half of the 129 rooms in the Cook Hotel overlook University Lake on the east side of campus. Rooms facing the west offer a picturesque view of the school's football home, Tiger Stadium, about six blocks away.

Ray not only got a firsthand look at the Cook Hotel but, upon the chancellor's urging, also flew to Blacksburg, Virginia, to inspect the Inn at Virginia Tech.

Upon reporting back, Ray told Sharp, "We can do better than both of those."

Indeed, the Doug Pitcock '49 Texas A&M Hotel and Conference Center has earned a reputation as one of the nation's premiere facilities of its kind. The hotel has garnered AAA's Four Diamond Ranking, putting it in the top 5 percent of full-service hotels in North America. In 2020, the Northstar Meetings Group, the leading meetings and conventions media group, named the A&M hotel the Best Hotel/Resort in the Southwest over the likes of the Broadmoor, the Gaylord Texan Resort and Convention Center, the Park Hyatt Beaver Creek Resort and Spa, and the University of Texas at Austin AT&T Hotel and Conference Center.

Just read a few of the recent reviews from the travel website TripAdvisor.com:

Whether you're an Aggie or not, this hotel is a GREAT place to stay.

Our room on the 8th floor was perfect. If you are a light sleeper be warned you will hear the train going by.

The hotel is amazing! Such attention to detail to the Aggie spirit. Very nice place and very clean. We enjoyed the decor. There were earplugs provided as the hotel is very close to the train tracks. But that is just part of how campus life is.

My wife and I were visiting College Station for the first time to attend a sporting event. Even though we were proudly sporting attire from the opposition team, we were welcomed with open arms! The property was beautiful and well-appointed.

My co-worker and I attended a conference for gardening educators this last week and Texas A&M Hotel and Conference Center exceeded all of our expectations. We come from South Dakota and were impressed with how friendly everyone was. The conference meeting rooms were excellent and the food outstanding. We got a "Howdy" everywhere we went! Our room was clean and comfortable. The train did not bother me at all. In fact I loved hearing the sound as I fell asleep! Great hotel and highly recommend it to others!

The "charm" of those railroad horns blaring in the night was significantly mitigated with the creation of a "quiet zone" in the campus area. That project, approved by the Texas A&M University System Board of Regents on May 14, 2020, required a $5 million investment to "channelize" vehicle and pedestrian travel paths near the tracks. Also added were median gates, a wayside horn, and a loudspeaker system with a reduced sound footprint pointing directly at approaching vehicles rather than campus buildings located to the east and west of the tracks.

As for those "$100,000 hotel rooms," an August 2018 *Forbes* story detailed that piece of the Texas A&M Hotel's revenue-generating puzzle: "The initial revenue opportunity for the university came in the form of donations required in order to enter a lottery last fall for a 10-year option to reserve one of the hotel's rooms or suites. Deposits ranged from $5,000 to $10,000, with opening bids ranging from $125,000 to $475,000 for the best rooms on the first day of the auction. Successful bids were considered a non-profit donation like any other donation to the university."

When plans for the hotel were officially unveiled, system administrators also projected naming rights for the facility could generate tens of millions of additional dollars. Instead, that honor went to a member of the Aggie Class of 1949. Doug Pitcock is cofounder and longtime CEO of the Houston-based Williams Brothers Construction

Company and has been a strong financial supporter to his alma mater for many years.

"It's a privilege to emblazon the name of a great Aggie and generous man upon Texas A&M's hotel and conference center," Chancellor Sharp said in a statement. "Doug Pitcock's support of Texas A&M University and his participation in creating the nation's roadways will be remembered for generations to come."

Student Success

One of the most prestigious opportunities available to undergraduate and graduate students within the Texas A&M University System is the position of "student regent." Since 2005, state law has authorized a yearly appointment of one student to each of the state's university system boards of regents. While the student regent is given no voting rights on the board, the position "provides a fresh perspective and an important voice in key discussions that determine the future," according to Texas A&M System Chancellor John Sharp.

Students interested in becoming student regents from any of the A&M System's eleven schools begin the process by completing and submitting an online application form. From those numbers, each regional institution puts forth recommended candidates. Ultimately, the names of at least two finalists are forwarded by the chancellor to the governor's office, where the ultimate decisions are made. The governor is not bound to select a student regent from the pool of finalists provided by each of the state's chancellors, but almost without exception, that is the course through which appointments are made.

In the fall of 2015, friends and faculty strongly encouraged Stephanie Martinez to pursue becoming a student regent prior to her senior year at Texas A&M International University in Laredo. Martinez was student body vice president, well liked by her instructors, and well respected by her peers. Of Stephanie, one fellow student said, "She seemed the kind of person you would want to sit next to in class, since she would probably help you without a 'price tag.'" Martinez, apparently, is not the kind of person looking to advance her own self-interests at the expense of others.

She just likes helping people.

When her senior advisor asked whether she would be interested in pursuing the student regent opportunity, Martinez was lukewarm to the notion.

"I told him I needed to work," Martinez says today from her office in the Senator Judith Zaffirini Student Success Center at Texas A&M International (TAMIU). Martinez is now a member of Vice Pres. Minita Ramirez's staff, with both bachelor's and master's degrees in communications from TAMIU.

"I told my advisor that I needed to spend my senior year looking for the full-time job I would move into after graduation," Martinez says. "He told me, 'Money shouldn't be the reason you don't apply for this.'"

However, as a first-generation college student and an only child of a single mother, work and the money that is the reward from work were the driving forces in Martinez's existence. For many lower-income students, money is also the primary obstacle, not just in obtaining a college education, but even in considering college as a viable life option. And that's the case not only at TAMIU but also throughout the A&M System for first-generation students.

"Do student regents get paid?" Martinez asked her advisor.

"No," he told her.

"Then that's not something I can really think seriously about," she replied.

Although Martinez was born in Laredo, she grew up in Nuevo Laredo, Mexico. She attended school there until the age of twelve, when rampant crime prompted Martinez's single mother, Alma, to seek a better life for her daughter across the border.

That process began by shuttling Martinez back and forth every day to a private school for immigrant children in Laredo. By the end of that school year, in 2007, Martinez and her mother established permanent residency in a Laredo hotel where Alma found employment as an events coordinator. Martinez's first job—at the age of thirteen—was washing dishes at night after many of the hotel's events.

Since then, Martinez and her mother have constantly held jobs, both sometimes holding two, three, or four jobs at the same time.

A few days after discussing the student regent position with her advisor, Martinez was invited to meet with Vice President Ramirez.

"We want you to be our school's student regent nominee," Ramirez told Martinez. "No one from here has ever been selected to that position. We think you'd make an outstanding candidate."

Martinez remembers thinking, "Great. No added pressure there."

When she later discussed matters with her mother, Martinez was encouraged to pursue the opportunity.

"Mom said, 'Look, we can work this out. I can get another part-time job. We're going to make this work.'"

"I don't know why I ultimately said yes, but I finally submitted my application a few days later," Martinez says, "just before the deadline."

Prior to Martinez's face-to-face interview with Chancellor Sharp, Ramirez took her protégé shopping for shoes and clothes and supervised proceedings at a hair salon. A Laredo native herself and a graduate of Laredo State University before it became TAMIU, Ramirez was keen to do everything possible to give Martinez the chance to succeed. Martinez impressed Chancellor Sharp, who put forth her name as one of the system's two student regent candidates for the 2016–17 academic year.

Two weeks before graduating from TAMIU—and on the precipice of becoming a graduate student at the school—Martinez learned she had been chosen to become the student regent for the Texas A&M University System. She was asked not to reveal the news until an announcement came from Gov. Greg Abbott's office. As it turned out, Martinez's appointment was first made public at her graduation ceremony on May 20, 2016.

Stephanie Martinez's story exemplifies how "student success" does not come easily for many students in today's world. "There certainly are 'at-risk' students throughout our system," says Dr. James Hallmark, the A&M System's vice president for academic affairs. "That holds true even on the flagship campus in College Station. But the regionals have a much higher percentage of those socioeconomically challenged students who are the first in their families to attend college.

"Thus there are 'student success' initiatives on almost all of our campuses, all patterned to some extent on the groundbreaking program at A&M International."

Of the 53,235 undergraduate students on the Texas A&M flagship campus for the fall semester of 2020, approximately one-fourth were first-generation students. At Texas A&M International, almost two-thirds of undergraduate students identified as first generation.

Minita Ramirez has been working to level the playing field for at-risk A&M System students in Laredo since arriving on campus in

2001 as executive director of enrollment management. Today, as vice president of student success, Ramirez is in charge of the entire gamut of student services, from recruitment to admissions to retention. Her quest, as is the goal of most universities in the United States: graduate students within six years.

Today, Ramirez's oversees the following departments at TAMIU:

- Office of Admissions
- Office of Housing & Residence Life
- Disability Services for Students
- Office of Financial Aid
- Recreational Sports
- Office of Recruitment and School Relations
- Office of the University Registrar
- Office of Student Counseling Services
- Office of Student Health Services
- Office of Student Orientation, Leadership and Engagement
- Office of Student Conduct and Community Engagement
- Office of Outreach and Precollege Programs
- Office of International Engagement

As you can see, Minita Ramirez's work touches the life—and college experience—of virtually every student on the TAMIU campus. She knows firsthand the challenges her students face. As a senior in high school, Ramirez's counselor told her she wasn't college material and that she needed to go to beauty school.

At the time, the Ramirez family was struggling financially. Ramirez's father was in poor health, and she chose to stay close to home and attend Laredo State to help keep the family's flower and bridal shop open. She graduated with a degree in history and political science, and her first job out of college was that of a Laredo teacher. Wanting more from her life, Ramirez eventually landed a job with Simon & Schuster, selling textbooks as the company's South Texas regional representative based out of San Antonio.

The contacts she made among school administrators in South Texas made her an attractive candidate for the TAMIU student recruitment position that opened up in 2000. "Pretty quickly I figured out there were a lot of processes that we had in place that were very counterproductive to student enrollment," Ramirez says today. "And quite frankly, we didn't have much of an enrollment to manage, so we changed the name of my department to 'Recruitment and High School Relations.'"

Rebranding was just the beginning of a cultural shift at Texas A&M International. Change, for the better, has been a constant under Ramirez under both her current boss, Pres. Pedro Arenaz, and his predecessor, Ray Keck.

"Dr. Keck and I had a very open, direct line of communications," Ramirez says, "and he had faith in the job I was trying to do. It seemed every time he called me into his office, he gave me another area of responsibility to manage.

"After he'd been here as president for about a year"—previously Keck had been provost at the school and before that chair of the TAMIU Department of Language, Literature, and Art—"he took part in a presidents' retreat at Harvard University. When he got back, he called me into his office again."

Keck told Ramirez his chief takeaway from the Harvard conference was that Texas A&M International was doing "much more than other universities."

"He said, 'We're really making an impact with your programs,'" Ramirez remembers. "'Why don't we come up with a new name for your department? What is it that you're promoting?'

"I said, 'I'm promoting the success of students. That's what I'm trying to sell. I'm telling parents that their kids are going to be successful if they become students at our university.'

"Dr. Keck thought a moment and then said, 'Why don't we call it the Division of Student Success?'"

The year was 2005, and that is where the concept of "student success," at least by name within the Texas A&M University System, officially began.

It would be another five years, however, before Ramirez would be able to coalesce the wide range of programs and offices that provided TAMIU's "one-stop shopping" for students under one roof.

While Ramirez has been an internal champion for student success for many years, Elaine Mendoza has been doing her part to bolster education in Texas from an external perspective.

On May 17, 2019, Mendoza was elected chair of the Texas A&M

University System Board of Regents, the second woman and first Hispanic to hold that position. Gov. Rick Perry first appointed Mendoza to the board in 2011. Gov. Greg Abbott reappointed her for a second term in 2017.

A native of San Antonio—where she lives and works today—Mendoza is a member of the Texas A&M's Class of '87. There was little question she would attend college. Her parents had paved that path.

"Both my father and mother worked themselves through school," Mendoza says, "and even though they had all the odds against them, they got their education."

Mendoza's father was a high school dropout from the small South Texas town of Premont. Like many young men with limited resources and opportunities, he joined the navy, and upon discharge, he hoped to use the GI Bill to secure a college education.

"When he first tried enrolling at St. Mary's University here in San Antonio," Mendoza says, "he was told that he'd be wasting his money."

Likewise, Mendoza's mother wasn't encouraged to attend college.

"My mother's father didn't believe that women should go to college," Mendoza adds, "but despite those obstacles, both of my parents finished school. Mom was an educator and Dad was a civil engineer."

From an early age, Mendoza wanted to follow her father's career path. She earned her aerospace engineering degree from Texas A&M University. "I was fascinated by the space program when I started college. I wanted to be an astronaut."

Instead, just three years after graduating from college, Mendoza started her own company, Conceptual MindWorks, a research, consulting, and software engineering firm providing services to the health care industry. She is still the president and CEO of the venture.

According to the Conceptual MindWorks website, Mendoza's initial corporate vision rested on making a "positive difference . . . today and tomorrow." She has made good on that promise in her benevolent endeavors, too, with a passionate focus on enhancing educational opportunities.

As a result of her volunteer work locally in San Antonio, Mendoza was asked in 1999 to chair a congressional commission supported by the National Science Foundation to explore ways that women, minorities, and persons with disabilities could more easily enter into

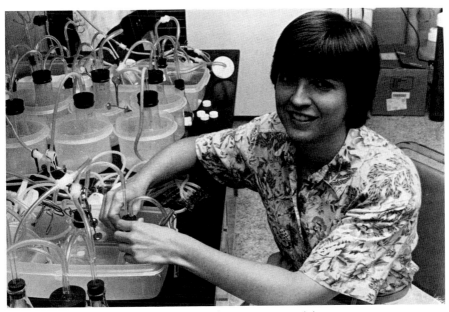

A young Kathy Banks conducting research in a university lab.

Growing up in Kentucky, Kathy Banks worked in her grandmother's general store, similar to this one.

Since coming to Texas A&M in 2011, Kathy Banks served as vice chancellor and dean of engineering. In the spring of 2021, she was named president of Texas A&M.

Every class of Hagler fellows is introduced at the annual Hagler Institute Gala beneath the saber arch provided by the Texas A&M Aggie Corps of Cadets Ross Volunteer Company. Hagler fellow Yonggang Huang is accompanied by Lily Zhou at the 2019 event.

Billy Hamilton, deputy chancellor and chief financial officer.

The Texas A&M Hotel and Conference Center, located adjacent to Kyle Field and the Memorial Student Union, is named for longtime financial supporter Doug Pitcock '49.

The hotel has earned AAA's Four Diamond ranking, which puts it in the top 5 percent of full-service hotels in North America. In 2020, the Northstar Meetings Group, the leading meetings and conventions media group, named the A&M hotel the Best Hotel/ Resort in the Southwest.

John Sharp '72 credits the Corps of Cadets for his leadership skills and campus politics for his interest in public service. At Texas A&M, Sharp was a member of the corps staff of the Corps of Cadets and was elected student body president.

In 2017, Gov. Greg Abbott asked Texas A&M System Chancellor John Sharp to lead the Governor's Commission to Rebuild Texas in the aftermath of Hurricane Harvey.

Gov. Greg Abbott, Texas A&M System Chancellor John Sharp, and FEMA regional administrator Tony Robinson convened meetings with local officials throughout the hurricane-damaged regions of the state.

Chancellor John Sharp uses his media skills to raise the profile of the Texas A&M University System as well as its eleven universities and eight state agencies.

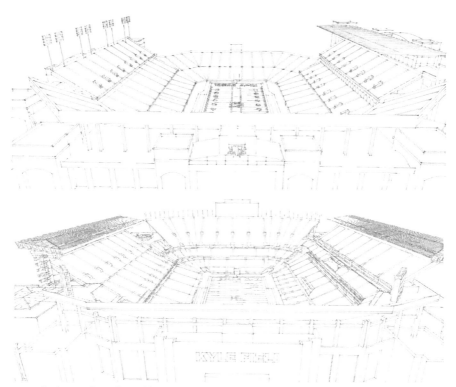

An early design for Kyle Field reminded Chancellor John Sharp of "a glorified high school stadium." At the chancellor's insistence, the final design was a true stadium bowl, and Kyle Field became the largest college football stadium in Texas.

An aerial rendering of Kyle Field.

Minita Ramirez, vice president of student success (seated), has been working to level the playing field for at-risk students at Texas A&M International University since arriving on the Laredo campus in 2001. She mentored her protégé and former student regent Stephanie Martinez.

The arrival of Ruth Simmons as president of Prairie View A&M University in 2017 has sparked excitement among students and increased enrollment. President Simmons congratulates Maduforo Eze at commencement and poses with Joyann Jerriho.

In 2016, Chancellor John Sharp announced the creation of the RELLIS Campus—formerly a World War II army airfield—that has become home of the RELLIS Academic Alliance as well as many research facilities, including for the Army Futures Command. The site is more than two thousand acres.

The RELLIS Academic Alliance is a unique partnership between ten A&M System universities, Blinn Community College, and Stephen F. Austin State University.

Fireworks at the RELLIS Campus are quickly becoming a tradition.

A RELLIS Campus entrance at dusk.

Texas A&M Extension Service personnel inspect damage from a 2013 explosion at the West Fertilizer Company, eighteen miles north of Waco. Fifteen people were killed, more than 160 were injured, and more than 150 buildings were damaged or destroyed in the community of West.

A Texas A&M Task Force 1 search-and-rescue technician, working aboard a Texas Military Department UH-60 Blackhawk, conducts a hoist rescue over Houston during Hurricane Harvey.

The Texas A&M Engineering Extension Service offers realistic, large-scale, and hands-on training for firefighters at the TEEX Brayton Fire Training Field in College Station. Each year, the 297-acre facility attracts more than forty-five thousand emergency responders from all fifty states and more than forty-five countries.

The half-billion-dollar Texas A&M Innovation Plaza is a 5.5-acre site adjacent to the Texas Medical Center in Houston. Scheduled to be completed in 2024, the plaza will be home to several Texas A&M System medical-related programs, including its groundbreaking EnMed program that blends engineering with medicine.

The year 2011, the hottest year in fifty years and the driest year on record in Texas, saw 351 days of continuous fire season. Though the Texas A&M Forest Service fought fires across the state, the most destructive was the Bastrop County Complex fire, as seen here from the state capital, Austin, some forty miles away. *Photo Credit: Kerri West.*

When the Texas A&M Forest Service isn't fighting fires in Texas, the firefighters are available to other states. The Texas agency sent firefighters to help Californians during the 2020 fire season.

s the head of a biotechnology and medical informatics company, doza was uniquely positioned to lead the system into a new age derstanding. But the challenge persists.

We still need to step up our game," Mendoza says. "We learned one of the things underrepresented students lacked is relevant rmation about what the college experience is really about. If you're gacy student, if your parents went to A&M, then you've grown up h an inherent understanding of higher education. But when you ve no one in your life with this frame of reference, it can be daunting hone the skills and develop the habits it takes to succeed in college.

"That's why academic advisors in our high schools are key, and at's why we've created the 'We Teach Texas' initiative within the mpowerU program. As the state system which sends the largest umber of teachers into our schools, we have the responsibility to prepare our educators for a state which is growing in both its diversity and its poorest population."

It is one thing to know help is out there, another to be able to find it conveniently. At Texas A&M International, the gamut of student services, from recruitment and admissions to housing and financial aid, can be found in one place: the Senator Judith Zaffirini Student Success Center.

Judith Zaffirini is a longtime Laredo politician, business executive, and community activist. She became the first Mexican American woman to hold a seat in the Texas State Senate when she was elected to represent the twenty-first district in 1987. She now owns the distinction of passing more bills than any legislator in state history.

Among her many honors, Zaffirini is a member of the Texas Women's Hall of Fame and was named a "Hero of Hope" by the *Laredo Morning Times*. In addition to the Student Success Center at TAMIU, Zaffirini's name can also be found on a Laredo elementary school as well as the library at Laredo College, the area's two-year institution for higher education.

"I remember having a conversation with Senator Zaffirini after we'd launched our Student Success program," Ramirez says. "When she asked about our greatest challenge, I told her that our various offices were spread all over campus. She looked at me and said, 'Why don't you build your own building?'

"And that's where the idea started."

The Texas A&M Transportation Institute uses everything from driving simulators to crash tests to save lives.

The Zachry Engineering Education Complex, the largest academic building on the Texas A&M University campus, is part of the $7.6 billion building boom across the Texas A&M System since 2011.

Chancellor John Sharp (*right, back row*) is with the five chairs who led the board of regents from 2011 to 2021: Clifford Thomas, Richard Box, Charles Schwartz, Elaine Mendoza, and Phil Adams.

the fields of science, technology, engineering, known collectively as STEM.

"What we learned was that we couldn't mal ing people into these skill areas if we tried to beginning at the high school level. That was ju. meaningful difference.

"But we found that even middle school was commission discovered was that to create an effe. the sciences, we had to go back all the way to early tion and look at the whole educational continuum, i unintentional bias against underrepresented grou] science did not exist."

Thus the A&M System Board of Regents found a t for education when Mendoza was brought onto the b What she quickly discovered was a reality she called "qui

Of the 13,500 students who entered into the A&M Syste schools in 2004, nearly 5,000 of those individuals ha graduate by the year 2010. Those students had received $50 million in financial aid, yet by not acquiring a degree, accumulated an average of nearly $11,000 of student debt would be ill prepared to repay through jobs in the workplace

"Those are hard numbers to look at and admit to," Mend. the *Texas Tribune*, "but the first thing we had to do was admit i had a problem so we could solve it."

Thus did Mendoza become the board of regents' lead on a syste tiative that would come to be known as EmpowerU. While the prog has evolved and grown since its launch in 2012 under Chancellor Sh the objective for the initial endeavor sought to "gather comprehens data" from all system institutions to provide "public accountability" the achievement of student retention and graduation goals.

"Back then," says Mendoza, "there was mounting skepticism abou higher education and the levels of debt many students were incurring without receiving a degree. At the time, there wasn't any place par- ents or legislators or even the schools themselves could go to better understand the problem.

"EmpowerU, initially, was a website through which we could pub- licly disseminate the data on learning outcomes so that we could understand where we were and how we could do better."

Legislative funding for the project came, in large part, thanks to the efforts of Zaffirini. The building was opened in 2010, but it was not until two years later that it received its current name, thanks to one of Zaffirini's former political associates and longtime professional admirers.

"There is no bigger champion of higher education in our state than Senator Judith Zaffirini, and certainly no larger influence on the campus of Texas A&M International University," Chancellor Sharp said at the time. Sharp left the Texas State Senate just as Zaffirini arrived in January 1987. The two became colleagues and friends during Sharp's time as Texas railroad commissioner and then comptroller of public accounts.

Of naming the new building for Zaffirini, Sharp added, "This recognition is a tribute to her work for students and our immense gratitude to her."

The Zaffirini Center was officially christened on September 20, 2012.

"If you can effectively share your story with people who are afraid of a process that is unknown to them, they're going to believe you, and they're going to trust you," Ramirez says of TAMIU's recruitment and retention efforts.

"If you lead them down the right path, people will work hard. If we can educate them, we can change how they live. With the right education and the steady income that comes from a steady profession, our graduates can enjoy their lives, and we can impact the cycle of poverty that has existed in this area for so many years."

Stephanie Martinez calls her time as an A&M System student regent a "life-changing experience."

"Since I saw my role as being the voice for all students throughout the system schools, my goal was to visit every campus and report back to the board of regents on what I had learned."

"The meetings were usually long," Stephanie says with a laugh, "but they were always very productive. I'm confident my opinions were heard and that I made a true contribution to the proceedings."

Without question, the most meaningful relationship Stephanie forged was with Regent Elaine Mendoza.

"She was my biggest supporter during that year and a huge mentor for me," she says. "One of the things that impressed me most about her was that every time I saw her, she had her husband and children with her, and I thought that was beautiful."

It is no surprise that those feelings are mutual.

"She's going to be a university leader someday," Mendoza says of Martinez. "She already understands the dynamics and complexity of higher education. I look forward to being able to say someday, 'I knew Stephanie when . . .'"

14

Rebuilding Texas

The lot of a Texan's life, particularly if he or she lives within proximity to the Gulf of Mexico, is the inevitable day when skies darken ominously and torrential rain begins to fall. Along the coastal shoreline, the sea turns an angry gray, and from its midst whitecaps grow tall and surge onto a defenseless land. With a fury that pummels everything that stands in its path, a wall of wind quickly follows.

Such is the wrath of a hurricane. Since statehood, more than sixty hurricanes have made landfall in Texas from the waters of the Gulf of Mexico.

Spanish explorers, in what would come to be called Texas, first chronicled this most savage manifestation of nature in 1527. In 1553, a hurricane making landfall along the lower Gulf Coast claimed, according to estimates at the time, more than 1,700 lives, the most deadly storm ever—until September 7–9, 1900, when more than 8,000 people (perhaps as many as 10,000) died in a catastrophic storm that devastated Galveston Island. Thousands wisely evacuated in advance of the tempest. Many, many others stayed to witness the spectacle of the event, unaware of the potential for impending catastrophe. Not only did experts disregard reports of the storm's size and strength, but they had assured locals the island was uniquely situated out of harm's way.

Just before midnight on September 8, winds gusting up to 125 miles per hour pushed more than fifteen feet of water onto the island and washed away those who had remained behind.

More than a century later in the city of New Orleans, nearly two thousand people died as Hurricane Katrina overwhelmed the Crescent City in August 2005. The specter of that disaster was still fresh on the minds of Texans as another titanic storm, named Rita, barreled toward land just weeks later. More than three and a half million people, most from the greater Houston area, moved inland in advance of the storm, the third-largest peacetime evacuation in global history from the fourth-most-intense Atlantic hurricane ever recorded.

Rita ultimately veered east and missed Houston entirely. One hundred twenty fatalities were attributed to the storm, but only seven of those took place in its actual wake. More than one hundred people died in the evacuation, including twenty-four who were killed when a bus carrying residents of a Houston-area nursing home caught fire and exploded on Interstate Highway 45 near Dallas.

Just three years later, Hurricane Ike pummeled the area surrounding Houston again. More than one hundred people were killed after the eye of the storm made landfall near the Houston Ship Channel. Ike caused more than $38 billion in damages. Jack Colley, head of emergency management for the Texas Department of Public Safety, said, "Hurricane Ike will go down in history as the most costly and destructive storm ever to hit Texas."

Then Harvey struck in 2017—the hurricane that would not go away.

As is the case with most tropical storms and hurricanes that reach the Eastern Seaboard and Gulf Coast regions of the United States, Harvey began as a tropical wave off the North Atlantic coast of Africa. Drawing energy from the warmth of ocean waters, Harvey transformed into a tropical storm and made initial landfall on August 18 over the Caribbean islands of Barbados and St. Vincent, bringing heavy rain and some flooding. As it continued to move west over open waters, the system weakened and appeared to be little cause for further concern.

Six days later, though, on August 24, Harvey had again gained strength and was officially categorized as a hurricane. On August 26, the storm made landfall near Rockport, Texas. It quickly weakened again, then did something unusual: it bounced back into the Gulf of Mexico, and three hours later, it made landfall a second time as a tropical storm.

Harvey continued to linger, dumping once-in-a-thousand-year rainfall amounts over much of southeastern Texas—more than fifty inches of rain in some places.

In all, Harvey made landfall five times during its unwelcome stay along the Gulf Coast.

Damage totals, mostly from unprecedented flooding throughout the region, totaled more than $125 billion, exceeding the devastation from Ike by nearly a factor of four.

This unparalleled catastrophe called for an unparalleled response.

In the wake of Harvey's devastation, Gov. Greg Abbott announced on September 7, 2017, the formation of the Governor's Commission to Rebuild Texas. To lead recovery endeavors, Abbott chose Texas A&M University System Chancellor John Sharp.

At an Austin news conference announcing the appointment, Sharp cited the devastation Harvey had brought to a large swath of southeast Texas, including his hometown of Placedo.

"I know well the charms and challenges of living on the Gulf Coast," Sharp said. "The road to recovery is going to be long, but Texans are a tough breed. We will rebuild Texas, and we will build it even better than it was before."

In selecting Sharp to head up his commission, Abbott said he was looking "for someone who knows how to work with officials at all levels; has a natural, intuitive feel for the people in the affected communities; and possesses deep knowledge of the budget as well as state agencies."

According to a story in the *Houston Chronicle*, when Abbott first approached Sharp about the position, the phone conversation went something like this:

> "Look, Sharp," said Abbott. "You probably work ten to twelve hours a day right now [as chancellor], so there's another ten to twelve hours a day out there that you ain't doing s—."
>
> "Do I get to keep the job I have now?" Sharp asked.
>
> "Yes," Abbott said. "This [new job] is not a paid deal."

The *Chronicle* story went on to quote Sharp: "He didn't say 'Would you like to be?' He just said he needed me to do this. Of course I said yes. I mean, anybody would." Anybody, perhaps, who had overseen the historic Texas Performance Review as the state's comptroller of public accounts or marshaled the dramatic turnaround that took place within the Texas A&M University System after becoming chancellor.

Sharp was an inspired choice to "Rebuild Texas." Quickly he put together a series of marching orders for the large and diverse set of individuals, agencies, and organizations that he would manage on behalf of those Texans affected by Harvey.

His edict to those under his command was simple: "Respond immediately, fix the problem, cut red tape . . . and no surprises."

In the early days of the Rebuild Texas endeavor, Sharp cited past reporting in the aftermath of natural disasters: "Every time you turned on CNN, the mayor was bitching, the parish sheriff, all those people were bitching, and they just turned the whole tone of everything.

"You've got to be able to get to that mayor before he gets so frustrated that he just starts screaming and hollering about it. You don't wait around for things to happen.

"In instances like that, I'm not big on rules."

Even before Sharp took the helm of Abbott's commission, the Texas A&M University System had mobilized resources to come to the aid of those affected by Harvey's devastation.

Texas Task Force 1 Urban Search and Rescue, managed by the Texas A&M Engineering Extension Service, initially moved two seventy-person teams first to Corpus Christi and then to the Brazos River / Fort Bend County area to support evacuation efforts.

More than two dozen members of the Texas A&M Veterinary Emergency Team (VET) were dispatched to Fort Bend County to help care for injured, abandoned, or displaced pets. Those VET units transported medical platforms, refrigerated pharmacy trucks, water, food, tents, generators, forklifts, and decontamination units into flooded locales.

The squads also provided health care for search-and-rescue dogs working with Texas Task Force 1.

In response to the crisis, the Texas A&M Forest Service mobilized 168 emergency responders and managed additional crews whose personnel numbered more than 250 individuals. These teams were positioned throughout southeast Texas, from Victoria and Corpus Christi, to Austin and the Bryan / College Station area, to Houston and Galveston.

The Texas A&M AgriLife Extension Service deployed dozens of Extension Agents across the disaster area to disseminate information to the public and coordinate the response for livestock affected by the flooding. Their livestock specialists assessed agricultural damages and the storm's impact on livestock throughout the counties impacted by the hurricane.

Susan Ballabina was executive associate director of the Texas A&M

AgriLife Extension Service when she got a Sunday call from Billy Hamilton, the deputy chancellor and chief financial officer of the Texas A&M University System. The date was September 3, Labor Day weekend, just days after Harvey's wrath had ebbed.

"We had just gotten back from church when I got Billy's call," Ballabina remembers today. "When I saw his name on Caller ID, I let the call go to voicemail because I wasn't sure why he would be calling me on the Sunday of a holiday weekend. I have two children, so to keep them out of the background, I went outside and called Billy back.

"'Dr. Ballabina,' he said, 'I'm going to need your help with something. If you tell anybody about this, you'll be fired.'"

Obviously, this wasn't an invitation to a Labor Day barbecue.

"In the next day or so," Hamilton went on to say, "there's going to be an announcement that the chancellor is going to be appointed to lead a governor's commission related to Hurricane Harvey. The chancellor wants to use the Extension Service network in some way. We're still fuzzy on what we're going to do, but the expectations are going to be very high."

"We don't know how this is going to work. Our time is short. And you can't tell anybody," Hamilton reemphasized.

Over the next few days, Hamilton and Ballabina worked out details of how the Texas A&M AgriLife Extension Service would assist recovery as the floodwaters throughout southeast Texas began to recede. By August 23, Governor Abbott had declared forty-seven Texas counties disaster zones. The Texas A&M AgriLife Extension Service had a presence in each of those forty-seven counties.

Another thirteen counties were eventually added to the disaster declaration.

"From the outset," Ballabina says today, "a key part of the work done by the Governor's Commission to Rebuild Texas would involve our extension workforce, our agents and their staffs in the field, to help identify the needs in the local communities they served."

Chancellor Sharp thought using Texas A&M AgriLife Extension agents made more sense than hiring consultants. During the recovery from Hurricane Katrina, Louisiana spent tens of millions on consultants—a waste in Sharp's view.

Once Abbott had announced Sharp as his "recovery czar," Ballabina began the process of mobilizing the Texas A&M AgriLife Extension Service network.

"What I told our people was that the governor had put his faith in the chancellor and the A&M System, and we as a group would help lead the response because that's what we do," Ballabina said. "We have a reputation of responding to the needs of our communities, and there was no need now greater than the need to begin recovery from the devastating thing that had just happened."

Many agents and Extension workers in the affected area had lost homes of their own or seen homes severely damaged by the hurricane. In addition, several Extension offices were damaged or destroyed, adding to the challenge of the mission. Yet the mandate was clear: the Texas A&M AgriLife network of county agents would serve as the official liaisons between county judges, city mayors, school superintendents, and those within state government charged with orchestrating the recovery objectives.

The Hamilton-Ballabina plan called for agents to put together a daily report on the needs of their local constituencies. Those reports would be due to Ballabina by 2 p.m. each day.

"We were pretty unsophisticated in our reporting that first week," Ballabina says. "While the reports were due to me by 2 o'clock, I had to have my report finished for the chancellor to then forward to the governor's office by 6 p.m.

"Fortunately, one of our sister agencies, the Texas A&M Forest Service, told me they thought they could covert one of their existing apps and make our reporting efforts much easier. We had that in about a week."

Ballabina is a product of the Texas A&M University System herself. Born and raised in Paris, Texas, Ballabina earned her undergraduate degree in family and consumer science with a minor in journalism from Tarleton State University, the system school located in Stephenville, Texas, near Fort Worth. With thoughts of working for a women's magazine after graduation, Ballabina did a journalism internship at the Texas Cooperative Extension's district research center in Stephenville. In that position, she wrote stories about the work of Texas Agriculture Experiment Station researchers and produced promotional materials for the Texas Cooperative Extension's educational programs.

After "a really great summer" of internship work, Ballabina was encouraged to seek a job as a county extension agent. After graduation, she landed a position in Rusk, Texas, with the Cherokee County

Extension office, coordinating the local 4-H Youth Development Program there.

While working full time with the Texas Cooperative Extension agency, Ballabina received her master's degree outside the system from Stephen F. Austin University in Huntsville. Later, while working in Williamson County, Ballabina began to give serious thought to pursuing a PhD in organizational leadership. With the University of Texas campus within easy driving distance, Ballabina set her sights on the doctoral program there, but Extension administrators convinced her to become county agent for Dallas County.

"For about three and a half years in Dallas," Ballabina says, "I worked full time, got my PhD in public affairs from UT Dallas, and used my coursework to study organizational development and leadership. I wanted to see if the Extension model could change to better suit the needs of a changing demographic in Texas."

Yet another promotion moved Ballabina into a midmanagement position in Dallas, where she was put in charge of Extension programming for sixty-eight Texas counties. Thus did the churchgoing wife and mother of two become the ideal organizational mastermind to help Chancellor Sharp and Vice Chancellor Hamilton rebuild Texas.

Ultimately, Ballabina helped set up a Rebuild Texas Assistance Center in one of the first-floor conference rooms in the system's headquarters building in College Station. It was there that Ballabina's team, working in tandem with Texas A&M AgriLife Extension staff in the field, helped local authorities resolve issues associated with recovery efforts in Harvey's aftermath.

Texas A&M AgriLife Extension personnel from virtually every outpost in the state also aided in cleanup efforts. The network supported displaced families and individuals and worked with farmers, ranchers, agricultural suppliers, and others to establish an animal supply points (ASP) network to provide food and shelter for affected livestock and pets.

"We had more than $1.3 million in hay and feed donations that came into the ASP thanks to the generosity of the people of Texas and of many other states," said Dr. Jeff Ripley, Texas A&M AgriLife Extension's associate director in charge of county operations.

Through the Texas A&M VET, more than one hundred state medical professionals were mobilized to offer care at the ASPs. They worked alongside VET staff and volunteers; members of the Texas Animal Health Commission, the Texas Department of Agriculture, and the US Department of Agriculture; and the military to distribute thousands of tons of hay, cattle cubes, horse feed, and all-stock feed. More than 230 tons of pet food was also distributed in the disaster areas.

Even more dramatic were the statistics generated by search-and-rescue efforts in association with the storm. On August 24, 2017, the Texas Division of Emergency Management activated Texas Task Force 1 (TX-TF1) to prepare for Harvey's initial landfall. That initial response lasted twenty-two days, with 257 TX-TF1 personnel deployed to support the early emergency response.

In all, TX-TF1 coordinated 2,433 other personnel from 103 state and national agencies to conduct search and rescue. According to the TX-TF1 website, 841 rescues were conducted by air, 19,050 rescues were conducted by ground or water, and 37,758 people were evacuated from flood zones. In addition, 4,354 welfare checks were conducted, and 2,055 pet rescues or evacuations were made.

Another staggering statistic associated with Hurricane Harvey was the number of students attending the Texas A&M System's universities impacted by the storm. At Texas A&M–Corpus Christi, some 8,800 students, representing more than two-thirds of the school's total undergraduate enrollment, were identified as being from counties in the disaster area. It became evident that intervention would be necessary to help those students return to and remain in school. Classes at several system schools were delayed in the weeks after the hurricane, and faculty and staff were mobilized to meet the needs of struggling students after they returned to campus or connected via distance-learning channels.

Many students were forced to withdraw from school. Others who did manage to return to their campuses did so with newfound financial challenges resulting from property damages back home and loss of parental livelihood. A sizable number of impacted students came from economically disadvantaged circumstances, further complicating recovery. Nearly a year after Harvey, a Kaiser Family Foundation / Episcopal Health Foundation study found that almost one-third of the residents in counties most severely affected by the storm reported that their lives "remained disrupted."

Through grants from the Rebuild Texas Fund and the Qatar

Harvey Fund, scholarships were created to help underwrite tuition and fees, textbooks and supplies, room and board, and general living expenses for students most affected by the devastation and its aftermath.

Since 2003, the Texas A&M flagship has operated a branch campus in Al Rayyan, Qatar, offering undergraduate degrees in the fields of chemical, electrical, mechanical, and petroleum engineering.

The Qatar Harvey Fund was created by Sheikh Tamim bin Hamad Al Thani, emir of the State of Qatar. According to the Qatar Harvey Fund website, $30 million was set aside not to underwrite emergency assistance in the immediate aftermath of the storm but to provide funding in areas that would have an enduring impact, such as housing, community development, and education.

Hundreds of system students have benefitted from proceeds from the Qatar Harvey Fund.

The Governor's Commission to Rebuild Texas created a 178-page report analyzing the storm and its devastation, assessing recovery efforts, and—most important—detailing recommendations for what can be done in the future to prepare for the next inevitable hurricane-related catastrophe.

Contributors to the report included more than twenty representatives from the A&M System, including Billy Hamilton and Susan Ballabina, now deputy vice chancellor of agriculture and life sciences. Also contributing to the report were staff and faculty from the Texas A&M flagship as well as graduate and undergraduate student researchers.

In the foreword, Sharp writes,

Before the difficulties our communities faced because of Harvey fade from memory, it is critical that we examine what happened and how our preparation for and response to future disasters can be improved.

In this report, we try to create as clear a picture of Hurricane Harvey as possible. We document how the storm developed and how it affected our state. We also offer a frank assessment of the federal, state, and local response and recommendations for how Texas can be better prepared to withstand future disasters. The report is both a record of a milestone event in the state's history and a guide to "future-proofing" our state to mitigate the impact of future Harveys.

Among the recommendations:

- Reorganize emergency management functions to unify the most critical emergency response and recovery functions.
- Emphasize to emergency management personnel the importance of working out partnership agreements and contracted services before a disaster strikes.
- Examine ways for the state to apply data analytics to improve disaster management through more effective and timely information.
- Continue to cultivate relationships with private technology providers to coordinate their assistance in the early days of a disaster when communications systems are damaged or destroyed.
- Investigate the possibility of creating a state case-management program administered by the Health and Human Services Commission.
- Determine the feasibility of developing a single intake form for disaster victims to complete to determine their eligibility for disaster programs.
- Create a catastrophic debris management plan and model guide for local use.
- Ensure the state is prepared to quickly develop and present a well-reasoned report to the federal government listing projects requiring federal funding after large-scale disasters.
- Grant the Texas Department of Transportation (TxDOT) authority to prepurchase food and water and stockpile these essentials for each hurricane season.
- Establish a single, well-publicized state website at the Texas A&M University System that is easy to use and presents important postdisaster information about response and recovery activities.

Recognizing the good work under Chancellor Sharp, Governor Abbott and the legislature transferred the Texas Division of Emergency

Management (TDEM), which had been part of the Department of Public Safety, to the Texas A&M System as its eighth state agency. TDEM joined the other A&M System agencies that respond to disasters.

"Hurricane Harvey was an inestimable tragedy for many Texans," said Sharp in the conclusion to his foreword in the *Eye of the Storm* report, "but the lessons it taught us should not be forgotten or ignored."

15

RELLIS

The RELLIS Campus was for many years "a land that time forgot."

Founded as one of America's most vital military installations during the first years of World War II, the RELLIS site—under other names—fell victim to more pressing priorities of administrators running the Texas A&M University campus.

Permanently affiliated with the Texas A&M main campus since 1962 and known as an annex to the college for decades, RELLIS has only recently lived up to the potential promise often foretold in its historic past.

Occupying what was once mostly cotton fields in the bottomland of the Brazos River, today's RELLIS Campus exists atop the footprint of the old Bryan Army Air Field. The base both played an important role globally in training Allied aviators for combat and provided a substantial economic boon locally to the nearby community from which it took its name. Thousands of soldiers and civilian workers toiled at the site during the war years, and many graciously shared their financial remuneration from Uncle Sam with Bryan-area merchants, landlords, nightclub owners, and young ladies looking to pass time with a young man involved in the war effort.

Bryan Field was the US Army Air Forces' primary instrumentation flying school. The base's mission was to teach those in charge of training army aviators the science—and art—of safely piloting aircraft in low visibility conditions.

The man who developed the manual for military instrumentation flight and who served as the commander at Bryan Field was Col. Joseph Duckworth. He himself proved the worthiness of his instrumentation protocol in the summer of 1943, shortly after the base was opened. Prompted by an officer's club wager with a British flight instructor training at the base, Duckworth flew a T-6 Texan aircraft from the flight line of his home field and, solely on the readings of its instrument panel, piloted the plane into and out of the eye of a hurricane off the Texas Gulf Coast west of Galveston.

And survived.

No one had ever intentionally done that before.

Under Duckworth's command, the training that took place at Bryan Field proved pivotal to the Allied efforts in both the European and Pacific theaters of war.

Cadets from the nearby Agricultural and Mechanical College of Texas (AMC) also played a key role in the US triumph in World War II. US Gen. George Patton famously said of AMC's fighting spirit, "Give me an army of West Point graduates and I'll win a battle. Give me a handful of Texas Aggies and I'll win a war!"

After the war, many of those cadets returned to campus to complete their schooling. In addition, military veterans who fought alongside Aggies and learned of the fine education to be had at AMC boosted enrollment numbers, as did recent graduates from high schools across Texas, once again college bound with World War II finally at an end.

The dramatic increase in the numbers of students created a dilemma for A&M administrators: where to put all those young men hungry for knowledge.

Thus did Bryan Field—on loan to Texas A&M from the federal government—become "the Annex." The base proved to be an ideal, if not picturesque, setting to accommodate A&M's postwar enrollment boom.

For four years, from 1946 to 1949, new students—called "fish" within the ranks of the Corps of Cadets—lived and learned on the site of Bryan Field. In doing so, they avoided, at least somewhat, the special welcome upper-class cadets had for their kind. The term "fish" came from the world of the Texas criminal justice system. Prisoners had a special name for those who were newly incarcerated: fish out of the waters of their old, familiar, crime-ridden ways.

Those who matriculated through their first year at Texas A&M on the grounds of the Annex experienced the hardships of living in Spartan-like conditions, where the tarpaper walls of abandoned military barracks were no match for the bitter cold of a Brazos Valley winter or the sweltering heat of its summer. Yet these hardships were but a small price to pay to limit the hazing and harassment typically due newcomers to A&M's Corps of Cadets.

In fact, in the bountiful free time made available to those who lived and learned at the Annex, enterprising fish started their own marching band and a drill team whose standards of excellence endure today.

About the time that new dormitories were completed on campus and first-year students abandoned the Annex, a new conflict of global significance erupted on the Asian peninsula of Korea, thus returning the old Bryan Field to active military status under a new name.

Under Pres. Harry Truman, the air force had become a separate branch of the military in 1947. So when Bryan Field was reopened for military flight training in 1951, it was renamed Bryan Air Force Base.

Millions were spent to upgrade the site. Two new runways were constructed to accommodate the faster-flying jet aircraft used by the new ranks of military aviators. One of the early students at Bryan Air Force Base was a young lieutenant by the name of Edwin Aldrin. He would later go by his nickname, "Buzz," and become one of the first human beings to travel to the surface of the moon.

No fewer than five future astronauts were stationed at Bryan Air Force Base. Gus Grissom, the second American to fly into space, was a cockpit instructor, and in ceremonies held at the base, he received his Distinguished Flying Cross for services as a combat pilot in the skies over Korea.

Grissom's youngest son, Mark, was born at the base hospital on the second-to-last day of 1953. Three other astronauts—Ted Freeman, Charlie Bassett, and William Pogue—were also stationed at Bryan Air Force Base either during or after the Korean War.

As was Don Ho. Before he became a well-known entertainer and poster boy for his homeland of Hawaii, Ho learned to fly at Bryan Air Force Base, nearly dying when he crash-landed his plane into a local farmer's barn.

After the active "war" part of what came to be known as the Korean conflict ended, Bryan Air Force Base continued its training mission until the base was permanently shut down in the summer of 1958.

When the property now called the RELLIS Campus was initially seized for military use in 1942, the four dozen local landowners, mostly European immigrants who were evicted from their homes under the terms of eminent domain, were collectively compensated $126,000. When the US General Services Administration put the base up for sale, the initial asking price was set at $18 million.

There were neither buyers nor prospects.

Eventually, the Department of Surplus Property reached back out to the local college to see whether the school had any interest in the venue. The year was 1961.

By this time, A&M's postwar enrollment boom had ended. In fact, by the early 1960s, student numbers were significantly down, and faculty morale was on the decline. This was due, in large part, to an absence of wide-ranging academic curricula at the school, coupled with the compulsory military training required of the all-male student body.

The Texas A&M Board of Directors—as the school's controlling body was known before becoming the board of regents in the early 1970s—saw the "reacquisition" of the Bryan Air Force Base site as a means by which research activities at the college could be increased. They insisted, however, that no money be spent to acquire the property.

Remarkably, Pres. Earl Rudder soon received an offer neither he nor the system's board could refuse. The federal government, as it turned out, was willing to lease the vacated air force base to the college, and for every year the school made productive use of the venue, 5 percent of the asking price, which had been reduced to $3.6 million, would be discounted.

After twenty years, the base could belong to A&M outright, a deal that the board of directors eagerly accepted.

Over the course of the next two decades, Texas A&M "University"— Rudder's request to upgrade the school's name had been approved—made "splendid" use of the property. Livestock were located on the site, including, for a short time, a colony of baboons used for research purposes. The university also built a cosmic-ray telescope in one of the vacated aircraft hangars left over from the wars. In an innovative use of one of the old barracks—upgraded to solid siding under the air force's domain—a "nautical archeology" laboratory was created to study ancient ocean-faring boats. In addition, the Texas Transportation Institute began crash-testing vehicles on the flight line of the old base.

Runways at the old base were eventually leased to the US Dairy Association to conduct crop-dusting research activities, which included, in the mid-1960s, testing that led to the development of a military defoliant called Agent Orange. That toxic compound not only killed trees and other jungle vegetation during the Vietnam War but also poisoned hundreds of thousands of civilians and soldiers on both sides of the conflict.

All this and more took place at the Texas A&M Research Annex. A&M gained full ownership of the property in 1982.

Although the university and system state agencies were making productive use of the base, a lack of upkeep and updating of the local infrastructure began taking a toll. In desperate need of an overhaul, a new master plan was created in 1988 in an effort to freshen up the Research Annex's ever more "tawdry" reputation.

Thus was born the Texas A&M University Riverside campus.

With the new name, a grandiose new vision also was laid out. The new developers hired by university and system administrators stated in their report, "The former Air Force base is burdened with an image problem, a seemingly remote location, and an unattractive appearance."

They went on to say, "The Annex is a place where few go, and then only out of necessity."

"I knew nothing of the Research Annex when I was in school," says Chancellor John Sharp. "I guess I was aware that there was an old air base somewhere in the area, but I never made the association with nor even heard the term 'Research Annex' in conjunction with Texas A&M."

Not long after Sharp's return to College Station as chancellor in 2011, he was talking to Gary Sera, the director of the Texas A&M Engineering Extension Service (TEEX).

"By that time, our offices had been located at the Riverside campus for many years," Sera says, "and after I took over as director of the agency, I became aware of how many people coming to the Bryan / College Station area along State Highway 21 were confusing Riverside for the main campus.

"I asked the chancellor to come and see the place for himself."

Of that occasion, Sharp reports, "I was embarrassed." And that was the nicest thing he had to say on completing his first inspection.

Sera told the chancellor, "Sometimes parents bringing their kids to College Station to check out the school pull in here wondering, 'Is *this* Texas A&M?'

"The Riverside campus doesn't make a very good first impression."

"It was *terrible*," says Kathy Banks, vice chancellor and dean of the A&M College of Engineering. "It was in terrible shape when I first got here in 2011, and I was appalled.

"The roads were impassable in many places, the sewage system was nonexistent, and many of the buildings were, literally, falling down. Some of the buildings had actually been invaded by snakes, and people were still asked to work in them!"

"When I first visited Gary out there," Sharp continues, "I asked him, 'Who is in charge of this place?' He explained the site was administered by the flagship, and he had been repeatedly told other priorities existed that were more important than maintaining the Riverside campus.

"What he also said was this could be something really special if we could figure out what to do with it. 'It's a shame,' Gary told me, 'to have nearly two thousand acres going mostly unused.'"

Five years later, with new president Michael Young in place on the flagship campus, Sharp suggested, "Let me take Riverside off your hands."

Young might have felt like he'd be swindling his new boss, but handing over control of the old air base to the system was a no-brainer. The deed to the property was once again transferred at no cost.

Ever conscious of the importance of branding, Sharp knew a name change was in order . . . again.

The name RELLIS was a pneumonic invention of A&M Regent Cliff Thomas, Sharp says.

"I asked Cliff one day, completely unrelated to the old air base, how he remembered the Aggie core values. Cliff told me, 'RELLIS,' which stands for respect, excellence, leadership, loyalty, integrity, and selfless service. After I had a chance to sleep on that for a night, I called Cliff the next day and told him, 'You've just renamed the Riverside campus.'"

Not only do these core values represent the finest aspects of the Aggie Spirit, but they also symbolize, as it turns out, the legacy that has endured at the site of today's RELLIS Campus. That legacy was first forged and fostered by servicemen of all ranks and colors serving their country over the course of two wars and again embodied during "the Annex" years by students who called the place their college home.

Then, beginning in 1962 and stretching over the next half century, the aging site continued to showcase advancements, breakthroughs,

and accomplishments in the areas of research, education, and training. And now, thanks to the vision of John Sharp—and an infusion of
hundreds of millions of dollars—RELLIS builds anew on its legacy
of learning, leadership, and discovery.

"When you think about how far, finally, we've come from the old
Bryan army airfield," says former RELLIS executive director John Bar-
ton, "RELLIS could be as impactful to the local community and this
part of the state as was the original Texas A&M campus. What we've
done since the system took control of the property in 2016 is pretty
exciting and a game-changing experience in many ways."

The biggest initial building boom on the new campus involved the
RELLIS Academic Alliance. This partnership between Blinn College,
the A&M System, and its ten regional institutions enables students
to receive four-year degrees at RELLIS.

"Blinn's history changed forever on April 28, 2016, when the concept for the RELLIS Campus was laid out to me," says Blinn chancellor
Mary Hensley. "That idea focused not on the past but on the future
of how RELLIS would impact our children, and their children, and
their children."

Blinn's buy-in ignited the RELLIS Academic Alliance. The community college located an eighty-three-thousand-square-foot classroom
building at RELLIS, bestowing two-year degrees from the site. Those
students, as well as others transferring in from community colleges
across the state, are continuing coursework toward more than forty
different undergraduate degrees offered at RELLIS by the regional
schools of the Texas A&M University System and Blinn College.

In addition, technical training and certification courses are also
part of the RELLIS Academic Alliance plan. These are offered through
not only Blinn College but also state agencies such as TEEX and Texas
A&M Engineering Experiment Station (TEES). TEEX headquarters
have been moved to RELLIS, with plans to locate the TEES headquarters building there at some point in the future.

"RELLIS has quickly become a small city of its own," says Kelly
Templin, the former College Station city manager who became director
of the RELLIS Campus in early 2018. "When you look at the intended
student presence here, and then you look ahead at the research which
will be conducted here with graduate students, doctoral candidates,
and postdoctoral researchers, those will be some impressive numbers."

The RELLIS Academic Alliance, with Blinn and ten A&M System universities on board, quickly attracted two thousand students—ten times more than early projections.

Templin also cited government and industry interest: "When you factor on top of that the future interaction with the Department of Defense, Department of Energy, and private industry which also will be locating at RELLIS, it becomes a little hard to imagine what this place is going to look like twenty years from now."

All of which will be good for the local area . . . just like back in the early days.

"Bryan Air Force Base was a large part of the local community," says Bryan mayor Andrew Nelson, "not only in its mission to protect our freedoms but in the payroll that was generated and spent here in the Brazos Valley."

"RELLIS is a big deal," says state representative John Raney, who attended Texas A&M and runs a local business in the Northgate retail development next to the main campus. "Look at its proximity to Houston, Dallas, and Austin. It will attract business, industry, and research."

In fact, it already has: one of the Army Futures Command's main research and testing sites is located on the north side of the RELLIS Campus.

More on that to come.

16

The Lab

Prior to beginning his academic career at the University of California in Berkeley, Robert Oppenheimer spent several weeks in New Mexico convalescing from a mild case of tuberculosis. During his recovery in such a picturesque setting, Oppenheimer wrote to a friend, "My two great loves are physics and desert country. It's a pity they can't be combined."

The son of a wealthy New York textile importer, Oppenheimer first discovered the high desert of northern New Mexico at the age of eighteen when his father sent him on a "Western adventure" that would help harden his bookish boy.

The teenaged Oppenheimer took both to the New Mexican countryside and to exploring the local environs on horseback. It was on a trail ride one day that he first came upon the Pajarito Plateau of northern New Mexico and the nearby canyon called Los Alamos, named for the cottonwood trees that grew along the stream running through the base of the canyon.

At the time, the only human inhabitants in that vicinity lived at the Los Alamos Ranch School, a private enclave that offered a college preparatory curriculum uniquely modeled on the Boy Scout experience.

Oppenheimer is best known for his work on the Manhattan Project, so named because the United States' quest to realize an atomic bomb during World War II began in the heart of New York City under the watch of the US Army Corps of Engineers' Manhattan Engineer District. The project was tagged originally as the Development of Substitute Materials, but then colonel Leslie Groves, who later, as a general, oversaw supervision of the creation of the atomic bomb, felt the name might raise suspicion.

Thus the project was given the alternative code name "Manhattan."

Groves ultimately named Oppenheimer—who by the early 1940s was a highly regarded physics professor at Berkeley—the civilian lead on the top-secret endeavor. When it came time to locate the research laboratory for the Project Y component of the mission—the actual assembly of the bomb—Oppenheimer was given a significant voice in the decision. As the group looked for a remote, isolated outpost far from curious minds and prying eyes, the search ultimately centered on New Mexico. At Oppenheimer's urging, the Los Alamos Ranch School was assessed, chosen, and ultimately seized by the government under eminent domain to become the top-secret location for bomb design.

It became known by those who worked there as simply, "The Hill." Oppenheimer's two great loves had become one.

Today, the historic Los Alamos National Laboratory, still a critical element in the United States' nuclear arsenal, is managed by an alliance called Triad National Security, which includes the Texas A&M University System. The group's five-year contract with the US Department of Energy, which began in late 2018, is worth $50 million per year, and the lab's annual budget is $3.7 billion.

Marvin Adams was a graduate student at the University of Michigan when he made his first trip to Los Alamos National Laboratory in the summer of 1984. Today, Adams is a professor of nuclear engineering at Texas A&M University and director of research and education to advance laboratory missions for the A&M System.

"I was first assigned to the Los Alamos lab," Adams says, "thanks to a fellowship from the DOE [Department of Energy]. I had my choice of summer-internship locations, but I chose Los Alamos mostly because there were people there doing what I wanted to do, and I wanted to meet them."

Adams grew up in rural Mississippi. He attended Mississippi State and worked his way through college on a co-op program. For every semester of school he attended, he worked a semester. His summer job while in Starkville was at the Sequoyah Nuclear Plant near Chattanooga, Tennessee.

"I worked there for five summers," Adams says. "When I started out, I was kind of a gopher, but by my fifth summer, I was given more important responsibilities. It was that year, 1982, [when] the reactor went critical."

For those who are not nuclear engineers, a reactor going "critical" sounds like something to get worried about.

"That is exactly what you want it to do," Adams laughs. "It signifies that you've achieved a self-sustaining chain reaction which makes the plant operational. I was in the control room when it happened at the Sequoyah facility, which was really cool and hugely beneficial for my education."

In that same vein, Adams's academic career "went critical" a decade later in 1992 when he joined the nuclear engineering faculty at Texas A&M.

Today, A&M's nuclear engineering program is ranked among the best in the country.

"When I first came here, we weren't ranked that highly yet," Adams says. "I was just one piece of the puzzle which elevated our department's reputation. We all pitched in, looked around, and hired a lot of good people."

Good people are a key reason why the Texas A&M University System, as part of the Triad National Security consortium, now plays a key role in the management of the Los Alamos National Laboratory.

In addition to the A&M System, other principals in the Triad partnership include Battelle and the University of California (UC) System. Battelle calls itself "the world's largest, independent non-profit research-and-development organization." Currently, the company manages six national laboratories.

Not only was Oppenheimer a member of the faculty at UC Berkeley, but the UC System itself also played a supportive role in the launch of the Los Alamos lab in 1943. The first successful detonation of an atomic bomb occurred on July 16, 1945, at the Alamogordo Bombing Range 210 miles south of Los Alamos.

Less than a month later, the US military deployment of two atomic bombs over Japan ended World War II.

"Los Alamos remains one of the most important nuclear security assets in the world," Texas A&M System Chancellor John Sharp said as Triad took the helm of Los Alamos on November 1, 2018. "We are committed to working with our partners to enhance safety and security at the lab while advancing its world-class science and executing its vital mission."

The mission of the Los Alamos National Laboratory has broadened since Oppenheimer's work in the 1940s. Today, Los Alamos is a "multidisciplinary research institution dedicated to enhancing national security by ensuring the safety and reliability of the US nuclear stockpile, developing technologies to reduce threats from weapons of mass destruction, and solving problems related to energy, environment, infrastructure, health, and global security concerns."

The journey that led to the A&M System's oversight of the Los Alamos lab echoes Oppenheimer's own personal sojourn to the facility. For the A&M System, according to Adams, the story begins as far back as 2004.

"The Department of Energy held a 'competition' to select a managing and operating contractor to run the Idaho National Lab which was being formed at that time," Adams says. "The Bechtel Corporation contacted us, and we ended up teaming with them on a bid-demand on the Idaho project. We didn't win, but that was our introduction into this crazy world of proposal competitions for national laboratory management.

"It is a crazy world you cannot imagine."

Some years later, under the watch of Kathy Banks, vice chancellor and dean of the College of Engineering, a new opportunity arose regarding the management of the Sandia National Laboratories. Named for a mountain range outside Albuquerque, New Mexico, Sandia got its start at the end of World War II as a sister facility to Los Alamos.

In 2015, the Sandia contract was put up for open bid following an investigation that revealed that Lockheed Martin, which oversaw the management of the facility as the parent company of the Sandia Corporation, used operational funds to lobby government officials *not* to open contract renewal to outside bidders.

As far back as 2012, the Department of Energy had openly considered making a change, and newly appointed system chancellor John Sharp was intrigued by that possibility.

"Kathy hadn't been here very long," Sharp says, "but she was up for the challenge. She's not shy about things."

As Banks conducted due diligence on the matter, she unknowingly fell victim to a campaign attempting to rebuff potential newcomers.

"I sat in on Dean Banks's initial briefing about Sandia," Adams says, "and it was apparent to me she had been given a lot of 'misinformation.' Later, I explained to her it would be difficult to cite my concerns in a short amount of time regarding the 'huge potential for embarrassment' if A&M didn't fully understand what it took to run a nuclear lab.

"Things were very different from what she had been told."

Banks led the necessary course correction, and the A&M System put out word regarding its interest in pursuing the Sandia contract.

"Kathy did the groundwork, and I handled the politics," Sharp says today. In time, the system was approached by Battelle, the global non-profit research and development management company based in Ohio.

"From the beginning," Adams says, "it was apparent that Battelle's commitment to integrity and national service was the same as ours. We agreed to partner with them, but the DOE shut down the process temporarily. By the time the contract was finally put up for open bid in 2015, we had learned a lot and had an attractive corporate partner in Battelle."

Also added to the mix—called "Together Sandia"—was Boeing, the University of New Mexico, and the University of Texas System. Gov. Greg Abbott was instrumental in facilitating the partnership between his state's two major university systems.

"From the moment Chancellor Sharp first approached me about bidding on the Sandia National Laboratory," Abbott wrote in a press release announcing the Sandia bid, "we have worked hard to build a coalition to take advantage of this unparalleled research opportunity."

In the end, the Together Sandia team put together a thousand-page proposal that cost upward of $5 million to create, a cost that Chancellor Sharp assures was picked up by the corporate entities involved in the proposed partnership.

"It's an enormous undertaking," Adams says. "Before you submit the proposal, you have to have your key leadership group lined up. Oftentimes, those individuals have to resign their current positions, and if you're not awarded the contract, you have to have a place for them to land. All told, it takes a group of about a hundred people working full time for two months or more to create the proposal."

The reward is a DOE contract worth billions of dollars to the winning partnership group. It costs a tremendous amount of money to keep a national nuclear laboratory safe and operational.

The Together Sandia alliance fell short in its quest to secure the Sandia contract, but another, even more prestigious opportunity soon presented itself: Los Alamos. That prize was sufficiently alluring to heighten interest again from both the A&M and UT Systems. This time, though, the two rivals would go their separate ways.

In putting together their bid, Battelle and the A&M System rolled the dice and welcomed the UC System as a partner. The move was risky for several reasons. As part of Los Alamos National Security LLC, the UC System had lost its previous management contract at the lab due to a series of poor performance ratings, primarily over safety concerns.

But there were other reasons why the University of California needed the A&M System more than Texas A&M needed Cal.

"Teaming with the UC System in the height of the Trump administration was also a risk," says Scott Sudduth, whom Sharp had hired in 2011 to head up the system's Washington, DC, office. "The California System had just filed suit against the Trump administration over DACA"—the Deferred Action for Childhood Arrivals immigration policy that the Trump administration opposed and the UC System supported—"and we were very careful about not looking like political neophytes and putting energy secretary Rick Perry in an embarrassing situation.

"We were able to pull off that delicate balancing act thanks in part to John Sharp's political savvy."

Chancellor Sharp had hired Sudduth because of his previous experience in DC representing the UC System, the University of Texas System, and the University of Chicago.

Sharp's instincts, as usual, served him well.

Since the University of California had played a role in the operation of the Los Alamos lab since, literally, the beginning, when the lab's contract came up for open bid, Sudduth brought a wealth of experience to the system cause—and knew where the landmines would be buried.

"In putting together our team for the Los Alamos bid," Sudduth says, "we really wrestled with whether or not to include the University of California as part of our alliance. Yes, they were the incumbent, but they also were being terminated for a second time. For a while, I thought we might want to decouple from them."

On June 27, 2017, the National Nuclear Security Administration (NNSA), an agency of the DOE, announced its intent to conduct a competition for the management and operations contract at Los Alamos.

According to an Associated Press story at the time, the Center for

Public Integrity, a watchdog group, had released documents "outlining federal regulators' concerns over the years about safety lapses at the lab."

Since 2006, the UC System had partnered with Bechtel in managing the Los Alamos lab. When the DOE chose not to renew that contract in 2017, the UC System chose to sever its ties with its corporate partner. In doing so, the California System levied harsh criticisms against Bechtel and, surprisingly, Secretary of Energy Rick Perry, a former governor and presidential candidate, and an Aggie.

Despite concerns about collaborating with the UC System, Texas A&M System and Battelle joined with the longtime incumbent institution overseeing the Los Alamos lab.

"The way the government scores these competitions," Sudduth says, "they give an enormous amount of weight to what's called 'past performance.'"

In the end, the California and Texas A&M Systems made a bit of an odd couple in pursuit of the Los Alamos contract, but together, they proved a winning team.

Sudduth disputes any speculation that Secretary Perry's ties to Texas A&M played a major role in the A&M System's Los Alamos win.

"Those decisions are more technical in nature and made at a level lower than the department secretary," says Sudduth. "Having been through several of these, I can say the DOE is fairly well insulated from direct political influence.

"You've got to score, and you've got to score well. Politics only plays on the margin."

In addition to Sudduth and Adams, the third key player in the A&M System's quest to manage the Los Alamos National Laboratory was one of its own: an Aggie with long-standing ties to the university.

Today, Diane Hurtado is associate vice chancellor for national laboratories management under the Texas A&M Engineering Experiment Station. As such, she serves as the A&M System's primary liaison with the Los Alamos lab.

Growing up in Temple, Texas, there was little doubt Diane would become an Aggie. Although neither of her parents attended college, her father, Don McCrae, had already sent one daughter to A&M. An army veteran, McCrae valued Texas A&M's military traditions and conservative mindset, according to Diane.

"I wasn't sure what I wanted to study at Texas A&M," Hurtado says today, "but when an advisor brought up the subject of astronomy, that sounded interesting to me."

But not to her father.

"What exactly is astronomy?" McCrae asked. The advisor explained astronomy was mostly the study of the night sky.

"You mean looking up at the stars?" Diane knew by the tone of her father's voice that he was skeptical regarding the direction the conversation had taken.

"There's more to it than that," the advisor assured.

"And that's a paying job?"

"Yes, sir," McCrae was told.

"How many astronomers are working in Texas?"

The advisor paused to contemplate the question. "I don't know," came the answer. "Maybe a dozen?"

McCrae looked at Diane. "My daughter needs a practical education, something which will lead to her being able to get a job in the real world."

Diane McCrae chose to be an aerospace engineer—a satisfactory pursuit in her father's thinking—receiving both her bachelor's and master's degrees and eventually her PhD from Texas A&M.

It was in graduate school at A&M that Diane met a fellow aerospace engineering student by the name of John Hurtado. "He dressed better than the rest of us," Diane remembers with a chuckle. John had recently arrived on campus from California, where he had attended San Diego State University as an undergraduate.

"The first time I met Johnny was in a classroom. I had arrived early and was the only student there. When he came in, he saw me, walked up to where I was sitting, and asked if the seat next to me was taken.

"We eventually got married, and after he finished graduate school, we both took jobs at the Sandia National Lab."

Diane Hurtado spent seven years at Sandia, working in a variety of capacities.

"One of the things I liked most about working there," she says, "was that they liked for their technical people to be really versatile. I worked in materials, robotics, and even bioengineering.

"Both Johnny and I loved working and living there, but when it came time to raise a family, we decided to come back to Texas, and we both found jobs at A&M."

Today, Johnny Hurtado is the deputy director of the Bush Combat Development Center, leading the A&M System's involvement with the Army Future's Command at the RELLIS Campus.

Working for Kathy Banks, both Hurtados have held a variety of key positions under the dean's guidance. Given her experience at Sandia coupled with work for the university in federal relations, Diane was a natural fit to help direct the system's bid for the Sandia lab contract.

The same held true for the Los Alamos opportunity when it arose.

"To be honest, we were smarting a little after losing on the Sandia bid," Diane says. "I wasn't sure we would have much interest in Los Alamos, but Chancellor Sharp and Dean Banks felt like it was consistent with where they saw the system heading."

As to how and why the Triad bid proved successful, Diane says, "The only people who know that for sure are the NNSA. But I can tell you why I think we should have won.

"We had the best leadership team. They're all people who are doing this for the right reason. And when you're in charge of a nuclear weapons laboratory, you want people doing it for the right reasons.

"It's a way to serve our country. They believe in the deterrent."

And by "deterrent," Hurtado means deterrent to global nuclear war. At the height of what was then called the nuclear arms race of the 1950s, 1960s, and 1970s, the deterrent against the world's other nuclear superpower, the Soviet Union, was referred to by the acronym MAD, which stands for "mutually assured destruction."

With the long-ago end of the Cold War, Los Alamos has broadened its research mission to include numerous peaceful purposes, but make no mistake: a key element of its mission remains maintaining a functional and formidable nuclear deterrent against potential aggressors.

As for the roles and responsibilities of the three principal partners in the Triad alliance, Hurtado explains each of the partners is responsible, both individually and collectively, for the entire statement of work.

"The Department of Energy made that very clear from the outset," Hurtado says. "The reason they care so much about that now is that in the past, when 'poop has hit the fan'"—as will happen from time to time in such a potentially dangerous environment—"there has been a tendency for partners to point fingers at each other."

Of the shared responsibilities of the Triad team, Hurtado goes on to say, "The DOE prefers that if poop hits the fan, all of us have poop on our faces."

Thom Mason, a former executive with Battelle, serves as president and CEO of Triad National Security and holds the position of director of the Los Alamos National Laboratory. Both Kathy Banks and Scott Sudduth sit on the Triad board of governance. Several members of Texas A&M's Department of Nuclear Engineering have regular engagement with the lab, but one of the key elements of the A&M System's role at Los Alamos, says Hurtado, comes through the Texas A&M Engineering Extension Service (TEEX).

"TEEX is a big component of what we've brought to the table. Their experience with security and training is vital to the Los Alamos mission. The many and varied emergency response and preparedness work that TEEX does, as well as workforce development training, is something the lab has taken advantage of."

"Securing the Los Alamos management contract is a lot bigger deal than most people realize," Sudduth says today. "In the history of use of nuclear weapons in this country, the University of California has, until recently, been the only name in the game. Now we can honestly say, they're not the only name in the game. The only other university in the nuclear weapons game—although it's hardly a game—is Texas A&M."

As the A&M System was formulating a strategy to bid on the Los Alamos National Laboratory contract, Chancellor Sharp approached the leadership of the University of Texas System. As the two had collaborated previously on the Sandia proposal, Sharp welcomed the involvement of his school's intrastate rival.

"We asked them if they wanted to partner with us again," says Sharp, "but they said no."

The UT System put together their own Los Alamos proposal and positioned themselves as the lead partner in the bid, but just as they had done in 2005 as part of a partnership with Lockheed Martin, UT lost out on Los Alamos. More disturbing to UT alums, their alma mater lost to Texas A&M.

On the day Triad was selected as the winning bidder for the Los Alamos National Laboratory management contract, Governor Abbott proclaimed the award "links Texas with one of the world's premier R&D institutions, and I am proud of the expanded contributions our state will make toward our nation's defense. I commend Chancellor Sharp and the Texas A&M University System for securing this contract that will provide significant opportunities for skilled workers trained in Texas to make lasting contributions to our national security."

To that end, the Texas A&M University System established a National Laboratories Office soon after Triad won the Los Alamos contract. Both Hurtado and Adams have important roles there.

That office serves as "a conduit for expanding engagement of the Texas A&M System['s] faculty, students, and staff with the national laboratories, helping potential research collaborators determine the best fit for ongoing or proposed research interests."

Adams says the future looks promising.

"I think with the National Laboratories Office, and with the experience we're gaining through our affiliation with Los Alamos, we're going to be positioned if opportunities arise in the future to serve the country in a way that we think we have the ability and responsibility to do.

"We want to be positioned so that we can do that. We want to be ready for other opportunities as they arise."

Of the more than 130,000 people who worked on the Manhattan Project during World War II, 300 of those were scientists and technicians stationed at Los Alamos. Family and support staff increased the number of those living at the lab to more than 8,000 by the end of the war.

Today, the city of Los Alamos, incorporated in 1957, has a population hovering around 15,000 people. The lab employs more than 13,000 workers, nearly 10,000 of whom are a part of the Triad team. More than 1,300 students are engaged with activities conducted at the site.

During a television broadcast in 1965, Oppenheimer was asked to recall the moment twenty years before in which the work of his Project Y team was affirmed with the initial test detonation of an atomic bomb: "We knew the world would not be the same. A few people laughed, a few people cried. Most people were silent. I remembered the line from the Hindu scripture, the Bhagavad Gita; Vishnu is trying to persuade the Prince that he should do his duty and, to impress him, takes on his multi-armed form and says, 'Now I am become Death, the destroyer of worlds.' I suppose we all thought that, one way or another."

Seventy-five years later, the work at Los Alamos continues, both in harnessing the "destroyer of worlds" and for more peaceful purposes. The Texas A&M University System has entered into that critical realm ably and willingly as a service to both the country and the future of all humanity.

17

Ruth Simmons

Around the Prairie View A&M campus, she is known as "Ruth the Truth."

In the rarified air of American college and university administrators, Ruth Simmons is recognized as a pioneer and a trendsetter in higher education.

In the opinion of Texas A&M University System Chancellor John Sharp, she is a "rock star and a really great human being."

From 2001 to 2012, Simmons served as president of Brown University, the first African American to head up an Ivy League school. Upon stepping down from that post, she returned to her hometown of Houston, intent on making a difference within the communities that made a difference in her own life as a school-aged girl.

She planned to enjoy retirement back home and close to family.

In June 2017, longtime Prairie View A&M President George Wright announced his plans to retire as head of the school and return to teaching and research duties as a member of the faculty. His intent was to remain as school president only until an interim successor could be named.

One month later, Sharp shocked the academic world by announcing that Simmons would fill that role at Prairie View.

"Soon after George Wright announced his retirement, Ruth's name kept popping up," Sharp says today. "I didn't know anything about her, but several regents kept mentioning her. When I did a Google search, I said, 'Wow! We need to talk to this woman.'"

Sharp reached out to Simmons and asked whether she would be interested in meeting with him to discuss possible candidates for the Prairie View A&M position. She agreed. The two met in Houston where, as you might guess, Sharp played his real hand.

"I lured you here on false pretense," Sharp says he told Simmons. "I want you to be the president."

"When he told me that, I thought the idea was completely ridiculous," Simmons says today. "I knew I was going to say no to him, but I didn't want to be rude."

So Simmons told Sharp, "I won't say no immediately."

If you don't close and lock the door on the chancellor, chances are he is going to barge right through and make you an offer you can't refuse.

"I was actually shocked at his offer," Simmons says of the initial agreement Sharp proposed. "All those years I'd worked as an administrator in higher education—vice provost at Princeton, president at Smith, president of Brown—not one time did I ever get an offer to come back to Texas. So, maybe that's why I didn't immediately say no to John."

After the meeting, Simmons called her brother, Clarence Stubblefield.

"Can you believe all this?" Simmons told her sibling. "I've been a university president twice. I'm retired! I don't want to do anything like that again."

To which Stubblefield replied, "You have to do it."

Stubblefield had attended Prairie View and is a member of the school's athletic hall of fame. In 1962, he and future NBA great Zelmo Beaty led the Panther basketball team to the National Association of Intercollegiate Athletics national championship.

"My brother is a dyed-in-the-wool Prairie View supporter," Simmons says. "The school means everything to him. When he told me I had to take the job, I realized I was in a dilemma with my family. The biggest mistake you can make in my family is to think that you're too good to do something important."

Like her brother, Simmons was also a first-generation college student and a graduate of an HBCU—Historically Black Colleges and Universities—Dillard University, in New Orleans. She went on to earn her master's and doctoral degrees in the study of Romance literature from Harvard University.

After further discussions with Clarence and other members of her family, Simmons agreed to take a tour of the Prairie View campus. Sharp insisted he be her tour guide.

The two met at the superconvenience store, Buc-ee's, on US Highway 290, just south of Prairie View. Sharp promised their tour would be kept secret.

"As we were driving around on campus, I made a wrong turn and went down a street I wasn't supposed to," Sharp remembers, "and a campus policeman came up to me and started screaming, 'Get the hell out of here!' Of course, he had no clue, nor did he care, who I was or who I had with me in the car.

"In the midst of all this, Ruth smiled and said, 'You've got a lot of influence around here.'

"'Yes, I don't,' was my reply as I scrambled to do a U-turn and make the campus officer happy."

Seeing the campus and its students made a big impact on Simmons. She was reminded of her own time on "The Hill," attending her older brother's basketball games.

"How am I going to be able to go back and tell my family that I won't do this because I think I'm too good for it?" she contemplated.

Then she gave thought to just how far she had come from her own youth.

While Simmons was president of Brown, the publishing house Simon & Schuster wanted her to tell her life story. Well known and well regarded in the academic world, Simmons received a sizable advance on future projected royalties for the book, and in a short amount of time, she completed her manuscript. But the process of creating a book doesn't end with a first draft. When Simmons realized how much more of her time would be taken in bringing a book about her life to publication, she returned the advance, explaining to the publisher that her top priority must remain her duties as a school president.

Another casualty of Simmons's dedication to Brown was her position on the board of the global banking firm Goldman Sachs. During the Great Recession of 2008–9, the Goldman board on which Simmons sat received criticism for the sizable bonuses it had authorized for top executives of the company while the firm was receiving bailout money to stay afloat.

In a 2010 *New York Times* story, a nineteen-year-old Brown student said Simmons's actions had "brought shame on the university." Simmons told the *Times* she was used to "lively debate on campus" but offered little more in the way of explanation or comment. The truth was that by the time the story was published, Simmons was no longer a member of the Goldman board. The firestorm had become a sizable distraction for her and required much more time than she was willing or able to give to the crisis. At considerable financial cost, she stepped down from the Goldman board.

Seven years later, with a desire to continue impacting young lives, Simmons accepted the Prairie View job on an interim basis. She began her new duties meeting with faculty, staff, and students. At one gathering, a group broke out T-shirts in the school's purple and gold colors that read "Ruth the Truth."

That handle has stuck.

Beverly Copeland, a Prairie View graduate and now associate professor and assistant to the president at the school, remembers her first meeting with Simmons.

"We had a get-together in the president's dining room, and it was a lovely occasion," Copeland says. "Her shared presence emanated something magnificent, and one got a feeling that we had landed someone exceptional. I introduced myself and made small chat with her about the refreshments that were being served. I walked away knowing that something good had just happened to Prairie View.

"I had been on the faculty at that point for close to five years, and for the first time, I felt I had a leader whom I wanted to follow. I don't know why; maybe it was the way she humbly conversed with me about seemingly insignificant matters. Whatever it was, I felt at ease.

"But if you know Ruth Simmons, she has a natural gift of making people comfortable in her presence."

Ruth Stubblefield was the youngest of twelve children raised by parents Isaac and Fanny Stubblefield. Ruth was born July 3, 1945, in the small East Texas town of Grapeland.

"We worked on a very large plantation on the banks of the Trinity River," Simmons says. "I'm told there were as many as a hundred families living on the plantation, toiling as 'sharecroppers.'"

They weren't slaves, Simmons says, "but just barely."

"We had a very basic existence, going into the fields and picking cotton all day," Simmons recalls. "That included children, whose labors were vital to the industry, but it meant that kids didn't spend a lot of time at school when crops needed to be brought in."

As the Stubblefield children came of age, most moved away to larger towns and cities where economic opportunity was greater and more diverse. Ruth's oldest siblings moved to Houston. Three of her older brothers enlisted in the army during and after the Korean War.

"My brothers made it clear their goal was to get my parents off the plantation," Simmons says. "My brothers often sent their paychecks home, and eventually, my parents and the rest of our family were able to move to Houston, too."

Grapeland had been "deeply segregated," says Simmons, who left the area when she was seven. "There was a long list of things we couldn't do. We were taught to step off the sidewalk when a white person approached."

Things were not much better when she moved to Houston.

Simmons and her parents settled into a home her older siblings had found in Houston's Fifth Ward. Once known as one of the "proudest Black neighborhoods in the US," by the 1950s, the segregated community two miles north of downtown Houston had become deeply impoverished due to the large number of residents, like the Stubblefield family, who were able to find only low-paying jobs.

But the schools within the Fifth Ward, although also segregated, opened up a whole new world for young Ruth.

"The most marvelous thing happened when we moved to Houston," Simmons says. "The community center down the street from where we lived had a library, and the schools I attended had libraries, and so I made it my goal to read every book ever written. I've concluded that my motivation then was to try to escape the 'self-imprisonment' of a segregated world that didn't make much sense to me as a child.

"I found that escape in books."

Simmons says the idea that a child wanted to read books all the time was alarming to her family and friends. "They thought I was touched in the head, but what I found in books gave me strength.

"One thing that happens when you read a lot is you begin to be very good at language. I started speaking in ways that became infuriating to others because they said I was using 'fancy words.'

"My father protected me from feeling ostracized until my teachers started taking care of me."

Simmons describes her younger self as "kind of a geeky kid who just loved learning."

Perhaps her greatest influence growing up was her young debate instructor at Wheatley High School.

"All of the schools I attended in Houston were segregated, and it may not have been until I joined the debate team under Vernell Lillie that I really spent any time around white people," Simmons says. "She took us to debate tournaments throughout Texas where we competed against white students. She also took us to plays at the theaters in downtown Houston.

"I graduated from high school in 1963, and it was about then the integration movement was starting to become a big deal."

Lillie strongly encouraged Simmons to attend college and recommended the school from which she had received her teaching degree, Dillard University in New Orleans. Lillie helped Simmons get a scholarship from Dillard, while Houston's Worthing Foundation also provided much-needed financial aid.

"While the racial landscape was beginning to change in the mid-1960s, Historically Black Colleges were still about the only option that high-ability Black students had at the time," Simmons says. "People sort of scoffed when I decided to major in French. They told me I needed to major in something practical because society was on the cusp of important change."

Such was Simmons's love of language that after her first year at Dillard, she got on a bus, traveled to Mexico, and spent her summer living with a Mexican family to learn Spanish.

Simmons also became an activist during her college years. "A real nuisance," she describes her younger self. So, it was not surprising that one day she was called to the Dillard president's house. "I figured I was in trouble."

Simmons didn't realize that college presidents don't usually mete out discipline from the living room of their residences. Instead, the school's then president, Albert Dent, had other news for her.

"We have an exchange program with Wellesley College," Dent told Simmons, "and every year we get to send a student there. We'd like you to go."

"At first I wasn't sure if he was trying to get rid of me or what," Simmons says today with a laugh.

Wellesley was and remains one of the most highly regarded all-women's colleges in the country. Located in Wellesley, Massachusetts, the school offered Simmons a new outlook on her world.

"I spent my junior year at Wellesley," Simmons says, "and that was a very eye-opening experience for me. I lived on a hallway with all these young white women. For the first time in my life, I studied alongside what society considered 'normal' people."

Simmons smiles and shakes her head at her words.

"I had one friend from Switzerland, and I got to meet her family on a trip we made to Europe. Another friend was a Jewish girl from Philadelphia. And I had a friend whose family lived on a farm in Connecticut. I got to go to all these different places and meet all these different people."

The most important lesson Wellesley instilled in Simmons was how to understand her own potential.

"I grew up in a very patriarchal family. My father made all the decisions. I never really considered that I deserved to be at the forefront of anything because that was for my brothers. Yet at Wellesley, something very strange happened. I saw a woman, Margaret Clapp, who was actually the president of the school.

"That disrupted all kinds of notions I had about my 'proper place.'"

Returning to Dillard, Simmons became an even more passionate activist, and when it came time to graduate, she was told she would not receive her degree for boycotting chapel services. At the same time, she had received a Fulbright Scholarship and was admitted into graduate school at Harvard.

"That created a conundrum for Dillard," Simmons says today. "Since I'd already been admitted into Harvard and that was a positive reflection on Dillard, administrators at the school decided to look the other way, and I was able to graduate."

By the time Simmons was in her early thirties, she was associate dean of graduate studies at the University of Southern California (USC). It was obvious she was on a rapid ascent into a senior position in university administration. Then came three critical decisions that friends and colleagues told her were career killers.

"The position I held at USC was a wonderful job, a wonderful environment," Simmons says, "but I really wanted to be in undergraduate education because that is the formative experience for young people. So, for about one-third the pay I was making, I took a job as director of undergraduate studies at Princeton.

"Everyone told me that was a step in the wrong direction.

"While I was at Princeton, I got an offer to become director of

African American studies at the school. At first, I told them I wasn't qualified, but they insisted I consider the position. When I decided I would take the job, my friends told me I was making yet another bad decision.

"'You'll be typecast,' they said. 'You're a French professor; you don't need to do that. If you do, you'll never be able to pursue an administrative job.'

"I took the position, which led to my biggest promotion at Princeton. They said, 'What you've done in African American studies, we now want you to do across the entire university.' That's how I became associate dean of faculty at Princeton."

By that time, Simmons realized people, despite their good intentions, often give bad advice because they cannot look inside a person's heart.

"I was doing all the 'wrong' things—at least in other peoples' minds—because I was making choices based on things I valued, like helping the African American community. That's why I made my third career-killing decision."

She left Princeton to become provost at Spellman College, a historically Black liberal arts college for women in Atlanta.

"Don't do it!" people implored Simmons. "You could be president of a major university someday; you don't need to be working at a *women's* college."

Two years later, Simmons was back at Princeton, and in 1995, she was named president of Smith College, the first African American woman to preside over a major American university.

In 2001, she became president of Brown.

After her visit to "The Hill," when Simmons considered her career trajectory, she realized accepting the Prairie View A&M job was a perfect fit with the decisions that had benefited her in the past.

"I realized that pursuing opportunities that meant a lot to me personally had shaped my life in really valuable ways. If I had listened to any of the advice I got through the years, I'm certain I wouldn't be where I am today."

Soon after assuming the presidency at Prairie View, she realized much work needed to be done and that an "interim" president probably was not going to accomplish much.

"I reached the conclusion those changes were important enough, both to the institution as well as to its students, that it might be best if I was able to hang around for a while."

Simmons texted Chancellor Sharp with a pointed question: "How complicated would it be to remove [my] interim designation?"

Twenty-seven minutes later, Sharp replied: "Simple."

In early 2018, Simmons was again featured in a *New York Times* piece, this one entitled "Cultivating the Next Generation of College Students":

> My aspirations for Prairie View are to essentially make sure the university is continuing to do the same thing for students today that it did for my brother—and Dillard did for me. And that is to offer the advantage of a strong education that will prepare students for the careers they want, in a social and cultural context that helps them develop the confidence to perform after graduation.
>
> As president, that means focusing on time-honored strategies to success that apply to universities everywhere: worrying about the faculty who are recruited here, the campus experience, and whether we are providing the leadership and internship opportunities that students need. It means worrying about the reputation of the university. It's obviously a much more competitive world today than it was when I was a student, but the underlying work to move the university to a level of achievement that makes students and alumni proud is the same.

Maduforo Eze was a member of Prairie View's first graduating class after Simmons became the full-time president of the school. Prior to his senior year, he interned in the Office of the President and watched as the transition from President Wright to President Simmons unfolded.

"On her first day, in meeting with everyone who worked in the president's office, the first thing she said was, 'Why isn't there any art on the walls of this building?' We all sort of laughed nervously, but her persona, from the very beginning, was welcoming and open. At the same time, you realized she was 'all about business' too.

"I was heavily involved in the Student Government Association during my time at Prairie View A&M, and when student leaders came to Ruth—she wanted everyone to call her by her first name—she was always very open to what we had to say, as long as we had thought through things thoroughly. If an idea seemed 'half baked' to her, she would ask thought-provoking questions to help us come up with better ideas.

"She was always very student centered and always wanted a student in the room when decisions were being made."

Simmons's impact on "The Hill" has been dramatic and far reaching. A drive past Buc-ee's today reveals a building boom within the town of Prairie View, as multiple student housing facilities are being added to accommodate the school's "Ruth the Truth" enrollment boom.

One of Simmons's most important initiatives at Prairie View A&M is to attract and retain top-notch faculty. For her, the modern-day "Historically Black College" experience means her students should be on an equal footing with other universities across the country.

It is difficult not to describe the Ruth Simmons of today as an "academic cult figure," as she was at Spellman, Smith, and Brown, but in speaking with the *New York Times* after landing her job at Prairie View, Simmons did not subscribe to a model of "hero-worship" leadership:

> People look at the institutions that I have led and they see dissimilarities. I see similarities. When people think in terms of leadership, they're often thinking about the kind of specific skills needed for different types of enterprises. I think of leadership as more of a disposition—the ability to step into a situation to learn about the history of the enterprise, the opportunities that it faces, the culture that exists and the people who are served by it. To look at all of that, to listen to stakeholders and then to think about how that enterprise or institution should best be served. There is no one model of leadership if you approach it that way.
>
> What I have tried to do wherever I go is to start where the institution is rather than try to import particularly rigid constructs from other places. In that sense, I think a leader is more than anything else a facilitator, a person who is able to come in to show a community a picture of what it is, to provide some insight into what it could be—how it could be different or improved perhaps—and then enlist the help of people who are there and others who support that institution in order to move forward together.

18

A Healthy Texas

Texas A&M graduated its first doctors—of veterinary medicine—in 1920. Since then, the A&M College of Veterinary Medicine and Biological Sciences has established itself as one of the top programs of its kind in the world.

Some sixty years later, in 1981, A&M graduated its first class of future physicians trained in the treatment of humans. Mark Sicilio was a member of that "charter class" within the newly created Texas A&M College of Medicine.

"I grew up in College Station, and my father taught chemistry at A&M," Sicilio says. "Dad had the highest regard for the Vet School, but I didn't give much thought to becoming a vet. I thought it would be hard enough to learn how to treat just one species."

The A&M College of Medicine was launched in the fall of 1977. Discussions about starting a program had gone on for years. Texas congressman Olin Teague, A&M Class of 1932, led the charge for the establishment of a medical school at his alma mater. Teague was wounded six times during his service in World War II and was hospitalized for nearly two years before being discharged from the army—at the rank of colonel—in September 1946. Two weeks before his release from medical care, Teague won a special election for a seat among the Texas delegation to the US House of Representatives, a post he retained for the next three decades.

It was Teague's hope that Texas A&M would produce doctors who could care for Aggie veterans in need.

The Olin Teague Research Center became the first on-campus home of the Texas A&M College of Medicine. At the time, that building also housed the office of school president Jarvis Miller.

"There were thirty-two of us in that charter class," Sicilio remembers, "and all but one had received our undergraduate degrees from A&M."

The lone exception was a student from Tarleton State.

"In the two years we took instruction on the main campus, our cadaver lab was in the basement of the Teague building, right below President Miller's office. Every now and then, the president would hear the 'clang, clang, clang' of the chains in our cadaver tanks, inevitably followed by the strong smell of formaldehyde."

Sicilio laughs at the recollection. "That's why they moved the president's office to the Williams Building," he says.

Eventually, the College of Medicine, along with the Colleges of Nursing, Pharmacy, Dentistry, and Public Health, became part of the Texas A&M Health Science Center (HSC), today located southwest of the flagship campus along the Riverside Parkway, also known as State Highway 47.

Don Powell was chair when the A&M System Board of Regents approved the establishment of the HSC in 1999. Gov. George W. Bush had appointed him to the board in 1996. When Bush became president, he selected Powell, a longtime Amarillo banker, to become chair of the US Federal Deposit Insurance Corporation in 2001.

Now retired, Powell still calls Amarillo home. A 1963 graduate of West Texas State College, Powell says he "fell in love" with Texas A&M when he joined his sons on a tour of the school in the late 1970s. At the age of eighty, Powell recently earned an online master's degree from Texas A&M University.

"I'll finally get my Aggie ring," he proudly proclaims.

Powell says the establishment of the Texas A&M HSC came as a means to bolster both the flagship's and the system's academic reputations. Other in-state schools—including the University of Texas, Baylor, Texas Tech, and the University of North Texas—operated health science facilities at the time. When the system purchased the former Baylor College of Dentistry in 1996, bringing A&M's two major health initiatives together made sense.

The establishment of the HSC also aided the A&M flagship's quest to become a member of the prestigious American Association of Universities (AAU).

"That's a far sight better than the Good Housekeeping 'seal of approval,'" Powell laughs. "The AAU is the elite of the academic elite. I remember hearing a lot of discussion about what it would take to achieve that status, and the HSC fit into that equation.'"

A&M achieved membership in the AAU in 2001, joining the University of Texas at Austin and Rice University as the state's only AAU-affiliated institutions of higher learning. Nationwide, there are sixty-six AAU members.

Also key to the establishment of both the A&M College of Medicine and the HSC was the continuing quest for the university to meet its original mission as a land grant school. Many of A&M's early doctors sought to practice or affiliate themselves in small-town or rural settings. Today, that mission has been formalized under the umbrella of the A&M HSC in a program called the Rural and Community Health Initiative (ARCHI). The program is under the guidance of Dr. Nancy Dickey, who is also president emeritus of the A&M HSC, having served as head of the HSC from 2001 to 2012.

Dickey came to College Station in 1996 from private clinical practice in Richmond, Texas, near Houston, to become an associate professor at the A&M College of Medicine. In addition, she soon launched the college's Family Medicine Residency Program. Two years later, she became the first woman president of the American Medical Association (AMA).

"Someone had to be the first," she says in her typically self-deprecating way. "God bless the people I worked with here at A&M. I was on airplanes a great deal doing AMA work, and the folks back here helped carry on my work."

During her time at the helm of the HSC, Texas A&M added both a College of Pharmacy in 2004 and a College of Nursing in 2008. The A&M College of Medicine also expanded its network of clinical centers under Dickey to include venues in Bryan, Dallas, and Round Rock. Moreover, A&M's enrollment in health science fields doubled to more than two thousand total students.

From its inception in 1999 until 2012, the HSC remained under the purview of the Texas A&M University System. This ensured continued state funding but limited other outside funding opportunities for the HSC, which restricted its ability to grow.

"I was shocked to learn when I got here that the Health Science Center was under my control," Sharp says. "I'm not an academician."

However, Sharp is astute when it comes to financial matters. He knew research dollars generated is a principal indicator of a major university's academic prowess and helps maintain its AAU standing.

Sharp was aware that many schools generate sizable amounts of research funding through university-owned hospitals and medical centers, but the flagship would get no credit for medical research as long as the HSC remained under the system's control. The flagship sorely needed affiliation with the HSC, its on-campus neighbor.

Within months of Sharp's arrival, that change was made. The new administrative priority: research development.

Dickey saw the writing on the wall. As a clinician, Dickey's area of expertise was not fundraising.

"For the last eleven years, the administration of the health-related programs of the Texas A&M System has essentially been my life," said Dickey in the press release announcing her departure. "The impending merger of the Health Science Center into the university seems an appropriate time for new leadership to take the helm."

Dickey's successor as permanent head of the HSC, Brett Giroir, possessed an extensive research background, with medical training as a pediatrician. From 2004 to 2008, under the presidential administration of George W. Bush, Giroir served as both deputy director and director of the Defense Advanced Research Projects Agency (DARPA). Since the beginning of the Space Age in the late 1950s, DARPA has been the arm of the US Department of Defense responsible for the frequently classified development of modern military technology.

Giroir joined the ranks of the Texas A&M University System in 2008 as a vice chancellor for strategic initiatives. In that capacity, Chancellor Sharp charged him with spearheading an effort to turn the area surrounding the A&M flagship campus into a biotech hub. In 2012, under Giroir's watch, an A&M group won a $285.6 million contract with the Department of Health and Human Services to create "a new center for developing and manufacturing medicine and vaccines in the case of a pandemic."

Two years later, Gov. Rick Perry named Giroir to head up an Ebola task force after two cases of the sometimes fatal disease surfaced in the Dallas area.

Giroir left the HSC in 2015 shortly after Michael Young assumed the presidency of the A&M flagship. "I was given a 'resign-or-be-fired' mandate," Giroir told reporters. His permanent successor was Dr. Carrie Byington, a former A&M student who had spent more than twenty years in teaching and administrative positions at the University of Utah, where Young had served as president before his move to Texas A&M.

Byington's return to her alma mater proved short lived. She resigned from her position in the late summer of 2019 after less than two years on the job to lead the University of California System's health enterprise.

When told the search for a full-time leader of the Texas A&M HSC resembled Pres. Abraham Lincoln's quest to land a general to lead Union forces during the Civil War, Sharp responded, upon reflection, "That's true. But we've found our Ulysses Grant in the person of Greg Hartman."

Following in the footsteps of a clinician, a researcher, and an academic, Hartman assumed the HSC helm in 2020 as a management expert with extensive experience in health care. Before joining the A&M System, Hartman served in a number of executive roles with Seton Healthcare, a $2 billion hospital network based in Central Texas. His responsibilities with Seton included serving as CEO of the company's two largest hospitals.

Like many among the system's current executive ranks, Hartman has long-standing ties with Sharp, whom he worked for in political campaigns and at the state comptroller's office before turning to health care management as a career.

"After I graduated from college, I was working for a political consulting firm in Austin," Hartman says in explaining his ties to Sharp. "One day, one of the principals of the firm called me into his office and asked me if I would be interested in working on the campaign for a client who was going to run for railroad commissioner. When they told me who it was, I said I wasn't really interested.

"I'd heard some things and I didn't think I liked Sharp."

"Well, just meet him before you make up your mind," the young Hartman was told.

"So, I did," he says, "and it turned out I really liked him. He was a good guy."

Hartman became Sharp's campaign manager, and together they won the race for railroad commissioner. Hartman later guided Sharp's successful run for state comptroller. Hartman spent the next six years of his life working for Sharp in the comptroller's office.

"John Sharp is by far the most intuitive politician I've ever known," Harman says, "but he's also intuitive enough to know when somebody else has a good idea. I think that's been a key to his success everywhere he's been."

Eventually, Hartman wound up with Seton, where, as its CEO, he was one of the primary drivers in bringing a medical school to the University of Texas in Austin.

After some fifteen years there, he decided it was time for a change. He considered taking an executive position with a nonprofit organization in his hometown of San Antonio. Hartman's father, Glen, had worked as a TV meteorologist there and had served on the San Antonio City Council.

In his "spare time," Glen Hartman also conducted overseas operations within the US intelligence ranks—as a spy.

"He got his start translating Russian communications during the Cuban Missile Crisis," Hartman says of his late father. "When I was a kid, Dad would go off on these trips for a month or two at a time. They always gave him time off at the television station, so none of us thought much about it. Not until years later did we discover he had been spending time on the other side of the Iron Curtain spying on the Soviets."

Whether or not Sharp knew his former protégé had espionage in his DNA, he stayed in touch with him. One night in late 2018, Sharp placed a call to find out how Hartman's job search was going.

"I'd stayed in touch with John and Billy [Hamilton] and Ray [Bonilla], but the chancellor's call that night surprised me," Hartman says. "He told me, 'I've got some programs that need somebody to kind of do some stuff on.' I wasn't sure exactly what that meant, but then he shared, 'There's the Healthy Texas program and a few other things.'"

The ongoing Healthy Texas initiative merges the expertise and resources of Texas A&M Health with the Texas A&M AgriLife Extension Service's statewide network to educate families and provide them with resources to create healthier lifestyles. The pilot program launched in 2015, called Healthy South Texas, operates in a twenty-seven-county region of South Texas striving to reduce the highest-impact diseases found in the area, including diabetes, respiratory illnesses, and infectious disease.

"After the chancellor explained all that, he offered me a job,"

Hartman says. "It sounded sort of interesting to me, so I told him I'd take the job. I moved to College Station at the beginning of 2019 to become vice chancellor for strategic initiatives."

Before the end of that same year, the university named Hartman the acting head of the A&M HSC. That role became permanent in April 2020, when Hartman was named chief operating officer of the HSC.

"When I first took the HSC job on an interim basis," Hartman says, "I told the leadership group, 'I enjoy being around academics and I'll enjoy being in the clinical world, but I barely passed chemistry class in high school, and I never could have been a doctor. I have a son who's a doctor, but I never could have been a doctor.'

"Fortunately, I had the support of the chancellor, and it didn't take long before I won the confidence of the provost. I told her, 'Look, the only way this works is if you want me to run things operationally, I'll do that. And I'm going to leave the academic stuff totally to you.'"

Texas A&M University Provost Carol Fierke came from the University of Michigan in 2017.

Before her departure at the end of 2020, Fierke proved to be a top-notch administrator with a reputation as a consensus-builder. She sees similar qualities in Hartman.

"One of the directions the HSC wants to go," says Fierke, "is to provide more clinical care. Greg has management experience in the hospital world, the clinical arena, and that's been a real boon. He's also done a great job of helping us integrate the HSC into the university.

"He understands that I probably know more about academics than he does, and he absolutely knows more about health care than I do."

"We don't have our own hospital," Hartman adds. "In fact, compared to other schools, we have a relatively small clinical enterprise, and I think that's been seen as a weakness.

"I actually think given the reality of where we're at in the health care world right now [and] with the way the health care ecosystem is changing, we're going to need to figure out how to deliver more value-based care to underserved populations and in different kinds of settings."

The Texas A&M University System is leading by example.

In early 2020, Chancellor Sharp and the Texas A&M System announced a 5.5-acre campus adjacent to the Texas Medical Center in Houston that would serve multiple purposes. Included in the half-billion-dollar complex is the home of the A&M EnMed program,

Dean Kathy Banks's idea for an engineering-based medical school made possible by a cutting-edge partnership between the Texas A&M Colleges of Engineering and Medicine.

"The Houston medical scene is about to see the benefits of 'Aggie ingenuity,'" said Chancellor Sharp upon announcement of the project in 2018.

In addition to the construction of two new buildings—a nineteen-story student housing structure and a thirty-story medical office tower—the complex also includes a refurbished eighteen-story building that is the physical home of EnMed.

Dr. Roderick Pettigrew is the executive dean of the A&M EnMed program and the guiding force behind a new kind of doctor called the "physicianeer."

"That term describes someone who understands the blending of medicine with engineering," says Pettigrew. "They realize that the sciences of chemistry and biology and physics and engineering are seamlessly interwoven into the fabric of life. That's what nature is, and human life is an expression of that."

The entirety of Pettigrew's own postgraduate educational experience forged a union between medicine and science. After receiving his bachelor of science degree in physics from the historically Black Morehouse College in Atlanta, Pettigrew attended Rensselaer Polytechnic Institute and the Massachusetts Institute of Technology for his graduate studies, earning both master's and PhD degrees. From there, he attended the University of Miami in Coral Gables, Florida, becoming an MD through a unique program that only admitted students who already held PhD degrees in a field of scientific study.

Thus has Pettigrew spent most of his scientific life in pursuit of an EnMed-like dream. He is recognized globally for his pioneering work in cardiovascular magnetic resonance imaging. Pettigrew joined the Texas A&M University System in late 2017 after nearly fifteen years as the founding director of the National Institute of Biomedical Imaging and Bioengineering at the National Institutes of Health. In 2020, the National Science Board honored him with the prestigious Vannevar Bush Award in recognition of his scientific achievements in the field of medicine.

"Science has long recognized," Pettigrew says, "that when you bring an engineer, physicist, mathematician, biologist, microbiologist, geneticist, neurologist, and immunologist—or some combination of those people—together in the same room and sit them around a table, good things will happen. Chances are they will come up with bright ideas to solve problems."

"With 'physicianeers,'" he adds, "we're going to get the cross-functional thinking of both a physician and an engineer all in the same brain. By doing that, we'll greatly accelerate ideation, invention, and innovation, which will then accelerate improvement in health and health care delivery."

Pettigrew's physicianeers receive two A&M degrees upon completion of their EnMed studies: an MD from the College of Medicine and a master's of engineering from the College of Engineering. The length of the program is four years; engineering content is integrated within the College of Medicine courses.

Among those in the "charter class" of EnMed students is Priya Arunachalam, an Austin native who came to the A&M EnMed program from Johns Hopkins University, where she received a bachelor's in biomedical engineering and an MBA in health care management and entrepreneurship.

"EnMed has put me on the path to being an interdisciplinary mind in the future of medicine," Arunachalam says. "The integrated curriculum engages my engineering thought process . . . and is prepar[ing] me to innovate in clinical practice."

A key element of the health care continuum is wellness: motivating people to do the things they need to do to prevent them from getting sick.

"It sure looks like there's a lot of evidence that what we're putting into our body, the foods we eat, can significantly impact our health," said Chancellor Sharp. "The 'food pyramid' that a lot of us grew up with has turned out to be a fallacy."

Just as the A&M College of Engineering has channeled a part of its sizable resources toward launching the system's EnMed program, so too has the College of Agriculture and Life Sciences stood firm on its commitment to establish programs and conduct research to create a healthier Texas.

At the forefront of those initiatives is the vice chancellor for Texas A&M AgriLife and dean of the College of Agriculture and Life Sciences, Patrick Stover.

"The dean of agriculture here at Texas A&M has long been someone trained in the sciences of food production," Sharp says. "In Dr. Stover, for the first time, we have a nutritionist leading our AgriLife programs.

"I think that's a good thing."

As vice chancellor, Stover is in charge of all agriculture, academic, and research programs across the entirety of the Texas A&M University System. In his duties, he also oversees the work of four of the state agencies administered by the system: Texas A&M AgriLife Research, Texas A&M AgriLife Extension Service, Texas A&M Veterinary Medical Diagnostic Laboratory, and Texas A&M Forest Service.

And as AgriLife dean on A&M's flagship College Station campus, Stover directs more than seven thousand students and 330 faculty members across fifteen academic departments.

In his previous position at Cornell University, Stover was director of the Division of Nutritional Sciences. And in his interview with Stover, Chancellor Sharp liked the sound of that.

"We wanted to start an institute where people can go, whether they're producers or consumers, to understand what to eat to have a healthy life," Sharp says. "We actually talked with Patrick about that concept in our interview with him. We both agreed we needed to do that, and I believe that's part of the reason that he came here."

Stover explains his goal this way: "A&M will be the leader in producing the most rigorous nutrition science in the world to inform dietary recommendations and replace the decades-old, outdated approaches used today."

Stover's background prepared him for this job.

"I grew up on a small family farm in Pennsylvania," Stover says, "and my parents were committed to raising all of our own food. They were very connected to the idea that you grow good food that makes you healthy. We had a family garden of about three acres, and we grew cauliflower and cabbage and corn and broccoli and carrots and radishes and string beans and everything else. We grew all of our own fruit, and we always had about two hundred chickens, both for eggs and for meat.

"We did have a steer once, but he got a name, which turned out to be the wrong formula for putting beef on our dinner table. He became a member of the family."

It was as a postdoc at the University of California at Berkeley that

Stover got interested in the study of metabolism and the link between biochemistry and nutrition. During his twenty-three-year stay at Cornell University in Ithaca, New York, Stover focused his research on the question of why some women are susceptible to having a child with birth defects. What he learned was how a change in diet can put people on a healthier path.

Stover continues that work at Texas A&M.

"What we're looking to do is to ensure that we have a food system that is accessible but also healthy. And in developing this new science space, we must create trustworthy dietary guidelines that have a chronic disease endpoint. That was a big part of the attraction to come here, because if you're going to solve the divide between agriculture production and making healthy people, it's going to be in Texas, where you have one of the highest rates of diet-related chronic disease in the country coupled with a hundred billion dollars a year ag economy."

"I was very happy at Cornell," Stover goes on to say, "and I wasn't looking for a job. But after a bunch of calls, I told the chancellor, 'Okay, I'll come down.'

"When I talked to him, there was this meaningful exchange you don't get from a lot of people in his position. He's not just a visionary; he sees the world twenty years ahead of where the rest of us look."

"Nobody is more committed to Texas," Stover says of Sharp. "Nobody is more committed and passionate about Texas A&M University, and nobody has the sort of vision that he sees looking forward.

"He understands that when it comes to food and nutrition and creating a world where people are healthy and can stay healthy, we've got to get this right."

Army Futures Command

When the original Bryan Army Air Field opened in the early months of 1943, it rolled out a methodology designed to aid in the United States' efforts to wage war successfully.

Prior to the establishment of the Instrumentation School for Instructor Pilots at Bryan Field, army aviators flew by the seat of their pants when encountering inclement weather during missions. Training men to fly safely in low- or no-visibility conditions solely by the readings on their instrument panels—the chief mission at the Bryan base—leveled the playing field for Allied pilots in the air wars fought during World War II.

Seventy-six years later, the US Army returned to Central Texas and the banks of the Brazos River. The mission once again was to modernize the means by which America engages in armed conflict.

The Texas A&M University System's RELLIS Campus, once the site of the Bryan Army Air Field, is now the home of the George H. W. Bush Combat Development Complex, a major research and testing site under the US Army Futures Command (AFC).

"We're leveraging the strength of academics and intellectual freedom to position army modernization in a way to win the fight before an actual fight," says Gen. John M. "Mike" Murray, senior commander of the Army Futures Command. "The Combat Development Complex will bring together diverse partners from businesses, academia, and most importantly, our soldiers to test emerging technology in an operationally relevant environment. With soldiers providing feedback, we can evaluate [the proposed technology] early to ensure we're getting exactly what our troops need in the field."

Upon the announcement of the system's partnership with the AFC, Kathy Banks, vice chancellor of engineering and national laboratories for the Texas A&M University System, said of the collaboration, "Delivering this capability is a truly unique challenge."

"The Bush Combat Development Complex positions Texas A&M as a nexus for high-tech testing in service of the nation's security," Banks added. "Like other universities, Texas A&M is tapping into its formidable prowess in key fields of academic research to help deliver new capabilities faster than ever. Unlike other universities, however, Texas A&M is building a $200 million testing complex where the army's partners—and others—can demonstrate pilot technologies and engage key stakeholders."

Enticing the US Army to come to Aggieland was an "all-hands-on-deck" endeavor driven by the same novel vision that created the REL-LIS Campus and forged the system's management role with the Los Alamos National Laboratory in New Mexico. All are the by-products of the forward—some would call it "outside-the-box"—thinking that has been the hallmark of Chancellor John Sharp since taking the helm of the Texas A&M University System.

"Outside the box" would also describe the groundbreaking approaches being taken by the AFC, which officially came into existence on July 1, 2018. Two weeks later, the Pentagon announced that Austin, Texas, would serve as AFC headquarters, a true indication the army was looking to break the mold.

More than 150 cities were originally considered for AFC headquarters. Texas A&M put in its own proposal at the eleventh hour. Ultimately, five finalists were chosen: Austin, Boston, Minneapolis, Philadelphia, and Raleigh.

Never before had the army sought to locate a key command headquarters in a major metropolitan area. Criteria for choosing the location included proximity to science, technology, engineering, and math workers and related industries; proximity to private sector innovation; local investment in academic STEM and research and development programs; quality of life; price tag; and civic support for the military and the project.

The army had tried for years, with minimal success, to modernize its forces through its ties with its large defense contractors. Too often, the goods delivered were more in line with the expertise of the contractors than what the army actually needed. As General Murray has stated, AFC represents an attitudinal shift in fighting philosophy not seen since the immediate aftermath of the Vietnam War in the mid-1970s.

"We're in search of ideas and different ways of thinking about problems that we face," Murray said, calling himself the CEO of "a start-up managing a merger." "We understand that we're all a product of our environment, and left to our own devices, we'll continue to think about problems in the way we've always thought about problems."

"Partnerships should be a two-way road," he added. Concerning AFC's future collaboration with academia, Murray said, "If we invest our resources into a university, we should get something back in return. We knew this wouldn't work if the command was behind the gates at Fort Bragg or Fort Hood. The word 'proximity' mattered."

"The ability to work out of a location and quickly bump into that innate spirit that Austin is known for and the ability for people to get in to see us without having to go through a front gate played a part," Murray said of the decision to locate AFC headquarters in the Texas capital city.

Proximity to academia included more than just the research interests of the University of Texas. Other nearby schools, like Rice, the University of Houston, and Texas A&M, also made Austin the best fit in the minds of army decision-makers.

Despite Texas A&M's failure to make the army's short list for an AFC command center, Chancellor John Sharp knew A&M's RELLIS Campus would be an attractive environment for the kind of research and development AFC would need. Just as the location was ideal for training instructor pilots during World War II, the twenty-first-century RELLIS Campus offered both size and amenities of import to the AFC mission: ample space for a variety of testing grounds in close proximity to researchers and scientists affiliated with Texas A&M who could aid in technology development.

Sharp showcased the RELLIS site and the research capabilities of his A&M System institutions at a three-day gathering with AFC brass in November 2018. At a press event held during the visit, the chancellor emphasized the commitment Texas A&M stood ready to make.

"This is a place where we honor those who serve," Sharp told Murray. "We are mission-driven. There isn't a question you can ask us that the answer is not 'yes.' We will do everything we can to fulfill [your] mission."

Six months later, in May 2019, AFC held a five-day autonomous vehicle demonstration at RELLIS. The event not only gave weapons and defense industry contractors an opportunity to showcase their wares but also put the RELLIS Campus on display as a potential site for future AFC testing activity.

The army liked what it saw.

Just three months later, on August 8, 2019, the A&M System announced an agreement with AFC to create a research, development, and testing complex on the RELLIS Campus. Of that sum, the system would invest $80 million into the venture, with the state of Texas committing to an additional $50 million in funding.

To bring the AFC command to Austin, the University of Texas System donated two floors of office space at its headquarters in the downtown Austin area.

Of AFC's partnership with Texas A&M, General Murray said, "We are humbled and grateful to the people of Texas, the elected leaders of the state, and the Texas A&M University System for the opportunity to further develop our strategic partnership through the establishment of the combat development complex on the RELLIS Campus. This effort will certainly prove vital as we work together to discover, develop, and test ideas and concepts that will help our soldiers, and our future soldiers, to protect America's tomorrows—beginning today."

RELLIS is one of many sites at which AFC is building its overall command. As of early 2020, the program involved twenty-four thousand civilians and soldiers in twenty-five US states and fifteen foreign countries.

One example of how AFC will advance modern military thinking and technology development was implemented at the army's Aberdeen Proving Grounds northeast of Baltimore. Although originally outside the sphere of the AFC, the Warfighter Innovation Leveraging Expertise and Experimentation program (WILE-E) broke ground on improving lines of communication between scientists and soldiers, a key tenet of the AFC's operational model to encourage better and more frequent interactions pertaining to real-world challenges on the battlefield.

According to the US Army's official website, the initial charge given to WILE-E researchers, scientists, and engineers was simple: "Slime happens. How do we get back in the fight?"

The team ultimately narrowed its focus to the importance of communications both within the framework of initial development at Aberdeen as well as in actual combat.

"With this problem in mind," the army website states, "the WILE-E team moved to shortcut traditional channels of communication by hosting events bringing together war-fighters and [subject-matter experts] from commodity areas within the Center to collaboratively tackle the problem[s].

"WILE-E unofficially dubbed these events FOXCONs, or 'future oriented experimenter conventions.'

"The FOXCONs were the first solution or prototype developed by WILE-E in an effort to err on the side of action and fail early."

The notion of "failing early" is one being welcomed by AFC.

In addition to the development and testing of futuristic fighting technologies, another of AFC's mission priorities for the Bush Combat Development Complex is the implementation of what is called agile project management.

According to the website CIO.com, Agile is "a project management methodology that uses short development cycles . . . to focus on continuous improvement in the development of a product or service."

At the helm of the Bush Combat Development Complex's Agile team is Dr. Nancy Currie-Gregg, a member of the Texas A&M College of Engineering faculty. Like General Murray, Currie-Gregg is a product of the Ohio State University's ROTC program. She is a retired army colonel and a former astronaut. During her thirty-year career at NASA, Currie-Gregg flew four times as a mission specialist on the space shuttle. As the robotic arm operator on her flights, she played a key role in assembling the first pieces of the International Space Station as well as repairing the Hubble Space Telescope.

Currie-Gregg's flying career at NASA ended in 2003 following the explosion of the Columbia orbiter and the loss of its crew. She personally participated in search-and-recovery efforts in the immediate aftermath of the tragedy, and then led reform initiatives within the shuttle program's Safety and Mission Assurance Office. After retiring from NASA, she joined the Texas A&M faculty in 2017 and currently holds the Donald Lummus '58 Professorship of Practice Chair in Engineering, as well as serving in her leadership role at the Bush Combat Development Complex.

As for the value of the AFC adopting Agile methodology, Currie-Gregg says, "Historically, the development of nearly every major Pentagon weapons system included a multimillion-dollar horror story involving something overlooked until close to the end. Often, it was something that could have been corrected with the early involvement of real-world operators.

"Our mission on behalf of the Army Future's Command is to ensure that the researchers and engineers we employ to develop new technology understand the value of doing things differently than they may be accustomed to."

That difference in approach, as well as Texas A&M's highly regarded aerospace engineering program, are two key reasons the US Department of Defense selected the system, through the Texas A&M Engineering Experiment Station (TEES), to create and lead a University Consortium for Applied Hypersonics.

TEES manages the five-year, $100 million consortium contract, which includes MIT, Purdue, UCLA, Cal Tech, Georgia Tech, the University of Tennessee Space Institute, Morgan State University, the University of Minnesota, the University of Illinois, and the University of Arizona.

Hypersonic speeds are those faster than five times the speed of sound, or "Mach 5." That is nearly four thousand miles per hour. One of the biggest advantages of modern hypersonic missiles is not simply speed. The "holy grail" of hypersonic research is to create pinpoint maneuverability at those speeds, thus making the missiles desirable as both offensive and defensive weapons.

The development of hypersonic weapons technology is a top priority for the US military.

"Investment in the future is vital," said former national security advisor Robert O'Brien.

"We believe we're in a bit of a race right now," echoed Mark Lewis, the defense department's former director of research and engineering for modernization. That "race" is with both the Chinese and the Russians.

"The department is funding a good amount of basic research in hypersonics," said Gillian Bussey, director of the Pentagon's Joint Hypersonics Transition Office. "But we're finding that tests [in] some of the more applied areas are not bringing fresh blood into the industry. The gold standard [for the University Consortium] will be to have the team develop a vehicle and fly it."

For fiscal year 2021, the Department of Defense requested more than $3 billion for research, development, testing, and evaluation related to hypersonic weapons.

"Our ability to predict and understand hypersonic is relatively immature," says Ed White, a member of the Texas A&M National Aerothermochemistry and Hypersonics Laboratory. The challenge, White explains, "is putting fins on a vehicle and having those fins survive at Mach 10"—ten times the speed of sound, or more than 7,500 miles per hour—"so you can steer with precise accuracy."

Even before the University Consortium of Applied Hypersonics announcement came in October 2020, construction on the RELLIS Campus had already begun to create the nation's only kilometer-long hypersonic test facility.

Leading innovation at the Bush Combat Development Complex as deputy director and chief technology officer is John E. Hurtado, whom friends and colleagues affectionately call "Johnny."

Hurtado calls work with the AFC "the chance of a lifetime," not only for himself, but also for his team as well as the Texas A&M University System. "This is a grand opportunity to change the type of research that we do and the way in which we do it."

"Specifically," he adds, "conducting AFC research is an opportunity to do applied research that can have a near-term impact, done in a way that leads to well-defined progress while being open to new research directions."

Hurtado is a native of Bakersfield, California. It was near there, in California's Central Valley, that Hurtado's immigrant grandfather worked alongside the displaced "Okies" in the vegetable fields and fruit orchards made famous in John Steinbeck's epic novel *The Grapes of Wrath*. A first-generation college student himself, Hurtado earned an undergraduate degree in aerospace engineering from San Diego State and then decided to further his education at Texas A&M.

"As a native Californian," Hurtado says today, "I was a bit more tan and my language a little more salty than most other students in

Aggieland. It took some time, but eventually, I was able to fit into the local culture."

Ultimately, Hurtado pursued both master's and PhD degrees in aerospace engineering while working under the tutelage of John Junkins. Hurtado received his doctorate from Texas A&M in 1996.

"Dr. Junkins taught me how to be a good researcher, how to be inspired by an open research problem, and how to appreciate the work of others," Hurtado says today. "As I neared graduation, Dr. Junkins helped me land my first position as a researcher at Sandia National Labs. I was at Sandia for five years, and my wife, Diane, and I were very happy there."

The Hurtados, as mentioned in Chapter 16, met in graduate school at Texas A&M. Diane Hurtado is associate vice chancellor for national laboratories management for TEES and head of A&M's management team at the Los Alamos National Laboratory.

Returning to College Station in 2001, Johnny Hurtado assumed a position as an associate professor in aerospace engineering. Working his way to a full and tenured professorship, Johnny eventually caught the attention of Kathy Banks. She brought him onto her staff within the College of Engineering in 2014. Since that time, Hurtado has served, in a manner of speaking, as consigliere to Dean Banks and her administrative staff, much in the same manner that the fictional character Tom Hagen guided the day-to-day activities of the Corleone family in the Oscar-winning films *The Godfather* and *The Godfather Part II*.

Hurtado laughs at the comparison.

"Dean Banks and I love those movies," he says.

"I see Dean Banks as someone with a grand vision, which is not something that I see in myself. I see myself as someone whose job it is to put structure around her vision and then implement her vision to a successful outcome.

"I consider myself a closer, meaning that I will take a task to its completion. Dean Banks afforded me wonderful opportunities at a time when I was ready to tackle them."

Thus Hurtado would seem to be the right man in the right place at the right time to move forward one of Chancellor John Sharp's most significant initiatives as leader of the Texas A&M University System.

"We consider serving the military of our nation to be the highest of honors and responsibilities," Sharp says. "Having the Army Futures

Command at RELLIS is also a game-changer for both that campus and the Brazos Valley area."

On September 20, 2020, US Army Secretary Ryan McCarthy visited the construction site of the Bush Combat Development Complex, calling the project "beyond any expectation [he] could have had."

"There is a tremendous opportunity here," said McCarthy, "for industry to come, establish a footprint, and vertically integrate research and manufacturing with the work of the Army Futures Command. The ceiling is very high."

Concurring with those thoughts the day of McCarthy's visit was Ross Guieb, US Army colonel (ret.), the executive director of the Bush Combat Development Complex.

"This will be a mini-research Pentagon, a high-tech hub for army, industry, and university-based experts to collaborate in one state-of-the-art location," Guieb said. "Together we'll develop next-generation defense capabilities to deter adversaries and convincingly win on any battlefield."

20

Chief Nim Kidd

Disasters come in many shapes and sizes.

Some are geophysical: earthquakes, landslides, tsunamis, and volcanic eruptions.

Climatological disasters include extreme temperatures, drought, and wildfires.

Avalanches and floods are examples of hydrological disasters.

Meteorological disasters stem from hurricanes and the storm surges that frequently accompany large-scale weather events in coastal regions, as well as outbreaks of severe thunderstorm activity, which can include large amounts of rain and high winds including the devastation emanating from the sudden arrival of a tornado.

Insect and animal plagues, affecting crops and livestock, are biological disasters, as are epidemics of human disease.

Disasters can also be manmade, such as environmental degradation, pollution, and accidents, often those stemming from the handling or transportation of hazardous materials.

And disasters come in all sizes. Those of more epic proportions include societal food insecurity, armed conflicts within and beyond national borders, displaced populations, and global pandemics.

According to the NASA website of its Synthetic Aperture Radar project—designed to take orbital measurements of earth's most complex processes—Texas ranks first in the United States "in the variety and frequency of natural disasters. Flooding, wildfires, tornados, hurricanes, hailstorms, sinkholes, erosion, and drought all occur in the state. Sometimes, even utilization of the state's natural reserves of oil, gas, and water can lead to subsidence and earthquakes."

The Texas A&M University System's Texas Division of Emergency Management, the newest state agency under system control, is responsible for coordinating rescue and recovery from the state's many and diverse catastrophes. The agency dates back to the early years of the Atomic Age and originally sprang forth from the threat of the ultimate manmade disaster.

In 1950, the National Security Resources Board created a nationwide civil defense framework in response to the simmering Cold War between the United States and the Soviet Union and the threat of nuclear war. From that, the Texas Civil Protection Act was instituted in 1951, establishing the Division of Defense and Disaster Relief under the administration of the governor's office. In 1963, control of the agency was split between the governor and the Department of Public Safety (DPS). In 2005, DPS assumed total authority of the organization, whose name was changed to the Texas Division of Emergency Management (TDEM) in 2009.

On August 28, 2019, TDEM became the eighth state agency of the Texas A&M University System, the system's first new agency in more than a half century. The move resulted in large part from the system's stellar efforts in leading Gov. Greg Abbott's Rebuild Texas initiative.

"I think he was happy with our work," says Chancellor John Sharp. "I think both the governor and the state legislature were pleased with the outcome of our response to Harvey and wanted the same thing to happen in response to future disasters."

Of the forty-four recommendations made in the system's *Eye of the Storm* report summarizing the state's Rebuild Texas efforts and the challenges the state faced in recovering from the devastation of Hurricane Harvey, forty-three were enacted into law upon the Texas legislature's return to session in 2019.

"The forty-fourth recommendation," says Chief Nim Kidd, the longtime director of the TDEM and now vice chancellor of the Texas A&M University System, "suggested the A&M Veterinary Emergency Team be more involved in the state's emergency medical plan. As the TDEM agency director, I had the authority to implement that without a legislative mandate."

Kidd has served as head of the TDEM since 2011, when he first took the job while retaining ties to the San Antonio Fire Department (SAFD), where he was a district chief. Early in his time as TDEM director, the *Austin American-Statesman* reported, "While Kidd supervises the state response to natural disasters for the Texas Department of

Public Safety, he technically remains a San Antonio firefighter, and the money for his salary comes from a third agency, the Texas A&M Engineering Extension Service."

"When my predecessor, Jack Collins, asked me if I had interest in his job," Kidd says, "I told him I was honored but that I was working on accruing my pension from the San Antonio Fire Department and I didn't think I wanted to give that up. He told me he was planning to retire in a year and hoped he could bring his successor on board to shadow him for a while."

A month after Kidd turned down the offer, Collins died of a heart attack.

Soon, Kidd got a call from Gov. Rick Perry's office asking whether he would reconsider his interest in the TDEM director's position. Out of respect to Collins, who had been an army colonel and tank battalion commander before going to work for the state, Kidd agreed and asked whether it might be possible to be "detailed" into the position while retaining active status with the SAFD.

"Law enforcement personnel do this all the time," Kidd explains. "Local law enforcement officers go to work for the state police or FBI and keep their jobs with their local agencies. So, during my first four years as chief of emergency management—until I was eligible to retire from the SAFD—we were able to do that."

How Chief Nim Kidd rose through the ranks of the SAFD to become a vice chancellor within the Texas A&M System and oversee emergency response for the nation's second-largest state is an intriguing tale.

Wesley Nim Kidd was born in Corsicana, Texas, in 1969. His family moved to San Antonio when he was two. No one has ever called him "Wesley." As for his middle name, Kidd laughs and explains, "The sixties were good to my parents."

Upon arriving in San Antonio, Kidd's father, Dale, went to work in the construction division for grocer HEB. Eventually, Dale became a construction contractor to the company, and by the time Nim was twelve, the son was working for his father.

After graduating from high school, Kidd found a summer job working construction for HEB. He enrolled at Southwest Texas State University and spent a year and a half there.

"It got to the point [where] the money working in construction was better than college," Kidd says today, "so, I dropped out and went to work full time." At nineteen years of age, Kidd was supervising a twenty-five-man demolition crew for HEB.

The year was 1988.

To pass the time on weekends, Kidd began playing pickup softball games in the tiny Texas town of La Vernia, a half hour east of San Antonio. During play one Sunday afternoon, an opponent suffered an ankle injury trying to make a leaping catch of a line drive. Kidd helped the player to the sideline, and as a group gathered to offer assistance, the injured man asked his daughter to fetch something from his car.

She dragged back a giant red bag bearing the logo of the SAFD. It turned out shortstop Joe Arrambide was a paramedic for the SAFD.

Arrambide would spend nearly thirty-seven years as a paramedic with the SAFD, rising to the rank of lieutenant before his retirement in 2017.

"I helped Joe wrap his ankle," Kidd says of that fateful day, "and as we were finishing up he said, 'The fire department in San Antonio is giving an employment test next month. You ought to take it.'"

Kidd deferred. "No, I've got a construction gig going. I'm good."

A week later, Arrambide returned to the La Vernia softball fields. Although still hobbled, he brought with him an SAFD application to give to Kidd. When Kidd asked how much money a rookie San Antonio firefighter could expect to make, he scoffed at Arrambide's answer.

"Joe, that's half as much as I make now."

But "as luck would have it," according to Kidd, during the recruitment pitch, Arrambide's pager went off.

"That's from the La Vernia Fire Department," Arrambide explained to Kidd. "I'm a volunteer firefighter there. Why don't you come on this call with me?"

The offer aroused Kidd's curiosity and he accepted. For the next five years, Kidd augmented his full-time construction job with volunteer firefighter duties for the City of La Vernia. He was eventually admitted to the San Antonio Fire Academy in 1993.

It turned out his construction background came in handy in his new pursuit.

"As a fireman, you kinda need to know how buildings are built," Kidd says. "You need to know how to pull them apart in order to find and extinguish fire. It's also important to know the right way to force entry and how to keep a building from falling down on you. So that's how I got into the fire service. I graduated from the academy in October '93, and I worked on a ladder truck on the west side of downtown San Antonio for the next three years."

During that time, the SAFD established a "technical rescue team." The unit employed specialized tools and skills for vehicle extrications, confined-space and structural-collapse rescues, as well as water and trench rescues.

"I wanted to be a part of that team," Kidd says, "but I wasn't accepted the first time I applied, and that made me a little mad. So I studied to become a fire department engineer, made engineer driver in 1996, and eventually got assigned to the technical rescue team as an engineer."

In an intriguing twist of fate, this led to Kidd's initial affiliation with the Texas A&M University System.

"I grew up in San Antonio and got busy doing my own thing when I was pretty young, so I didn't know a whole lot about Texas A&M," Kidd says today. "My parents didn't go to college. I dropped out of college, but in late 1996, not too long after I got involved with the technical rescue team in San Antonio, I learned of the establishment of Texas Task Force 1 [TX-TF1], an urban search-and-rescue team created by the Texas A&M Engineering Extension Service [TEEX] as a part of the Texas Division of Emergency Management.

"That sounded pretty exciting to me, so I applied, and along with about fifteen others from the SAFD, was accepted to be an original member of Texas Task Force 1. I was at Rudder Tower on Valentine's Day 1997 when we held our first organizational meeting."

Now called Texas A&M Task Force 1, the initiative was the brainchild of Kem Bennett, the former TEEX director who later became dean of the Texas A&M College of Engineering. Bennett was inspired by stories he had heard at a seminar where several first responders to the Oklahoma City bombing attended.

Knowing Texas would also have been ill prepared for such an event, Bennett engaged the TEEX resources at his command to create not only TX-TF1 but also the search-and-rescue training venue in College Station, which became known as Disaster City.

Today's TEEX website describes the complex, also established in 1997, as a "mock community [that] features full-scale, collapsible structures designed to simulate various levels of disaster and wreckage which can be customized for the specific training needs of any group."

Disaster City training helped set TX-TF1 apart. By June 2001, the team joined the FEMA National Urban Search and Rescue System. Its first assignment to a national incident came on September 11, 2001, when the terrorist attacks on the World Trade Center in New York.

"I was getting ready to go on my duty shift in San Antonio that morning," Kidd remembers, "when one of my firefighter buddies in San Antonio called me. He said, 'Hey man, turn on the TV.' I was like, 'All right, which channel?' He says, 'It doesn't matter. Just turn on the TV!'

"While I reached for the remote, I could hear his TV in the background. They were talking about big buildings and flames and smoke all across the skyline.

"And before I could get my TV on, I got mad because I thought there was a fire in a downtown San Antonio high-rise. I would have wanted to have been first in on that fire. Instead, by the time I'd be going on duty, I'd be doing cleanup, picking up hoses from the fire and things like that."

Kidd then finally got his television turned on.

"I saw it was New York City. And within minutes, the second plane hit. Mesmerized by what I was seeing in front of me, I said to my friend, 'I don't think I'll be coming in today.' And I was right. Texas Task Force 1 was activated shortly thereafter.

"We came to College Station that afternoon, and they held us here for a couple of days. We weren't sure if we were going to the Pentagon or to the World Trade Center.

"Eventually we wound up at Ground Zero."

As for Kidd's recollections of that deployment, he talks most about "the sights, the sounds . . . and the smells."

"I remember the looks on the faces of the New York City firefighters," Kidd says. "You could see the anguish in their eyes coping with the knowledge that so many of their brethren had lost their lives in the initial response to the attacks. When we got there, people were so glad to see us. All along the route from the Javits Center where we bivouacked to Ground Zero, New Yorkers held up signs showing their appreciation for the work we were there to do."

"And I remember five-gallon buckets," Kidd adds. "We sat on five-gallon buckets to rest, and also used them to remove debris."

Two months later, Kidd was promoted to the rank of captain within the SAFD. Soon after, he was offered the role of assistant emergency management coordinator for the City of San Antonio. Just thirty-two at the time, Kidd again said no.

"I'm not ready to go ride a desk," he replied in declining the job. "I want to be a captain in the field first."

After running the SAFD hazmat team for a year, Kidd was again offered a position within the city's emergency management department. Wisely, he accepted the role and held the position of assistant director for eighteen months. He spent much of his time managing post-9/11 grant money coming in from the Department of Homeland Security.

Kidd's subsequent return to active duty with the hazmat team ultimately led to him becoming a fire chief within the SAFD. Soon after, the director of the city's emergency management department announced his retirement. Chief Kidd was selected to be his replacement. Kidd held that position from 2004 until he became director of the TDEM in 2011.

Not bad for a college dropout.

It was at that point, mostly because of his desire to be eligible to move even further up the ranks of the SAFD, that Kidd decided he would resume work toward an undergraduate degree.

And he did so at a Texas A&M University System school.

"I discovered that Texas A&M–Commerce offered a degree program that I could do completely online," Kidd says. "Even though my job with the state was technically in Austin, I was still living in San Antonio, and so I was used to doing the 'long-distance' thing. So, thanks to the amazing bachelor of applied arts and sciences distance-learning program in Commerce, I was able to reconnect with my East Texas roots and get my undergraduate degree in about a year and a half."

At the age of forty-two.

A year later, Kidd began pursuit of his master's in public administration through another online program through Texas State University, previously known as Southwest Texas State, the school where Kidd had started college as a teenager more than twenty years earlier.

"That's the same MPA program that John Sharp completed. I knew of John then, but I'd never met the man."

That meeting would take place a few years later when the two collaborated during the Rebuild Texas initiative in 2017.

"The governor had John and me going all over the Gulf Coast," says Kidd. "Sometimes we hit fifteen cities in three days, just bam, bam, bam, one right after the other."

"And we worked great together," Kidd proclaims. "I love the chancellor. He takes care of business. He gets the job done. You either get on, get out of the way, or get run over."

The admiration is mutual.

"I think Nim's the best in the country at what he does," says Sharp. "He's very good at bringing both people and organizations together. You don't want to go through a disaster without him."

Under Sharp's Rebuild Texas leadership, the methodology the system developed and detailed in the *Eye of the Storm* report provided Kidd with an important contrast to the usual way emergency management is conducted.

"Under DPS, TDEM was an almost paramilitary organization," Kidd explains. "The state police and state law enforcement do well in the immediate emergency response, but when it comes time for the recovery and the mitigation, that's something that the law enforcement body just wasn't ever built to do.

"When I took the job as deputy emergency director for the City of San Antonio, I helped manage millions of dollars in federal grant funds. People usually think of emergency management as plans, training, exercise, and response, but that doesn't address the long-term issues of disaster recovery. You've got to recover from an event, too. And to recover stronger, to mitigate against the next disaster, you have to keep track of all the federal dollars that flow through in a disaster's aftermath and to know how to audit to the federal standard on how that money is ultimately used.

"The last thing you want to do is give money back later because you've failed to follow FEMA or HUD protocols."

The first official "meeting of the minds" after TDEM became a part of the Texas A&M University System came on October 17, 2019, in a daylong session at the Doug Pitcock '49 Hotel and Conference Center on the A&M flagship campus.

"This was the inaugural meeting bringing together the operational side of the Texas Division of Emergency Management and the academic, the scientific, the philosophical sides of the Texas A&M University System," Kidd said in a TDEM video highlighting the event.

"I think it was an amazing day with eleven universities and now eight state agencies present."

"There are a lot of people working on the problem," said A&M System Deputy Chancellor Billy Hamilton on the disaster management responsibilities facing not only the system's newest agency but also the system's collective body. "I think it's up to TDEM, up to Chief Kidd, up to the system to make sure everybody tries to pull in the same direction. Hurricane Harvey showed us all that we have a vulnerability in this state, but we also have a chance to do amazing things for the people of Texas."

One of Chief Kidd's top priorities as the A&M System's newest vice chancellor is the creation of what he calls Disaster University.

Kidd says, "When you ask first responders that are doing urban search and rescue—people from anywhere around the world—where to go to hone their craft, it's right here. It's Brayton Fire Training Field. It's Disaster City. It's the Texas A&M University flagship campus and the Texas A&M University System. If you're going to learn about firefighting and structural collapse and the technical requirements for trench and cave and confined space rescue scenarios, College Station is the place to go on this planet."

"But," and Kidd lingers for a moment on the word, "if I ask where to go to learn to manage billions of dollars in federal grant funds received in the aftermath of a disaster, the question gets a lot of shoulder shrugs.

"I want this to be the place to come for everything related to emergency management."

When Kidd speaks of emergency management, he speaks of the "scientific" and "philosophical" aspects to effective disaster response in the same breath as rescue and recovery. From his many years in the business, he knows one disaster follows another, and his vision for Disaster University addresses a gaping hole in the overall equation.

"We're already doing a great job here training firefighters and emergency response personnel, but no one is preparing local and state governmental entities [for] the 'disaster' which immediately follows. And that is properly managing the federal money that comes in after a disaster with very specific rules and regulations as to how it can be used.

"When we surveyed the 254 counties in Texas after Hurricane Harvey and asked them how many had a single individual whose full-time job, paid for with local government funds, was to do the paperwork necessary to manage FEMA funding, there wasn't a single person tasked with doing that. Not one.

"There's no place to go to learn contracting, auditing, grant compliance, and all of the things you need to do to finance a recovery. Communities can only recover if they have a plan to recover."

Kidd's excitement grows as he speaks of degree programs offered through the Texas A&M University System that train young people in all aspects of emergency management. A precedent for that was established in the recovery from Harvey.

"Chancellor Sharp put engineering students in Reed Arena during both the Christmas and spring breaks which followed Harvey so they could be taught how to do a FEMA disaster assessment. They then went back to their communities, and they helped do damage assessments as students.

"I know the FEMA workforce. They're not bad people, but many of the reservists that FEMA brought in didn't have as much training or education as our students that we put in the field. So when we see this again, when another disaster inevitably strikes, why wouldn't we continue to use the future leaders and businesspeople we're molding right here on our campuses?

"And why not teach them in the disaster moment? Let them go and learn from somebody else's disaster before they have to experience and manage one here themselves.

"This is how I want to see Disaster University play out over time. We're working with the engineering folks, working with the architecture folks, talking to the business school, talking to the Bush School of Government about how to start bridging this together."

Bringing the TDEM into the realm of the Texas A&M University System has created a unique dynamic, Kidd says.

"Other states aren't tied to university systems like Texas. Our critical state agencies are now tied together as a part of the emergency-management structure of the government. We have always had a good setup in Texas, but now being part of the A&M System gives us a superb arrangement because we're able to engage and integrate on a daily basis.

"I think one of the things the chancellor really impressed upon both the governor and the legislature was the fact the A&M System was the place for TDEM to be."

And just in time for the COVID-19 pandemic.

"People have told me, 'You can't treat this like a hurricane,'" Kidd says. "And I say, 'Why not?'

"Emergency management is a 'must-be-present-to-win' sport. By having all of our system agencies together, we're solving problems in seconds that would take most organizations a lot longer to even identify.

"You need people to respond to something like a pandemic. We do that all the time in incident management. You need stuff to respond with. We do that all the time in incident management. You need an organizational structure for those people and that stuff to operate. We do that all the time.

"You need management and incident priorities. Those are things that TEEX has been teaching for years. So we have the best people right here that have taught the world how to respond to disasters.

"It shouldn't be a novel response just because it's a novel virus."

Pandemic

Tai Lee first got word of the virus outbreak that would come to be known as COVID-19 from his brother-in-law's brother, who works in China.

"It was during the holidays, as I remember, that he told the family about the virus outbreak in Wuhan," says Lee, a native of South Korea who is known as Chef Tai in the Bryan / College Station area where he's run a quartet of restaurants and a mobile van, which earned the title of "America's Favorite Food Truck" on the *Food Network* in 2011.

Of the news from China that closed out 2019, Lee says, "All of us in my family thought, 'Here comes another SARS outbreak.'"

SARS, of course, stands for "severe acute respiratory syndrome." And, in fact, Lee's family was correct in their assessment.

Chef Tai is a member of the Texas A&M Class of '92. He followed his grandparents to the United States when he was twelve and explains his decision to become an Aggie this way:

"Most Americans take great pride in their independence. But for Asian people like myself, the group is seen as more important than the individual. That same thinking really stood out when I visited Texas A&M for the first time, so this felt like the place I needed to be."

In staying near his alma mater, Lee has become not only a top-notch restauranteur but also a respected member of the local community.

The SARS epidemic of 2003 also originated in China and affected about eight thousand people in twenty-six countries worldwide. Due to its immediate and all-encompassing response, South Korea, where many members of Lee's family still live, reported just three cases.

Only twenty-seven SARS cases were documented in the United States, although the concern of possible outbreaks of the exotic disease—in places like Dallas and Dyess Air Force Base near Abilene—generated near-apocalyptic headlines.

While SARS CoV, as the 2003 virus was named by the scientific community, turned out to be, for the most part, much ado about nothing, such has not been the case for its successor.

On March 1, 2020, South Korea's daily COVID-19 infection numbers topped one thousand. On March 2, when the Centers for Disease Control first began publishing statistics, twelve cases were reported in the United States.

The numbers then began to grow . . . and grow . . . and grow.

"I got a little worried by what was happening in South Korea," Lee says of the period before the coronavirus was much of a concern in the United States. "I asked my landlord from whom I rented space for our Veritas restaurant if he could work with me in case things got bad here. He said, 'Sure, that won't be a problem.'

"Neither one of us thought things would ever get to that point."

In early March, with COVID still mostly an "elsewhere" thing, Lee took a long-planned business trip to California.

"When I landed in Los Angeles, it was around five o'clock," Lee says. "Rush hour. Yet when I got my Uber and we drove onto the 405 Freeway outside the airport, we made it to Orange County in less than thirty minutes. That's a trip that can easily take two hours or more, even on a good day. My driver said people there were scared. They were already talking about shutting down schools."

Three days later as Lee prepared to return home, LAX was nearly a ghost town. By April, passenger numbers at the airport were down 95 percent from the previous year. Gradually, COVID became a global pandemic.

The Texas A&M student newspaper, the *Battalion*, put together a timeline of the early days of change on and around the flagship campus:

- *January 23, 2020:* Brazos County Health District announces a possible case of coronavirus in Texas A&M student; later confirmed negative.
- *January 29, 2020:* Texas A&M suspends university-sponsored travel to China for undergraduates.
- *February 28, 2020:* University cancels all Spring Break trips to Italy.
- *March 2, 2020:* Education Abroad trips in countries with

Travel Advisories canceled, students currently abroad sent home.

- *March 6, 2020:* SXSW canceled due to coronavirus fears; A&M plans to move its interactive exhibit to Aggieland.
- *March 9, 2020:* All university-sponsored international travel between March 16 and May 1 is canceled.
- *March 10, 2020:* Classes canceled Monday, March 16, and Tuesday, March 17, for teachers to adjust syllabi for potentially moving classes online.
- *March 11, 2020:* NCAA announces they will only allow essential staff and limited family to attend games. The Southeastern Conference (SEC) announces a similar ban.
- *March 12, 2020:* White House announces travel restrictions to most of Europe, causing many faculty and students abroad to quickly return home. Texas A&M cancels in-person classes for the remainder of the spring semester, and Spring Break is extended an extra week. The SEC cancels the remainder of the Men's Basketball Tournament, then later cancels all sporting events through March 30. The NCAA cancels all remaining winter and spring championships.
- *March 13, 2020:* The SEC extends suspension of sporting events through April 15.
- *March 16, 2020:* Big Event is canceled. All study abroad trips scheduled to depart on or before June 1 are canceled.
- *March 17, 2020:* The first positive case of coronavirus is confirmed in Brazos County: a woman in her twenties with no affiliation to Texas A&M or Blinn College. Bryan and College Station declare a state of emergency.

Since then, at least at the time of this writing, the pandemic has continued to dominate US lives, news, politics, and culture. Business as usual, for people like Tai Lee, has become an elusive target in most corners of the country.

"My first concern was our staff," Tai Lee says, explaining how he, as a business owner, began to prepare for the uncertainty of a COVID world.

"We made sure we had enough masks and hand sanitizer to keep employees as safe as possible. Soon, though, customers stopped coming, and then the governor ordered all eating establishments closed for in-person dining.

"That's when things became a little dire."

Although Lee would put his food truck to good use and offer delivery and curbside pickup at his brick-and-mortar establishments, the crown jewel of his restaurant group became unsustainable.

On August 6, 2020, Lee told his staff he would be closing Veritas.

That same day, 7,598 new coronavirus cases were reported across Texas. One week before, the nationwide death toll from the virus had passed the 150,000 mark.

The COVID-19 pandemic has affected the world in alarming, grievous, and unimaginable ways. Nearing the one-year mark of the original outbreak in Wuhan, the end appears to be nowhere in sight. The 1918 Spanish flu pandemic lasted more than two years and infected one-third of the world's population.

The coronavirus continues to infect Americans, but the varying nature of their illnesses—if they get sick at all—is problematic to recovery efforts and at the core of why this version of SARS is exacting such an enormous toll not just in lives lost but also in its destructive power over the collective consciousness.

After the magnitude of the COVID pandemic became apparent, the Texas A&M University System sought to fulfill its land grant mission by disseminating good and helpful information to the public. One means of achieving that was through a television series originating from the A&M-owned public television station KAMU located near Kyle Field on the flagship campus.

The half-hour show first aired in April 2020 as "COVID-19: The Texas A&M System Responds" and was hosted by Chancellor John Sharp. Over the course of its initial twelve-episode run, Sharp interviewed a number of system academic and agency experts about the nature of the COVID-19 virus, the means by which the scientific community was seeking to combat the disease, and the measures people should take to remove themselves from harm's way.

Among the system experts to appear with Sharp—albeit via the video-conferencing app Zoom—was Ben Neuman, at the time a biology professor at Texas A&M–Texarkana and an internationally recognized authority on coronaviruses.

Neuman kicked off his initial appearance on the show, which aired originally in April 2020, calling the virus "bad news that arrives in a little protein shell."

"All a virus really is," he said, "is a set of instructions that says copy these instructions an infinite number of times."

Near the end of the episode, Sharp asked Neuman, "Look into your crystal ball. When do you think this is going to be over with?"

"If you look at how long it's taken to knock out other coronavirus infections," Neuman said, "the answer is once they start coming down, once we pass peak, it's usually about two and a half to three months to get rid of most of the cases. Sometimes you'll have little tiny flare-ups after that."

Six months after making those remarks, Neuman admits things turned out a little differently than what he expected.

"Back when the virus outbreak was still reasonably small, it seemed like a thing we could probably shut down just by putting a quarantine period in place on people coming into the country. But there was a lot of reluctance to do that, particularly on Americans coming back from overseas or from cruise ships.

"Testing seemed easy because we had the sequence of the virus in January. It was close enough to SARS to give us a good head start. But then the US redesigned our test, and that was a little frustrating, given that in Europe, they already had a test. That cost us about a month and a half, but still the thinking here was that we've got control of it. We should be able to stop it."

"I won't call what followed a comedy of errors because what happened wasn't very funny," Neuman observes. "A lot of politicians probably don't get into politics because they were great at science somewhere along the way."

Neuman's own interest in science began at an early age and ultimately led him to the northeast Texas town of Texarkana. How he came to assume teaching and research positions within the Texas A&M University System and "star" on a Facebook page with more than four thousand young followers is a story worth noting.

Growing up in the small northern Ohio town of Niles, Neuman frequently spent weekends and summers at his grandparents' cottage on the nearby shore of Lake Erie.

"As a kid, I devoted a lot of my time to looking for treasures along the beach," Neuman says. "Sometimes I found fossils. During certain times of the year, there would be all these butterflies along the shore-line, grounded by heavy storms. I bought a microscope and really liked looking up close at the things I discovered."

Neuman's parents, an attorney and a paralegal, believed their son might one day become a doctor, and that was Neuman's intent when he enrolled at the University of Toledo to major in biology.

During college, Neuman participated in a one-year exchange program at the University of Salford in Manchester, England.

"Upon arrival, they whisked us off to a field camp in the south of Wales," Neuman says, "and they had all kinds of wonderful things there along the coast. One day we'd measure snails, and the next day we'd count the little air bladders on different kinds of seaweed. And while doing all this, I ran into this very nice girl."

That young woman, whose name was Nicola, ultimately lured Neuman back to the United Kingdom for his graduate studies. There, he decided to pursue a PhD degree from the University of Reading rather than become a doctor. It was also during this time that Ben and Nicola decided to get married.

Nicola Benning Neuman was an adjunct professor and biology lab coordinator at A&M-Texarkana, where her husband was head of the biology department. Nicola also spends time managing her husband's popular Facebook page, "Dr. Ben Neuman's Science Group."

"My wife set that up for me so that I could help kids make sense of the coronavirus," Neuman says. Among the more interesting questions that he has been asked there: "Are Santa Claus and the Easter Bunny essential workers?"

Neuman's reply: "They certainly must have been well connected with the government since they are allowed into our homes. So, yes, I would think they are a different sort of essential worker."

After earning his PhD, Neuman and his wife returned to the United States, where he did postdoctoral work at the Scripps Research Institute in La Jolla, California, and then served as an assistant professor at the prestigious medical research facility. During his time at Scripps, the SARS virus emerged.

"Before what became known as the 'SARS' outbreak, most coronaviruses mostly affected farm animals like cows, pigs, and chickens. The ones that occasionally infected humans were not really a big deal.

That all changed in late 2002, when SARS emerged from China. Why that happened, I think, is just a matter of bad luck."

Virology, Neuman's specialty, hinges on the ability to reproduce viruses in a laboratory for study. In the case of the original SARS—SARS CoV—no one has created more copies of the virus than Neuman.

"Yeah, I think so," he says. "When we first started studying the SARS CoV virus, we needed to get a real good picture of it, so I would grow as much virus as I could cram into our incubators at Scripps. That involved finding smaller and flatter platers on which I would put cancer cells and then attach a tiny bit of the SARS virus to those cells. Some cancer cells are particularly susceptible to virus attack. We'd then let them grow and harvested the end product. In that manner, I made probably ten viruses for every person on earth.

"Tiny, concentrated, milky pills of death."

Because of COVID-19's similarity to the original SARS virus, it is technically called "SARS CoV-2"

Neuman was on the committee that arrived at that name.

"Back in 2016, I discovered a couple of viruses that were related to coronaviruses. I then forwarded my findings to the international committee on the taxonomy of viruses. It turned out the committee head was a coronavirus person. After the Wuhan outbreak was made known, he invited me onto his committee, whose one job is determining the name and classification of new viruses."

While SARS CoV and SARS CoV-2 microscopically resemble each other, they do differ, says Neuman, in one very important way.

"With SARS, almost everybody who had the disease got a really high fever right away. And that fever appeared before they became contagious. So temperature checks worked really well in helping us stem the original SARS outbreak. With COVID-19, that's not the case. Less than half the people who contract the illness ever develop a fever, so they don't know they're sick themselves.

"That's what makes controlling the COVID pandemic so much harder. It's a case where we needed to change with the times, and we didn't really change. We just kept trying to do what we'd done before, and it didn't work."

This insight prompts innumerable questions, most of which don't come with easy answers. But there is one question to which Neuman can offer a straightforward reply.

How did someone considered a global expert on coronaviruses wind up in Texarkana, Texas, of all places?

"I left the Scripps Institute in 2006, and Nicola and I moved back to the UK, where I found a teaching position at the University of Reading. In 2016, about the time that Brexit became an issue for the Brits, we realized that we weren't making much headway over there. Things had gotten very expensive, and so we decided to look for a place back in the US that was a little more affordable.

"That obviously wasn't New York or San Francisco. As it turned out, of the couple hundred resumes I sent out, we got one reply: Texas A&M–Texarkana."

One must say "Bravo!" to the administrator who made that decision.

"David Allard," says Neuman, "is the one who hired me to come to the A&M System. David is the mainstay of our biology department here in Texarkana."

Talking with Neuman in early November 2020, COVID cases across the United States again were spiking. The optimism expressed in his April interview with Chancellor Sharp had vanished completely.

"Right now, I see it circling around me," Neuman said. "Every day it seems I'm getting notes from one of our schools here about how many new cases they have. Neighbors on both sides of where we live came down with COVID. I've been exposed and in quarantine myself. Thankfully, I haven't tested positive.

"At least not yet."

Here is the list of system administrators and health experts who appeared on Chancellor Sharp's COVID-19 series:

- Dr. Peter Hotez, a Hagler Institute Scholar at Texas A&M and a dean at the Baylor College of Medicine
- Dr. Gerald Parker, director of Pandemic Programs at the Texas A&M Bush School of Government and Public Service
- Dr. Christine Blackburn, deputy director of Pandemic Programs at the Bush School of Government
- Dr. Detlef Hallermann, director of the Reliant Energy Trade Center at the Texas A&M Mays Business School
- Dr. Raymond Robertson, director of the Mosbacher Institute for Trade, Economics, and Public Policy at the Bush School of Government

- Dr. Venky Shankar, director of Research at the Center for Retailing Studies at the Mays Business School
- Greg Hartman, chief executive officer and senior vice president, Texas A&M Health Science Center
- Dr. Jeff Cirillo, director of the Center of Airborne Pathogen Research at the Texas A&M Health Science Center
- Chief Nim Kidd, director, Texas Division of Emergency Management
- Dr. David Anderson, extension economist, Texas A&M AgriLife
- Dr. Bart Fischer, codirector, Texas A&M AgriLife Agriculture and Food Policy Center
- Dr. Patrick Stover, dean and vice chancellor, Texas A&M AgriLife
- Thom Mason, Director, Los Alamos National Laboratory
- Dr. Jon Mogford, vice chancellor for research, Texas A&M University System
- Dr. Jay Treat, principal investigator, Center of Innovation in Advanced Development and Manufacturing, Texas A&M Health Science Center
- Dr. James Hallmark, vice chancellor for academic affairs, Texas A&M University System
- Dr. Carol Fierke, provost, Texas A&M University
- Dr. James Samuel, Texas A&M College of Medicine

The idea to produce a television show in pandemic times seems a natural way to employ modern technology in achieving the A&M System's mandate of service to fellow Texans. Under the watch of his vice chancellor of marketing and communications, Laylan Copelin, Sharp had appeared in front of cameras for some time. His "Chancellor Videos," posted to both the system website and YouTube, generated significant viewership and media attention for initiatives and milestones the A&M System achieved.

However, it was one thing to send a videographer with Sharp into the field to put together a ninety-second news package; it is quite another to create a half-hour television show.

"After it became apparent COVID wasn't going away, the chancellor suggested doing a webinar with our public health experts," says

Copelin. "But as my staff and I talked about it, we decided to be a little more aggressive with the idea. We decided to team up with KAMU-TV and do a full-blown public service television show on how the A&M System was responding to COVID-19.

"What we learned producing those twelve episodes led to us to extending the concept into what became known as 'Around Texas with Chancellor John Sharp.' We began airing that series on KAMU in the spring of 2021 and offering it to other public television affiliates around the state."

Another pandemic-related initiative, which kept system institutions open and educating, was the government relations office's work to secure funding under the Coronavirus Aid, Relief, and Economic Security—or "CARES"—Act. That money, which totaled more than $86 million dollars for the Texas A&M University System, helped offset some of the financial losses and costs associated with providing campus safeguards during the pandemic.

During 2020, more than sixty thousand coronavirus tests were conducted systemwide in an attempt to contain asymptomatic spread. That included the deployment of free testing kiosks and mobile vans on the flagship campus in College Station. In addition, faculty from the A&M School of Public Health and a group of public health students volunteered both expertise and time to assist the Brazos County Health District set up a contact-tracing system.

The system's newest state agency, the Texas Division of Emergency Management, played a key role in coordinating the statewide response to COVID in conjunction with the Department of State Health Services. And, as they have always done in a time of crisis, the other state agencies under A&M System management—Texas A&M Engineering Extension Service (TEEX), Texas A&M Engineering Experiment Station (TEES), and Texas A&M Transportation Institute (TTI), AgriLife Extension, and the Texas A&M Forest Service—provided resources, expertise, and statewide logistical support.

Perhaps most significant on a long-term basis, the Texas A&M System and its pharmaceutical subcontractor, Fujifilm Diosyth Biotechnologies, were awarded by the federal government's Biomedical Advanced Research and Development Agency a $265 million contract to manufacture COVID-19 vaccines.

After canceling all in-person classes for the spring semester of

2020, Sharp was determined to bring students back to campus in the fall. While colleges and universities across the country weighed options and debated proposed safety protocols, Sharp drew a figurative line in the sand for his flagship campus.

"You can take classes online, but you can't become an Aggie online," he said, quickly adding, "and that sentiment applies to each of our other universities, too."

Carol Fierke was provost of the Texas A&M flagship in 2020. She took the job in the summer of 2017 after having served as dean of the graduate school at the University of Michigan, where she was also a highly regarded researcher in biochemistry.

As provost, she led the flagship's response to the viral villain, and she knows science enough to know of COVID's wily ways.

"There's no binder you can pull off the shelf to deal with something like this," Fierke says. "We took this seriously from the outset. Early on, the university leadership group began meeting twice a day to address the response. At that point, things were changing so fast that four hours was a long time."

The ultimate administrative goal, according to Fierke, was to keep the entire campus community as safe as possible. She knew there was no way to dictate every action of every person on the flagship campus—more than one hundred thousand including students, staff, and faculty—every second of every day. Many have gotten sick, but most have followed appropriate protocols in their recovery because respect, loyalty, and selfless service are the Aggie way.

Regarding the future, Fierke says the pandemic response will enable the university to offer a wider range of online courses while retaining the on-campus student experience so important to being an Aggie.

One story Chancellor Sharp told often, before his attention shifted to the wrath of a global pandemic, involved a 2012 email he received from an elderly woman after A&M's first home football game against newly minted SEC rival Florida. Sharp says that email vividly illuminated how Aggies are "a different breed of folks."

"Most every Monday after a game at Kyle Field, fans of our opponents reach out to let me know how much they enjoyed their time with us and what a fine student body we have. But this one lady painted a very clear picture of the nature of our young people.

"She wrote, 'I'm eighty years old and I never miss a Gator game. When I got off the bus outside your stadium, it was hotter than hell.'"

In the telling of this story, Sharp incorporates some of his own freewheeling turns of phrase.

"She went on to write," he says, "'I was slowly making my way to the stadium'"—aided, as Sharp explains, by a walker—"'when four of your students picked me up, carried me through the line, into the stadium, and took me all the way up to my seat.'

"'Like a whirlwind!'"

But the message did not stop there, as Sharp enjoys sharing.

"'After the game, these same four students came back to my seat and carried me and my walker all the way back to the bus.'"

Then comes the punch line as only John Sharp can deliver.

"She concluded her email with a simple question, 'What the hell kind of school are you running?'"

Ma'am, he runs an entire university system and eight state agencies in much that manner; and all of Aggieland, much of this great country of ours, and humankind in general are the better because of Aggie vision, determination, and leadership.

BIBLIOGRAPHY

INTRODUCTION

Bullock Museum. "American Indians." Accessed April 10, 2019. https://www
.thestoryoftexas.com/discover/campfire-stories/native-americans.

A&E Television Networks. "Texas." History, April 10, 2019. https://www.history
.com/topics/us-states/texas.

Wikipedia. "Spanish Texas." Accessed April 10, 2019. https://en.wikipedia.org/
wiki/Spanish_Texas.

Humanities Texas. "Moses Austin." Texas Originals. Accessed April 10, 2019.
https://www.humanitiestexas.org/programs/tx-originals/list/moses-austin.

Wikipedia. "Stephen F. Austin." Accessed April 10, 2019. https://en.wikipedia
.org/wiki/Stephen_F._Austin.

Wikipedia. "Texas Revolution." Accessed April 10, 2019. https://en.wikipedia.org/
wiki/Texas_Revolution.

Peshek, Sam. "The Morrill Act, Explained." Texas A&M Today, July 1, 2018. Accessed
April 10, 2019. https://today.tamu.edu/2018/07/01/the-morrill-act-explained/.

Borden, Robert. "Harvey Mitchell." RELLIS Recollections, Texas A&M University
System. Accessed April 10, 2019. http://www.rellisrecollections.org/harvey
_mitchell.html.

ecahn. "Today in Texas History: Jefferson Davis Turns Down the Presidency
of Texas A&M University." *MySanAntonio* (blog), June 14, 2010. Accessed
April 12, 2019. https://blog.mysanantonio.com/texas-on-the-potomac/2010/
06/today-in-texas-history-jefferson-davis-turns-down-presidency-of-texas-am
-university/.

Woolfolk, George Ruble. "Prairie View A&M University." Texas State Historical Association, *Handbook of Texas*. Accessed April 12, 2019. https://www
.tshaonline.org/handbook/entries/prairie-view-a-m-university.

Wikipedia. "Texas A&M University System." Accessed April 10, 2019. https://
en.wikipedia.org/wiki/Texas_A%26M_University_System.

Wikipedia. "Tarleton State University." Accessed April 12, 2019. https://en
.wikipedia.org/wiki/Tarleton_State_University.

Wikipedia. "Gibb Gilchrist." Accessed April 12, 2019. https://en.wikipedia.org/
wiki/Gibb_Gilchrist.

Aggie Network. "Distinguished Alumni." Accessed April 12, 2019. https://www
.aggienetwork.com/tribute/tributelist/?exhibitId=11&pageNum=28&pageSize
=10&sort=yearAwarded&desc=True.

Hatfield, Thomas. *Rudder: From Leader to Legend.* College Station: Texas A&M
University Press, 2011.

Office of the President, Texas A&M University. "History of the Office." Accessed
April 13, 2019. https://president.tamu.edu/administration/past-presidents/
index.html.

Texas A&M University System. "About / Universities." Accessed April 12, 2019.
https://www.tamus.edu/system/about/.

Burka, Paul. "Can Anyone Save the Aggies?" *Texas Monthly,* June 2009. Accessed
April 13, 2019. https://www.texasmonthly.com/articles/can-anyone-save-the
-aggies-hint-it-wont-be-rick-perry/.

Texas A&M Galveston. "Dr. R. Bowen Loftin 24th President of Texas A&M University." February 12, 2010. Accessed April 13, 2019. https://www.tamug.edu/
newsroom/2010articles/Bowen24thpresident.html.

Box, Richard. Interview with the author, May 1, 2019.

Sharp, John. Interview with the author, March 13, 2019.

CHAPTER 1

Wikipedia. "2011 Texas Wildfires." Accessed April 14, 2019. https://en.wikipedia
.org/wiki/2011_Texas_wildfires.

Mobley, William. "Effects of Changing Development Patterns and Ignition Locations within Central Texas." *PLOS One* 14, no. 2 (2019). https://journals.plos
.org/plosone/article?id=10.1371/journal.pone.0211454.

Dinish, Heather, and Sam Khan Jr. "Realignment Rewind: How the Latest Round
of Movement Affected CFB." ESPN, June 26, 2017. Accessed April 14, 2019.
https://www.espn.com/college-football/story/_/id/19718974/college-football
-realignment-look-back-winners-losers.

Gray, Rich. Interview with the author, August 21, 2019.

Jackson, Jessica. "Texas A&M Forest Service Celebrates a Century of Service."
Shelby County Today, February 12, 2015. Accessed August 21, 2019. https://
scttx.com/articles/texas-am-forest-service-celebrates-century-service.

Texas A&M Forest Service. "Wildfires and Disasters." Accessed August 21, 2019.
https://tfsweb.tamu.edu/WildlandFireResponse/.

Sharp, John. Interview with the author, March 28, 2019.

Huber, Mary. "Five Years after Devastating Fire, Bastrop County Still Recovering."
Statesman News Network, September 15, 2016, updated September 26, 2018.
Accessed August 21, 2019. https://www.statesman.com/news/20160915/five
-years-after-devastating-fire-bastrop-county-still-recovering.

Texas A&M University System. "Sharp Named Chancellor of Texas A&M System."

September 6, 2011. Accessed August 21, 2019. https://www.tamus.edu/sharp -chancellor-tamus/.

Grissom, Brandy. "Will Troubles Cut Deep for Perry Troubleshooter?" *Texas Tribune*, September 22, 2011. Accessed August 21, 2019. https://www .texastribune.org/2011/09/22/kimbrough-knife-incident-badly-timed-perry/.

Eagle (Bryan / College Station, TX). "Kimbrough Fired from A&M System, Pulls Knife." September 22, 2011, updated July 23, 2020. Accessed August 21, 2019. https://theeagle.com/news/a_m/kimbrough-fired-from-a-m-system-pulls -knife/article_cod c1d06-204b-5e28-b737-62d8a31c23ee.html.

Bonilla, Ray. Interview with the author, September 4, 2019.

CHAPTER 2

ESPN. "Texas A&M Officially Joins SEC." September 25, 2019. Accessed August 10, 2019. https://www.espn.com/college-football/story/_/id/7019493/texas-aggies -officially-get-accepted-sec.

Stallings, Gene. Interview with the author, June 5, 2019.

Wikipedia. "Gene Stallings." Accessed August 10, 2019. https://en.wikipedia.org/ wiki/Gene_Stallings.

Stephenson, Creg. "Alabama vs. Texas A&M in 1968 Cotton Bowl Featured Bryant vs. Stallings, Stabler's Swan Song." Advance Local, October 16, 2015. Accessed August 10, 2019. https://www.al.com/sports/2015/10/looking_back_alabamas _1968_cot.html.

Clark, Rob. "Survivors of A&M Coach 'Bear' Bryant's Grueling Training Camp Reunite in Junction on 60th Anniversary." *Eagle* (Bryan / College Station, TX), August 15, 2014. Accessed August 10, 2019. https://theeagle.com/news/ local/survivors-of-a-m-coach-bear-bryants-grueling-training-camp-reunite-in -junction-on-60th/article_87a14b0e-eda4-5ade-8446-c7f23ff876f3.html.

Wikipedia. "Bear Bryant." Accessed August 10, 2019. https://en.wikipedia.org/ wiki/Bear_Bryant.

Hinnen, Jerry. "The End for Now? A Realignment Timeline." CBS Sports, April 24, 2013. Accessed August 11, 2019. https://www.cbssports.com/college-football/ news/the-end-for-now-a-realignment-timeline/.

Thamel, Pelt. "Uncertainty Marks Start of College Football Realignment." *New York Times*, June 11, 2010. Accessed August 11, 2019. https://www.nytimes .com/2010/06/11/sports/11colleges.html.

Chittum, Ryan. "ESPN Obscures Its Own Role in the Conference Realignment Mess." *Columbia Journalism Review*, September 22, 2011. Accessed August 11, 2019. https://archives.cjr.org/the_audit/espn_obscures_its_own_role_in.php.

Adams, Phil. Interview with the author, July 17, 2019.

Peloquin, Matt. "Updates from the Pac-10 Meetings: Expansion Green Light, 4 Texas Schools?" College Sports Info, June 6, 2010. Accessed August 11, 2019.

http://collegesportsinfo.com/2010/06/06/updates-from-the-pac-10-meetings -expansion-green-light-4-texas-schools/.

Box, Richard. Interview with the author, May 1, 2019.

Schwertner, Jim. Interview with the author, May 1, 2019.

Loftin, Bowen. *The 100-Year Decision: Texas A&M and the SEC.* N.p.: Dog Ear, 2014.

Wikipedia. "Texas-Texas A&M Football Rivalry." Accessed August 11, 2019. https://www.google.com/search?client=safari&rls=en&q=texas+a%26m+texas +football+rivalry&ie=UTF-8&oe=UTF-8.

University of Texas at Austin. "History." Accessed August 11, 2019. https://www .utexas.edu/about/history.

Texas Legacy Support Network. "The Longhorn Teapot Saga." Accessed August 11, 2019. https://www.texaslsn.org/origin-and-story-of-the-longhorn-teapots.

Texas A&M University. "Aggie Traditions: The Aggie War Hymn." Accessed August 9, 2019. https://www.tamu.edu/traditions/gameday/aggie-songs/index.html.

My Aggie Nation. "Farmers Fight! Aggie Yells Date Back to 1896." July 29, 2013. Accessed August 9, 2019. https://myaggienation.com/history_traditions/yell _leaders/farmers-fight-aggie-yells-date-back-to-1896/article_029448e4-f85a -11e2-bb12-0014bcf887a.html. ,

Wikipedia. "Southwest Conference." Accessed August 11, 2019. https://en .wikipedia.org/wiki/Southwest_Conference.

Wikipedia. "Big 12 Conference." Accessed August 11, 2019. https://en.wikipedia.org/ wiki/Big_12_Conference.

Wikipedia. "Pac-12 Conference." Accessed August 11, 2019. https://en.wikipedia .org/wiki/Pac-12_Conference.

Pollack, Sam. "Pac-10 Expansion: Confusion Is the Name of the Game." SB Nation, June 14, 2010. Accessed August 11, 2019. https://arizona.sbnation.com/2010/ 6/14/1517523/pac-10-expansion-confusion-is-the.

Bleacher Report. "Big-12 Revenue Sharing: Why the Texas Longhorns Are Not to Blame." May 15, 2010. Accessed August 11, 2019. https://bleacherreport.com/ articles/392564-big-12-revenue-sharing-why-the-texas-longhorns-are-not-to-blame.

Hamilton, Reeve. "Aggies Poised to Revisit '100-Year Decision' in Print and Film This Year." *Texas Tribune,* June 1, 2014. Accessed August 11, 2019. https:// www.texastribune.org/2014/06/01/aggies-revisit-100-year-decision-print-and -film/.

Thamel, Pete. "The Key Player in the Pac-12's Expansion Outlook: It's Texas, Again." *New York Times,* September 5, 2011. Accessed August 11, 2019. https:// www.nytimes.com/2011/09/05/sports/ncaafootball/texas-is-key-player-in-pac -12s-expansion-outlook.html.

Wikipedia. "Larry Scott (Sports Administrator)." Accessed August 12, 2019. https://en.wikipedia.org/wiki/Larry_Scott_(sports_administrator).

Carlton, Chuck. "Baylor's Late Lawsuit Threat Stops A&M Short of Its SEC Goal." *Dallas Morning News,* September 7, 2011. Accessed August 12, 2019. https://

www.dallasnews.com/sports/2011/09/08/baylors-late-lawsuit-threat-stops
-am-short-of-its-sec-goal/.

Bragg, Roy. "Aggies Killed the Big 12 as Their Parting Gift." *San Antonio News-Express*, October 12, 2016. Accessed August 12, 2019. https://www.expressnews
.com/sports/columnists/roy-bragg/article/Aggies-killed-the-Big-12-as-their
-parting-gift-9963435.php.

Sharp, John. Interview with the author, May 12, 2019.

Hamilton, Reeve. "Branch: No Hearings Planned on A&M Conference Switch." *Texas Tribune*, August 31, 2011. Accessed August 12, 2019. https://www
.texastribune.org/2011/08/31/branch-no-hearings-planned-m-conference
-switch/.

Hamilton, Reeve. "Texas A&M President Loftin Stepping Down." *Texas Tribune*, July 12, 2013. Accessed August 12, 2019. https://www.texastribune.org/2013/
07/12/texas-m-president-loftin-stepping-down/.

Kruse, Nyssa. "'We Were Scammed': A Dozen Authors Say Dog Ear Publishing Owes Them Thousands." *Indianapolis Star*, August 7, 2019. Accessed August 12, 2019. https://www.indystar.com/story/news/investigations/2019/
08/07/dog-ear-publishing-accused-owing-thousands-self-published-authors/
1860676001/.

Watkins, Matthew. "Former A&M President Out as Chancellor at Missouri." *Texas Tribune*, November 9, 2015. Accessed August 12, 2019. https://www.texastribune
.org/2015/11/09/amid-controversy-former-m-president-will-exit-job-/.

Smith, Chris. "College Football's Most Valuable Teams: Texas A&M Jumps to No. 1." *Forbes*, September 11, 2018. Accessed August 12, 2019. https://www.forbes
.com/sites/chrissmith/2018/09/11/college-footballs-most-valuable-teams/?sh
=6e301da06c64.

Selcraig, Bruce. "UT's Decline Drags Longhorn Network with It." *Houston Chronicle*, December 27, 2015. Accessed August 12, 2019. https://www
.houstonchronicle.com/news/houston-texas/houston/article/UT-s-decline
-drags-Longhorn-Network-with-it-6723106.php.

CHAPTER 3

Humanities Texas. "Plácido Benavides." Texas Originals. Accessed April 17, 2019. https://www.humanitiestexas.org/programs/tx-originals/list/placido
-benavides.

Sharp, John. Interview with the author, March 19, 2019.

Geraghty, Jim. "How Five Years in the Air Force Shaped Rick Perry." *National Review*, April 28, 2015. Accessed April 19, 2019. https://www.nationalreview
.com/2015/04/how-5-years-air-force-shaped-rick-perry-jim-geraghty/.

Wikipedia. "John Sharp (Texas Politician)." Accessed April 19, 2020. https://en
.wikipedia.org/wiki/John_Sharp_(Texas_politician).

CHAPTER 4

Box, Richard. Interview with the author, May 1, 2019.

Texas A&M Today. "Thanks to Legislators, Texas A&M System Has Record Session." May 30, 2019. Accessed September 3, 2019. https://today.tamu.edu/2019/05/30/thanks-to-legislators-texas-am-system-has-record-session/.

Wikipedia. "John Sharp (Texas Politician)." Accessed September 3, 2019. https://en.wikipedia.org/wiki/John_Sharp_(Texas_politician).

Wikipedia. "Comptroller." Accessed September 3, 2019. https://en.wikipedia.org/wiki/Comptroller.

Texas State Historical Association. "Comptroller of Public Accounts." *Handbook of Texas*. Accessed September 3, 2019. https://www.tshaonline.org/handbook/entries/comptroller-of-public-accounts.

Texas State Historical Association. "Shaw, James B." *Handbook of Texas*. Accessed September 3, 2019. https://www.tshaonline.org/handbook/entries/shaw-james-b.

Sharp, John. Interview with the author, April 3, 2019.

Hamilton, Billy. Interview with the author, April 24 and April 29, 2019.

Reinhold, Robert. "Thinking the Unthinkable in Texas: State Income Tax on the Horizon." *New York Times*, April 6, 1987. Accessed September 3, 2019. https://www.nytimes.com/1987/04/06/us/thinking-the-unthinkable-in-texas-state-income-tax-is-on-the-horizon.html.

Texas State Historical Association. "Spindletop Oilfield." *Handbook of Texas*. Accessed September 3, 2019. https://www.tshaonline.org/handbook/entries/spindletop-oilfield.

Eaton, Collin. "1980s Oil Bust Left a Lasting Mark." *Houston Chronicle*, August 31, 2016. Accessed September 3, 2019. https://www.chron.com/local/history/economy-business/article/The-1980s-oil-bust-left-lasting-mark-on-Houston-9195222.php.

CHAPTER 5

Broder, David. "Dead Heat in Texas." *Washington Post*, January 18, 1998. Accessed September 25, 2019. https://www.washingtonpost.com/archive/opinions/1998/01/18/dead-heat-in-texas/cc83e96f-cc4f-4f5c-8da6-7a3a27e33751/.

Dave Leip's Atlas of U.W. Elections, LLC. "1998 Lt. Gubernatorial General Election Results—Texas." Accessed September 25, 2019. https://uselectionatlas.org/RESULTS/state.php?year=1998&off=6&elect=0&fips=48&f=0.

Sharp, John. Interview with the author, April 10, 2019.

Pederson, Jere. Interview with the author, September 23, 2019.

Bonilla, Ray. Interview with the author, September 5, 2019.

Brownstein, Ronald. "Texas 'Dream Team' Carries State's Democratic Hopes." *Los Angeles Times*, October 15, 2002. Accessed September 26, 2019. https://www.latimes.com/archives/la-xpm-2002-oct-19-na-dream19-story.html.

Wikipedia. "G. Brint Ryan." Accessed September 26, 2019. https://en.wikipedia.org/wiki/G._Brint_Ryan.

Ramsey, Ross. "Analysis: A Short History of Perry's Surprisingly Long Political Career." *Texas Tribune*, December 16, 2016. Accessed September 27, 2019. https://www.texastribune.org/2016/12/16/analysis-short-history-rick-perrys-surprisingly-lo/.

Wikipedia. "Politics of Texas." Accessed September 26, 2019. https://en.wikipedia.org/wiki/Politics_of_Texas.

Root, Jay. "Rick Perry: The Democrat Years." *Texas Tribune*, July 14, 2011. Accessed September 27, 2019. https://www.texastribune.org/2011/07/14/rick-perry-democrat-years/.

Adams, Phil. Interview with the author, July 17, 2019.

Texas A&M Educational System. "Minutes of the Special Telephonic Meeting of the Board of Regents of the Texas A&M University System Held in College Station, Texas, September 6, 2011." Accessed September 28, 2019. https://assets.system.tamus.edu/files/bor/pdf/Minutes/Telephonic/2011/2011-09-06F.pdf.

CHAPTER 6

Sharp, John. Interview with the author, March 28, 2019.

South Texas College of Law Houston. "History." Accessed October 8, 2019. https://www.stcl.edu/about-us/history/.

Spurlock, Joe. Interview with the author, October 18, 2019.

Fort Worth Star Telegram. "Bids for New Law Schools in Texas Rejected by Panel." March 3, 1973. Accessed October 5, 2019. https://www.newspapers.com/image/632893515/?terms=coordinating%20board%20jaworski&match=1.

Wikipedia. "Leon Jaworski." Accessed October 1, 2019. https://en.wikipedia.org/wiki/Leon_Jaworski.

Texas Attorney General. "Texas Higher Education Coordinating Board Opinion Letter." March 25, 1998. Accessed October 1, 2019. https://www2.texasattorneygeneral.gov/opinions/opinions/48morales/rq/1998/pdf/rq1111dm.pdf.

Marianist Universities. "Characteristics of Marianist Universities." Accessed October 1, 2019. https://marianistuniversities.org/wp-content/uploads/2019/10/CMU_2019_FINAL.pdf.

Slaybaugh, Fred. Interview with the author, October 1, 2019.

Ahdieh, Robert. Interview with the author, October 9, 2019.

Texas Wesleyan University. "Texas Wesleyan History." Accessed September 27, 2019. https://txwes.edu/about/university-history/.

Pham, Huyen. Correspondence with the author via email, October 25, 2019.

Franklin, Greg. Correspondence with the author via email, October 22, 2019.

CHAPTER 7

Sharp, John. Interview with the author, March 28, 2019.

Haye, Jeff. Correspondence with the author via email, August 8, 2019.

Walker, Patricia. Interview with the author, November 12, 2019.

Ray, Phillip. Interview with the author, May 1, 2019.

Wood, Patricia. "Outsourcing in Higher Education." Educational Resources Information Center (ERIC), 2000. Accessed November 18, 2019. https://www.ericdigests.org/2001-3/outsourcing.htm.

Carter, Chase. "Help Wanted." *Battalion*, February 27, 2012. Accessed November 18, 2019. https://issuu.com/thebatt/docs/thebattalion02272012.

Walker, Jake. "Sharp Questions." *Battalion*, March 1, 2012. Accessed November 18, 2019. https://issuu.com/thebatt/docs/thebattalion03012012.

Oliver, Bill. "A&M System Issues More Outsourcing RFP's." WTAW News Talk, March 2, 2012. Accessed November 17, 2019. https://wtaw.com/am-system-issues-more-outsourcing-rfps/.

Reed, Allen. "Texas A&M Staff Council Updated on Status of Outsourced Dining, Maintenance Efforts." *Eagle* (Bryan / College Station, TX), March 19, 2014. Accessed November 17, 2019. https://theeagle.com/news/local/texas-a-m-staff-council-updated-on-status-of-outsourced/article_ea25e7fd-e33a-5908-b435-35f9940e971b.html.

Villanueva, Stuart. "A&M Student Senate Tackles Outsourcing Issue." *Eagle* (Bryan / College Station, TX), April 6, 2012, updated July 23, 2020. Accessed November 17, 2019. https://theeagle.com/news/a_m/a-m-student-senate-tackles-outsourcing-issue/article_04c265f3-3286-50e4-b47d-803063426d63.html.

Eagle (Bryan / College Station, TX). "Employees, Vendors Wary about Outsourcing." July 27, 2012. Accessed November 17, 2019. https://theeagle.com/news/local/employees-vendors-wary-about-a-m-outsourcing/article_87738b22-acf3-5910-81e3-46c80f791f87.html.

Walker, Jake. "Dining Dispute Sparks Outcry." *Battalion*, September 19, 2012. Accessed November 18, 2019. http://www.thebatt.com/news/dining-dispute-sparks-outcry/article_98b95fbc-b712-503d-966d-a54a55828163.html.

Reed, Allen. "Details of Texas A&M System's Outsourcing Contract Released." *Eagle* (Bryan / College Station, TX), November 18, 2012. Accessed November 17, 2019. https://theeagle.com/news/local/details-of-texas-a-m-system-s-outsourcing-contract-released/article_33d6b58a-1599-5610-8112-0a7aa8fb6ad2.html.

TexasTowelie. "Facilities Services at Texas A&M May Be Outsourced, Officials Said." *Democratic Underground* discussion forum, February 23, 2012. Accessed November 17, 2019. https://www.democraticunderground.com/10781254.

Texas A&M University System. "Texas A&M System Awards Contract for Dining, Building Maintenance, Landscaping, and Custodial Services at Texas A&M."

June 21, 2012. Accessed November 17, 2019. https://www.tamus.edu/tamus
-awards-contract-compass/.

Texas A&M University System. "Texas A&M System and Texas A&M University Sign
Contract with Compass Group USA." August 5, 2012. Accessed November 17,
2019. https://www.tamus.edu/tamus-and-tamu-sign-contract-with-compass/.

Reed, Allen. "Texas A&M System Implementing Outsourcing at Other Campuses." *Eagle* (Bryan / College Station, TX), February 28, 2013. Accessed
November 17, 2019, https://theeagle.com/news/local/texas-a-m-system
-implementing-outsourcing-at-other-campuses/article_581a5c56-a751-56ca
-bbb0-27367dfcf42b.html.

CHAPTER 8

Junkins, John. Interview with the author, July 16, 2019.

Institute for Advanced Study. "Albert Einstein." Accessed November 5, 2019.
https://www.ias.edu/scholars/einstein.

Institute for Advanced Study. "Mission and History." Accessed November 5,
2019. https://www.ias.edu/about/mission-history.

Needleman, Alan. Interview with the author, December 8, 2019.

Texas A&M University Hagler Institute for Advanced Study. "Alan Needleman." Accessed December 9, 2019. https://hias.tamu.edu/fellow/dr-alan
-needleman/.

ShellBuckling.com. "Acceptance Remarks." Accessed December 9, 2019. https://
shellbuckling.com/cv/needleman.pdf.

American Society of Mechanical Engineers. "Alan Needleman: 2018 Honor-
ary Member." Accessed December 9, 2019. https://www.asme.org/topics
-resources/content/alan-needleman-2018-honorary-member.

Texas A&M University System. "A&M System Chancellor John Sharp to Announce
Creation of $100 Million Research Initiative." August 1, 2012. Accessed
December 11, 2019. https://www.tamus.edu/tamus-chancellor-john-sharp-to
-announces-100-million-research-initiative/.

Blackwell, Monika. "Texas A&M Foundation Receives $20 Million Commitment
to Name Hagler Institute for Advanced Study." Texas A&M Today, February 20,
2017. Accessed November 3, 2019. https://today.tamu.edu/2017/02/20/texas
-am-foundation-receives-20-million-commitment-to-name-hagler-institute-for
-advanced-study/.

Kuhlmann, Steve. "Texas A&M's Institute for Advanced Study Receives $20
Million Endowment." *Eagle* (Bryan / College Station, TX), February 21, 2017.
Accessed November 3, 2019, https://theeagle.com/news/local/texas-a-m-s
-institute-for-advanced-study-receives-million/article_c5d8e242-efd9-5ce9
-ac42-450cadcda85a.html.

Texas A&M University Corps of Cadets. "Jon L. Hagler '58." Accessed November 3, 2019. https://corps.tamu.edu/jon-l-hagler-58/.

CHAPTER 9

Eagle (Bryan / College Station, TX). "A&M Selects M. Katherine Banks to Lead College." October 1, 2011. Accessed December 29, 2019. https://theeagle.com/news/a_m/a-m-selects-m-katherine-banks-to-lead-college/article_8c840137-2f9a-5cdd-83f9-020dc68a7642.html.

Banks, Kathy. Interview with the author, June 26, 2019.

Texas A&M University Zachry Department of Civil and Environmental Engineering. "Robin Autenrieth." Accessed January 4, 2020. https://engineering.tamu.edu/civil/profiles/rautenrieth.html.

Texas A&M University Engineering. "Remembering Stephen A. Holditch." Accessed January 5, 2020. https://engineering.tamu.edu/news/2019/08/remembering-stephen-a-holditch.html.

American Institute of Mining, Metallurgical, and Petroleum Engineers. "Stephen A. Holditch." Accessed January 5, 2020. http://www.aimehq.org/programs/award/bio/stephen-holditch-deceased-2019.

Adams, Phil. Interview with the author, July 17, 2019.

Eagle (Bryan / College Station, TX). "G. Kemble 'Kem' Bennett Steps Down." August 24, 2011. Accessed January 5, 2020, https://theeagle.com/news/a_m/g-kemble-kem-bennett-steps-down/article_aaff97f6-a62b-591a-9f4e-498763e742b7.html.

O'Connor, John. "What Are Texas' Seven College Solutions?" National Public Radio, August 29, 2011. Accessed January 4, 2020. https://stateimpact.npr.org/florida/2011/08/29/what-are-texas-seven-college-solutions/.

Hamilton, Reeve. "Jeff Sandefer Opens Up on Higher Ed Debate." *Texas Tribune*, May 2, 2011. Accessed January 5, 2020, https://www.texastribune.org/2011/05/02/jeff-sandefer-opens-up-on-higher-ed-debate/.

Hamilton, Reeve. "Six Degrees of Jeff Sandefer: Reform and Texas Higher Ed." *Texas Tribune*, March 16, 2011. Accessed January 5, 2020. https://www.texastribune.org/2011/03/16/whos-behind-proposed-reforms-to-texas-higher-ed/.

Caudill, Harry. *Night Comes to the Cumberlands: A Biography of a Depressed Area.* Boston: Little, Brown, 1962; n.p.: independently published, 2017. https://www.amazon.com/gp/product/1973378442/ref=ppx_yo_dt_b_search_asin_image?ie=UTF8&psc=1.

Cornett, Jim. "What Is a Holler?" *Mountain Eagle* (Whitesburg, KY), May 23, 2018. Accessed January 6, 2019. https://www.themountaineagle.com/articles/what-is-a-holler/.

Texas Monthly. "Embracing Growth in Engineering." March 28, 2013. Accessed January 6, 2020. https://www.texasmonthly.com/articles/embracing-growth-in-engineering-education/.

Texas A&M University Engineering. "25 by 25." Accessed January 4, 2020. https://engineering.tamu.edu/25by25/index.html.

Bloom, Aubrey. "Texas A&M Engineering Ranked in Top 10 in Latest U.S. News Rankings." Texas A&M University Engineering, September 17, 2018. Accessed January 4, 2020. https://engineering.tamu.edu/news/2018/09/texas-am -engineering-ranked-in-top-10-in-latest-us-news-rankings.html.

Haurwitz, Ralph. "Group including Texas A&M System Wins Contract to Run Los Alamos Lab." *Austin American-Statesman*, June 9, 2018. Accessed January 3, 2020. https://www.statesman.com/news/20180609/group-including -texas-am-system-wins-contract-to-run-los-alamos-lab.

Halbert, Amy. "Banks Recognized for Dedication to Future Engineers." Texas A&M University Engineering, December 19, 2018. Accessed January 6, 2020. https://engineering.tamu.edu/news/2018/12/banks-recognized-for-dedication -to-future-engineers-influence-in-energy-sector.html.

Katz, Chelsea. "New Zachry Engineering Education Complex Officially Unveiled at Texas A&M." *Eagle* (Bryan / College Station, TX), September 8, 2018. Accessed January 3, 2020. https://theeagle.com/news/local/new-zachry-engineering -education-complex-officially-unveiled-at-texas-a-m/article_31ee8b49-f379 -5720-b0a2-235fc6ada7b3.html.

Website of Olafur Eliasson. "Biography." Accessed January 6, 2020. https://olafureliasson.net/biography.

Texas A&M University Engineering. "Art of the New Zachry." Accessed January 6, 2020. https://zachry.tamu.edu/art/.

CHAPTER 10

Sharp, John. Interview with the author, March 28, 2019.

Dallas Morning News. "Texas A&M Is Rebranding the Aggie Empire." March 29, 2012. Accessed December 11, 2019. https://www.dallasnews.com/news/2012/03/29/texas-am-is-rebranding-the-aggie-empire/.

Smith, Edward. Interview with the author, December 12, 2019.

Maberry, Sharon. "Agricultural College Adds New Twist to Previous Title." *Battalion*, March 29, 1989. Accessed February 21, 2020. https://newspaper.library.tamu.edu/lccn/sn86088544/1989-03-29/ed-1/seq-3/.

Huffman, Holly. "State and Regional News." *Eagle* (Bryan / College Station, TX), February 3, 2008. Accessed via Lexis-Nexis, December 10, 2019.

Wikipedia. "History of Texas A&M University." Accessed December 10, 2019. https://en.wikipedia.org/wiki/History_of_Texas_A%26M_University.

Wikipedia. "Texas A&M AgriLife Extension Service." Accessed December 10, 2019. https://en.wikipedia.org/wiki/Texas_A%26M_AgriLife_Extension _Service.

Wikipedia. "Texas A&M AgriLife Research." Accessed December 10, 2019.

https://en.wikipedia.org/wiki/Texas_A%26M_AgriLife_Research#cite_note
-garzapost.com-3.

Huffman, Holly. "Regents Debate Ag Name Change." *Eagle* (Bryan / College Station, TX), July 27, 2007. Accessed December 10, 2019. https://theeagle.com/
news/a_m/regents-debate-ag-name-changes/article_2e142af3-ca32-5f6d-a32d
-0e5dbfac5483.html.

Wikipedia. "Brand." Accessed December 7, 2019. https://en.wikipedia.org/wiki/
Brand.

Texas A&M University Brand Guide. "Logo Guidelines." Accessed December 11,
2019. https://brandguide.tamu.edu/visual-style/logos/guidelines.html.

Guthrie, Chris. "Tarleton Becomes Part of the Texas A&M College, 1917." Tarleton
State University, Historic Images Project. Accessed December 11, 2019. https://
www.tarleton.edu/library/crosstimbers/collections/tsucollection/TAN00045P
.html.

Texas A&M University–Commerce. "How Old E.T. Became A&M-Commerce."
Accessed December 11, 2019. https://www.tamuc.edu/aboutUs/historyTraditions/
1996.aspx.

Mahomes, Bill. Interview with the author, February 15, 2020.

CHAPTER 11

Khan, Sam. "New Name for the New Kyle Field?" ESPN, May 12, 2014. Accessed
December 22, 2019. https://www.espn.com/blog/colleges/tamu/post/_/id/
13163/new-kyle-field-the-house-that-johnny-built.

Wikipedia. "Edwin Jackson Kyle." Accessed December 22, 2019. https://en
.wikipedia.org/wiki/Edwin_Jackson_Kyle.

Heathman, Claire. "Aggie Profile: Edwin Jackson Kyle, the Namesake of Kyle
Field." My Aggie Nation, May 13, 2014. Accessed December 22, 2019. https://
myaggienation.com/aggie_profiles/aggie-profile-edwin-jackson-kyle-the
-namesake-of-kyle-field/article_ef670f78-dac0-11e3-8989-0019bb2963f4.html.

My Aggie Nation. "1894." Accessed December 22, 2019. https://myaggienation
.com/athletics_history/football/year_by_year/article_e9b5fec6-f705-11e2-a298
-0014bcf887a.html.

Schexnayder, C. J. "Texas vs. Texas A&M, the Historical: The First and the Last."
Vox Media / SBNation, November 24, 2011. Accessed December 22, 2019.
https://www.sbnation.com/ncaa-football/2011/11/24/2566344/texas-vs-texas
-am-game-rivalry-history-1894.

Wikipedia. "1900 Cornell Big Red Football Team." Accessed December 22,
2019. https://en.wikipedia.org/wiki/1900_Cornell_Big_Red_football
_team.

Cornell University. "150 Ways to Say Cornell." Accessed December 23, 2019.
https://rmc.library.cornell.edu/cornell150/exhibition/hail/index.html.

Texas A&M 12th Man. "Kyle Field Historical Timeline." Accessed December 23, 2019. https://12thman.com/sports/2015/7/30/kyle_timeline.aspx.

Wikipedia. "1919 Texas A&M Aggies Football Season." Accessed December 23, 2019. https://en.wikipedia.org/wiki/1919_Texas_A&M_Aggies_football_team.

Texas A&M University. "What Is an Aggie?" Accessed December 23, 2019. https://www.tamu.edu/about/faq.html.

College Gridirons. "Kyle Field." Accessed December 23, 2019. https://www.collegegridirons.com/stadiums/kyle-field/.

Wikipedia. "Kyle Field." Accessed December 23, 2019. https://en.wikipedia.org/wiki/Kyle_Field.

Schirmer Engineering Corporation. "Life Safety Code Compliance Survey: Kyle Field." January 13, 2004.

Zwerneman, Brett. "Kyle Field Reinforcement Swaying Aggies' Concerns." *Houston Chronicle*, July 24, 2015. Accessed December 23, 2019. https://www.houstonchronicle.com/sports/aggies/article/Kyle-Field-reinforcements-swaying-Aggies-concerns-6366773.php.

Texas A&M University Office of Safety and Security. Letter to Christopher W. Beasley, Deputy State Fire Marshal, July 30, 2008.

Watkins, Matthew. "A&M Athletics Reworks Budget to Pay Loan." *Eagle* (Bryan / College Station, TX), May 14, 2012. Accessed December 23, 2019. https://theeagle.com/news/a_m/a-m-athletics-reworks-budget-to-pay-loan/article_64806bd6-c97c-5c00-a6df-3eb2d076b694.html.

New York Times. "Texas A&M Hires Franchione." December 6, 2002. Accessed December 27, 2020. https://www.nytimes.com/2002/12/06/sports/college-football-texas-a-m-hires-franchione.html.

Barron, David. "Franchione Resigns as Texas A&M Head Coach." *Houston Chronicle*, November 23, 2007. Accessed December 27, 2019. https://www.chron.com/sports/college-football/article/Franchione-resigns-as-Texas-A-M-head-coach-1809971.php.

ESPN. "Mike Sherman Unhappy with Firing." December 2, 2011. Accessed December 27, 2019. https://www.espn.com/college-football/story/_/id/7308074/ex-texas-aggies-coach-mike-sherman-unhappy-firing.

Khan, Sam. "Timeline of Kevin Sumlin's Up-and-Down Career at Texas A&M." ESPN, November 26, 2017. Accessed December 27, 2019. https://www.espn.com/college-football/story/_/id/7308074/ex-texas-aggies-coach-mike-sherman-unhappy-firing.

Ramsey, Shawn. "Johnny Manziel's Texas A&M Timeline." Fox Sports, October 20, 2016. Accessed December 27, 2019. https://www.foxsports.com/southwest/gallery/johnny-manziel-s-texas-a-m-timeline-010114.

Hicks, Tommy. "Gene Stallings: Texas A&M Made Right Move to SEC, Might Take a While to Win." Advance Local, March 9, 2012. Accessed December 27, 2019. https://www.al.com/sports/2012/03/gene_stallings_texas_am_made_r.html.

Zerneman, Brent. "Former A&M Athletic Director Eric Hyman Was a Bad Fit from the Beginning." *San Antonio News-Express*, September 21, 2017. Accessed December 27, 2019. https://www.expressnews.com/sports/columnists/brent _zwerneman/article/Former-A-M-athletic-director-Eric-Hyman-was-a-bad -12219471.php.

Ray, Phillip. Interview with the author, May 1, 2019.

Wikipedia. "HOK (Firm)." Accessed December 27, 2019. https://en.wikipedia .org/wiki/HOK_(firm).

Ray, Phillip. Interview with the author, December 6, 2019.

Populous. "Populous Selected for Kyle Field Redevelopment by Texas A&M, 12th Man Foundation." February 2, 2012. Accessed December 27, 2019. https:// populous.com/populous-selected-for-kyle-field-redevelopment.

Sharp, John. Interview with the author, March 12, 2019.

Newcomb, Tim. "Texas A&M's Redone Kyle Field Is Now Largest in SEC, Full of New Amenities." *Sports Illustrated*, August 27, 2015. Accessed December 27, 2019. https://www.si.com/college/2015/08/27/redone-kyle-field-now-largest -sec-full-fresh-amenities.

McClure, Greg. Email interview with the author, December 16, 2019.

Vaughn, Bill. Email interview with the author, December 14, 2019.

Texas A&M College of Architecture. "College Honored Outstanding Alumni at October 14 Ceremony." July 26, 2016. Accessed December 28, 2019. https:// newsarchive.arch.tamu.edu/news/2016/7/26/college-honor-eight-outstanding -alumni/index.html.

Vaughn Construction. "Founded on Family Values and Craftsmanship." Accessed December 28, 2019. https://www.vaughnconstruction.com/about/history.

Zwerneman, Brent. "Redevelopment of Kyle Field Nears End of First Phase." *Houston Chronicle*, July 3, 2014. Accessed December 28, 2019. https://www .houstonchronicle.com/sports/aggies/article/Redevelopment-of-Kyle-Field -nears-end-of-first-5599517.php.

Mauss, Jeremy. "Renovations to Kyle Field Could Have Texas A&M Playing in Reliant Stadium in 2013." SB Nation, January 27, 2012. Accessed December 28, 2019. https://houston.sbnation.com/texas-a-m-aggies/2012/1/27/2753639/ kyle-field-renovations-texas-aggies-football.

Sacks, Adam. "The Economic Impact of Texas A&M Home Games." Oxford Economics via SlideShare, September 2012. Accessed December 29, 2019. https://www.slideshare.net/ColinKillian/kyle-field-study-oxford-economics.

Brown, Beth. "College Station Commits to Helping Fund Kyle Field Renovations." *Eagle* (Bryan / College Station, TX), July 12, 2013. Accessed December 29, 2019. https://www.slideshare.net/ColinKillian/kyle-field-study-oxford-economics.

Texas A&M Athletics. "Kyle Field Redevelopment Project Overview." YouTube, May 1, 2013. Accessed December 29, 2019. https://www.youtube.com/watch ?v=u5gcobC9Srw.

Fornelli, Tom. "Kyle Field to Be So Loud 'Someone Is Going to Wet Their Pants.'" CBS Sports, May 10, 2013. Accessed May 20, 2021. https://www.cbssports .com/college-football/news/kyle-field-to-be-so-loud-someone-is-going-to-wet -their-pants/.

Chambers, Randy. "Texas A&M's Goal for New Football Stadium Is to Make You Wet Your Pants?" Bleacher Report, May 10, 2013. Accessed December 29, 2019. https://bleacherreport.com/articles/1635373-texas-ams-goal-for-new-football -stadium-is-to-make-you-wet-your-pants.

O'Donnell, Paul. "Killed Irving Worker's Family Wins $53M Jury Verdict in Kyle Field Stadium Makeover Accident." *Dallas Morning News*, February 11, 2016. Accessed December 29, 2019. https://www.dallasnews.com/business/2016/ 02/11/killed-irving-worker-s-family-wins-53m-jury-verdict-in-kyle-field-stadium -makeover-accident/.

Texas A&M Today. "Kyle Field Redevelopment Came in on Time and under Budget." January 13, 2016. Accessed December 29, 2019. https://today.tamu.edu/ 2016/01/13/kyle-field-redevelopment-came-in-on-time-and-under-budget/.

Reid, Allen. "Students Not Feeling the Financial Pain of Kyle Field Renovation." *Eagle* (Bryan / College Station, TX), May 18, 2014. Accessed December 29, 2019. https://theeagle.com/news/local/students-not-feeling-the-financial-pain -of-kyle-field-renovation/article_d9ad9d40-2c39-57e3-8fd4-1b0e37879a41 .html.

Treadway, Dan. "Texas A&M Regent Wants to Rename Football Stadium 'Kyle Field: The House That Johnny Built.'" *Sports Illustrated*, May 13, 2014. Accessed December 29, 2019. https://www.si.com/extra-mustard/2014/05/13/kyle-field -the-house-that-johnny-built.

Schwertner, Jim. Interview with the author, May 1, 2019.

CHAPTER 12

Texas A&M University System. "Texas A&M System Regents Approve Construction Projects." April 11, 2019. Accessed April 22, 2020. https://www.tamus .edu/texas-am-system-regents-approve-construction-projects/.

Association of Former Students. "The Permanent University Fund." Accessed April 21, 2020. https://www.aggienetwork.com/media/guides/advocacy/puf .pdf.

Texas A&M University System. "Board of Regents of the Texas A&M University System Permanent University Fund (PUF) Debt." Accessed April 21, 2020. https://www.tamus.edu/finance/treasury-services/bondholder-information -2/puf/.

Senate of the State of Texas. "What Is a Tuition Revenue Bond?" Accessed April 24, 2019. https://senate.texas.gov/cmtes/80/c535/062508_THECB_Process_and _History_of_Evaluation_of_TRBs.pdf.

Britannica. "Public-Private Partnership." Accessed April 22, 2020. https://www
.britannica.com/topic/public-private-partnership.

Wikipedia. "Public-Private Partnership." Accessed April 22, 2020. https://en
.wikipedia.org/wiki/Public-private_partnership.

Ray, Phillip. Interview with the author, April 23, 2020.

Hardy, Michael. "Country Revival." *Texas Monthly*, July 2017. Accessed April 20,
2020. https://features.texasmonthly.com/editorial/country-revival/.

American Campus Communities. "Prairie View A&M." Accessed April 22, 2020.
https://www.americancampus.com/for-universities/case-studies/prarie-view
-management.

American Campus Communities. "Texas A&M University." Accessed April 22,
2020. https://www.americancampus.com/student-apartments/tx/college
-station.

Abernathy Roeder Boyd Hullett. "Are Public-Private Partnerships a Solution to
Your Organization's Financial Challenges?" Accessed April 20, 2020. https://
www.abernathyroeder.com/public-private-partnerships-solution/.

Peshek, Sam. "Texas A&M Unveils Plans for $360M, 3,400-Bed Park West Hous-
ing to Be Ready by Fall 2017." *Eagle* (Bryan / College Station, TX), July 31, 2015.
Accessed April 22, 2020. https://theeagle.com/news/local/texas-a-m-unveils
-plans-for-m--bed-park/article_6a93eb90-fc22-5817-a638-217b3c3c8b35.html.

National Campus Community Development. "Park West-Texas A&M University."
Accessed April 23, 2020. https://nccdevelopment.org/master-portfolio/park
-west-texas-am-university.

Eden, Greg. Interview with the author, April 20 and May 7, 2020.

Bond Buyer. "Moody's Downgrades $36.1M Texas A&M's P3 Housing Debt."
Accessed April 23, 2020. https://www.bondbuyer.com/news/moodys
-downgrades-361-million-of-texas-a-ms-p3-housing-debt-to-junk.

National Campus Community Development. "Cain Hall Redevelopment II."
Accessed April 23, 2020. https://nccdevelopment.org/master-portfolio/cain
-hall-redevelopment-ii.

Peshek, Sam. "Texas A&M Eyes Tearing Down Cain Hall to Make Room for
Possible On-Campus Hotel." *Eagle* (Bryan / College Station, TX), October 11,
2014. Accessed April 23, 2020. https://theeagle.com/news/local/texas-a
-m-eyes-tearing-down-cain-hall-to-make/article_dde7e1ae-0fe2-569d-a10c
-a157a5b823b5.html.

Higgins, Laine. "Coming Soon to Campus: The $100,000 Hotel Room." *Wall
Street Journal*, November 6, 2017. Accessed April 23, 2020. https://www.wsj
.com/articles/coming-soon-to-campus-the-100-000-hotel-room-1509983744.

Sharp, John. Interview with the author, May 1, 2019.

LSU Alumni Association. "The Cook Hotel." Accessed April 23, 2020. https://
www.lsualumni.org/cook-hotel.

Texas A&M Hotel and Conference Center. "Doug Pitcock '49 Texas A&M Hotel and Conference Center Receives AAA's Four Diamond Rating." June 24, 2019. Accessed April 23, 2020. https://www.texasamhotelcc.com/press/press _releases/AAA_Diamond_Rating/.

Northstar Meeting Group. "Stella Awards 2020: Best Hotel/Resort." Accessed April 23, 2020. https://www.northstarmeetingsgroup.com/Best-Of/The-Stella -Awards/2020-Stella-Awards-Best-Hotel-Resort.

Eagle (Bryan / College Station, TX). "Texas A&M's Luxury Hotel Named after Aggie Philanthropist Doug Pitcock, Class of '49." February 8, 2018. Accessed April 23, 2020. https://theeagle.com/news/a_m/texas-a-ms-luxury-hotel-named-after -aggie-philanthropist-doug-pitcock-class-of-49/article_2d33edcc-0d11-11e8-a415 -87152318bfd5.html.

Trip Advisor. "Texas A&M Hotel and Conference Center." Accessed April 23, 2020. https://www.tripadvisor.com/Hotel_Review-g55649-d13964174-Reviews -Texas_A_M_Hotel_and_Conference_Center-College_Station_Texas.html.

Dosh, Kristi. "New Hotel Opens at Texas A&M Overlooking Kyle Field." *Forbes*, August 31, 2018. Accessed April 23, 2020. https://www.forbes.com/sites/ kristidosh/2018/08/31/new-hotel-opens-at-texas-am-overlooking-kyle-field/ ?sh=199cf64b2edb.

CHAPTER 13

Tex. Educ. Code § 51.001. Accessed September 10, 2020. https://statutes.capitol .texas.gov/Docs/ED/htm/ED.51.htm.

Texas A&M International University. "Governor Selects TAMIU Student for Historic Role as Student Regent." May 12, 2016. Accessed September 11, 2020. https://www.tamiu.edu/newsinfo/2016/05/TAMIU%20Student%20Regent %205122016.shtml.

Texas A&M University System. "A&M System Student Regent." Accessed September 11, 2020. https://www.tamus.edu/academic/student-success/student -regent/.

Bridge. "TAMIU's First Student Regent." September 13, 2016. Accessed September 11, 2020. http://www.thebridgestudentnews.com/2016/09/13/tamius-first -student-regent/.

Martinez, Stephanie. Interview with the author, September 3, 2020.

Ramirez, Minita. Interview with the author, September 16, 2020.

Hallmark, James. Email interview with the author, September 28, 2020.

Texas A&M University System spreadsheet. "Fall 2020 First Generation Students." Provided by Vice Chancellor James Hallmark via email on September 15, 2020.

Texas A&M International University Division of Student Success. "Offices." Accessed September 16, 2020. https://www.tamiu.edu/studentsuccess/offices .shtml.

Texas A&M International University. "Keck Named President of Texas A&M

International University." Accessed September 16, 2020. https://www.tamiu.edu/kecknamed.htm.

Mendoza, Elaine. Interview with the author, September 14, 2020.

Texas A&M Today. "Elaine Mendoza Elected Texas A&M System Board of Regents Chair." May 17, 2019. Accessed September 15, 2020. https://today.tamu.edu/2019/05/17/elaine-mendoza-elected-texas-am-system-board-of-regents-chair/.

Conceptual Mindworks Inc. "Our Story." Accessed September 15, 2020. https://www.conceptualmindworks.com/our-story/.

Hamilton, Reeve. "Texas A&M System Launches EmpowerU Website." *Texas Tribune*, October 29, 2012. Accessed September 17, 2020. https://www.texastribune.org/2012/10/29/texas-m-system-unveils-new-accountability-website/.

Judith Zaffirini Texas Senator. Home page. Accessed September 18, 2020. JudithZaffirini.com.

Texas A&M International University. "TAMIU Names University Success Center in Honor of Sen. Zaffirini." June 11, 2012. Accessed September 18, 2020. https://www.tamiu.edu/newsinfo/newsarticles/2012-ZaffiriniCenter061112.shtml.

CHAPTER 14

Wikipedia. "List of Texas Hurricanes (Pre-1900)." Accessed March 19, 2020. https://en.wikipedia.org/wiki/List_of_Texas_hurricanes_(pre-1900).

Wikipedia. "1900 Galveston Hurricane." Accessed March 19, 2020. https://en.wikipedia.org/wiki/1900_Galveston_hurricane.

Burnett, John. "The Tempest at Galveston: 'We Knew There Was a Storm Coming, but We Had No Idea.'" National Public Radio, November 30, 2017. Accessed March 19, 2020. https://www.npr.org/2017/11/30/566950355/the-tempest-at-galveston-we-knew-there-was-a-storm-coming-but-we-had-no-idea.

Wikipedia. "Hurricane Katrina." Accessed March 19, 2020. https://en.wikipedia.org/wiki/Hurricane_Katrina.

Levin, Matt. "How Hurricane Rita Anxiety Led to the Worst Gridlock in Houston History." *Houston Chronicle*, August 25, 2017. Accessed March 19, 2020. https://www.chron.com/news/houston-texas/houston/article/Hurricane-Rita-anxiety-leads-to-hellish-fatal-6521994.php.

"Hurricane Ike Impact Report." December 8, 2008. Accessed March 19, 2020. https://www.fema.gov/pdf/hazard/hurricane/2008/ike/impact_report.pdf.

Wikipedia. "Hurricane Ike." Accessed March 19, 2020. https://en.wikipedia.org/wiki/Hurricane_Ike.

Svitek, Patrick. "Texas Gov. Greg Abbott Selects A&M's John Sharp to Lead Harvey Rebuilding Effort." *Texas Tribune*, September 6, 2017. Accessed March 20, 2020. https://www.texastribune.org/2017/09/06/abbott-selects-sharp-lead-harvey-rebuilding-effort/.

Texas A&M University System. "Governor Abbott Taps Chancellor Sharp to Lead Commission to Rebuild Texas." September 7, 2017. Accessed March 20, 2020. https://www.tamus.edu/governor-abbott-taps-chancellor-sharp-to-lead-commission-to-rebuild-texas/.

Ward, Mike. "John Sharp: An Unlikely Recover Czar Takes Over." *Houston Chronicle*, September 21, 2017. Accessed March 20, 2020. https://www.chron.com/news/houston-weather/hurricaneharvey/article/John-Sharp-an-unlikely-recovery-czar-takes-charge-12214949.php.

"Hurricane Harvey Deployment Statistics." Accessed March 22, 2020. http://texastaskforce1.org/wp-content/uploads/2019/08/2017_Hurricane-Harvey.pdf.

Texas A&M University System. "Texas A&M University System Scrambles Personnel to Help in Wake of Hurricane Harvey." August 28, 2017. Accessed March 22, 2020. https://www.tamus.edu/texas-am-university-system-scrambles-personnel-to-help-in-wake-of-hurricane-harvey/.

Governor's Commission to Rebuild Texas. *Eye of the Storm: Report of the Governor's Commission to Rebuild Texas.* November 2018. Accessed March 23, 2020. https://www.rebuildtexas.today/wp-content/uploads/sites/52/2018/12/12-11-18-EYE-OF-THE-STORM-digital.pdf.

Ballabina, Susan. Interview with the author, October 15, 2019.

Fannin, Blair. "Texas Agriculture Losses from Hurricane Harvey Estimated to Be More Than $200 Million." Texas A&M Today, November 8, 2017. Accessed March 23, 2020. https://today.tamu.edu/2017/11/08/texas-agriculture-losses-from-hurricane-harvey-estimated-to-be-more-than-200-million/.

Schattenberg, Paul. "AgriLife Extension Playing Key Role in Rebuild Texas Efforts." *Gilmer Mirror*. Accessed March 23, 2020. http://www.gilmermirror.com/view/full_story/27555065/article-AgriLife-Extension-playing-key-role-in-Rebuild-Texas-efforts?instance=news_special_coverage_right_column.

Bissett, Wesley. "Aggies Step Up: Texas A&M Veterinary Emergency Team (VET) Hurricane Harvey Response." Texas A&M University Veterinary Medicine and Biomedical Sciences, July 19, 2018. Accessed March 24, 2020. https://vetmed.tamu.edu/vet/wp-content/uploads/sites/56/2020/08/VETHarveyUpdate071918.pdf.

Texas A&M University–Corpus Christi. "Harvey Help." Accessed March 25, 2020. https://harveyhelp.tamucc.edu.

Kaiser Family Foundation. "Survey: One Year after Hurricane Harvey, 3 in 10 Affected Texas Gulf Coast Residents Say Their Lives Remain Disrupted." Accessed August 23, 2018. https://www.kff.org/other/press-release/one-year-after-hurricane-harvey-3-in-10-texas-gulf-coast-residents-say-lives-remain-disrupted/.

Qatar Harvey Fund. "About." Accessed March 26, 2020. https://www.qatarharveyfund.com/about/.

CHAPTER 15

Gregg, Tim. *RELLIS Recollections*. College Station: Texas A&M University Press, 2019. http://www.rellisrecollections.org.

CHAPTER 16

Conant, Jennet. *109 East Palace: Robert Oppenheimer and the Secret City of Los Alamos*. New York: Simon & Schuster, 2006.

Wikipedia. "J. Robert Oppenheimer." Accessed August 4, 2020. https://en .wikipedia.org/wiki/J._Robert_Oppenheimer.

Wikipedia. "Manhattan Project." Accessed August 4, 2020. https://en.wikipedia .org/wiki/Manhattan_Project.

Wikisource. "Los Alamos Ranch School Seizure Letter." Accessed August 4, 2020. https://en.wikisource.org/wiki/Los_Alamos_Ranch_School_Seizure_Letter.

Triad National Security, LLC. Home page. Accessed August 4–5, 2008. https:// www.triadns.org.

Texas A&M Today. "Texas A&M System, Partners Selected to Manage Los Alamos National Lab." June 8, 2018. Accessed August 5, 2018. https://today.tamu .edu/2018/06/08/texas-am-system-partners-selected-to-manage-los-alamos -national-lab/.

Adams, Marvin. Interview with the author, July 21, 2020.

Battelle. Various pages. Accessed August 5, 2018. https://www.battelle.org.

University of California Office of the President. "Los Alamos National Laboratory." Accessed August 5, 2020. https://www.ucop.edu/laboratory-management/ about-the-labs/overview-lanl.html.

Los Alamos National Laboratory. Various pages. Accessed August 4–6, 2020. https://www.lanl.gov.

Eagle (Bryan / College Station, TX). "Texas A&M-Involved Coalition Not Awarded $2.6 Billion Sandia Labs Contract." December 17, 2016. Accessed August 4, 2020. https://theeagle.com/news/local/texas-a-m-involved-coalition-not -awarded-2-6-billion-sandia-labs-contract/article_7d56c3c3-be35-5c95-9a86 -6f1f195750a5.html.

Tiefer, Charles. "The 10 Worst Things about Lockheed Martin's Alleged Lobbying Fraud." *Forbes*, August 31, 2015. Accessed August 5, 2020. https://www.forbes .com/sites/charlestiefer/2015/08/31/lockheed-fined-4-7-million-for-fraudulent -taxpayer-paid-lobbying-with-most-corrupt-ex-rep-wilson/?sh=2235a05646c0.

Sharp, John. Interview with the author, April 24, 2019.

Watkins, Matthew. "A&M, UT Will Vie to Co-manage Sandia National Laboratory." *Texas Tribune*, May 24, 2016. Accessed August 5, 2020. https://www .texastribune.org/2016/05/24/m-ut-will-vie-co-manage-sandia-national -laboratory/.

Texas A&M Today. "Texas A&M System, Partners Place Bid to Manage Nuclear Lab." May 24, 2016. Accessed August 6, 2020. https://today.tamu.edu/2016/05/24/texas-am-system-partners-place-bid-to-manage-nuclear-lab/.

Sudduth, Scott. Interview with the author, July 13, 2020.

Bryan, Susan Montoya. "Multibillion-Dollar Contract for Los Alamos Lab Up for Bid." *Seattle Times*, June 27, 2017. Accessed August 6, 2020. https://www.seattletimes.com/business/multibillion-dollar-contract-for-los-alamos-lab-up-for-bid/.

Hurtado, Diane. Interview with the author, August 25, 2020.

University of Texas System. "UT Regents Authorize Offer of Bid to Operate Los Alamos National Laboratory." November 27, 2017. Accessed August 6, 2020. https://www.utsystem.edu/news/2017/11/27/ut-regents-authorize-offer-bid-operate-los-alamos-national-laboratory.

Texas A&M University National Laboratories Office. Home page. Accessed August 5–7, 2020. https://nationallabsoffice.tamus.edu/.

Pontin, Jason. "Oppenheimer's Ghost." *MIT Technology Review*, October 15, 2007. Accessed August 12, 2020. https://www.technologyreview.com/2007/10/15/223531/oppenheimers-ghost-3/.

Wikipedia. "Los Alamos, New Mexico." Accessed August 12, 2020. https://en.wikipedia.org/wiki/Los_Alamos,_New_Mexico.

CHAPTER 17

Prairie View A&M. "'Ruth the Truth' Is All about the Students." Accessed February 10, 2020. https://www.pvamu.edu/blog/ruth-the-truth-is-all-about-the-students/.

Sharp, John. Interview with the author, May 6, 2019.

Brown University. "Eighteenth President: Ruth J. Simmons." Accessed February 10, 2020. https://www.brown.edu/about/history/timeline/eighteenth-president-ruth-j-simmons.

Wikipedia. "Ruth Simmons." Accessed February 10, 2020. https://en.wikipedia.org/wiki/Ruth_Simmons.

Watkins, Matthew. "Prairie View A&M President George Wright Says He's Stepping Down." *Texas Tribune*, June 13, 2017. Accessed February 10, 2020. https://www.texastribune.org/2017/06/13/prairie-view-m-president-george-wright-says-hes-stepping-down/.

Simmons, Ruth. Interview with the author, June 7 and 29, 2019.

Prairie View Athletics. "Clarence Stubblefield." Accessed February 10, 2020. https://pvpanthers.com/honors/prairie-view-am-university-sports-hall-of-fame/clarence-stubblefield/287.

Wikipedia. "Prairie View A&M Panthers Basketball." Accessed February 10, 2020. https://en.wikipedia.org/wiki/Prairie_View_A%26M_Panthers_basketball.

Stempel, Jonathan, and Steve Eder. "Goldman Sachs Charged with Fraud by SEC." *Reuters*, April 16, 2010. Accessed February 11, 2020. https://www

.reuters.com/article/us-goldman/goldman-sachs-charged-with-fraud-by-sec
-idUSTRE63F3JX20100416.

Graham, Bowley. "Questions at Brown on Ruth Simmons' Role at Goldman
Sachs." *New York Times*, March 1, 2010. Accessed February 11, 2020. https://
www.nytimes.com/2010/03/02/business/02brown.html.

Copeland, Beverly. Email interview with the author, August 13, 2019.

New York Times. "Ruth Simmons on Cultivating the Next Generation of College
Students." February 28, 2018. Accessed February 11, 2020. https://www.google
.com/search?client=safari&rls=en&q=Cultivating+the+Next+Generation+of
+College+Students&ie=UTF-8&oe=UTF-8.

Eze, Maduforo. Email interview with the author, August 13, 2019.

CHAPTER 18

Texas A&M University Veterinary Medicine and Biological Sciences. "College History." Accessed August 1, 2020. https://vetmed.tamu.edu/about-us/history/.

Texas A&M University College of Medicine. "History." Accessed August 1, 2020.
https://medicine.tamu.edu/about/history.html.

Sicilio, Mark. Interview with the author, July 27, 2020.

Watkins, Melanie. "Teague, Olin Earl [Tiger]." Texas State Historical Association, *Handbook of Texas.* Accessed August 1, 2020. https://www.tshaonline
.org/handbook/entries/teague-olin-earl-tiger.

Washington Post. "Ex-Rep. Olin E. Teague of Texas Dies." January 24, 1981. Accessed
August 1, 2020. https://www.washingtonpost.com/archive/local/1981/01/24/
ex-rep-olin-e-teague-of-texas-dies/5f3941d7-ce49-4aa1-aceb-b05607d0eb94/.

Vital Record: News from Texas A&M Health. "A History of Selfless Service."
May 30, 2017. Accessed August 1, 2020. https://vitalrecord.tamhsc.edu/a
-history-of-selfless-service/.

ISSUU. "Texas A&M Health Science Center College of Medicine." Accessed
August 1, 2020. https://issuu.com/tamhsccom.

Texas A&M University Health Science Center. "About." Accessed August 1, 2020.
https://health.tamu.edu/about/index.html.

Powell, Don. Interview with the author, August 5, 2020.

Wikipedia. "Donald Powell." Accessed August 6, 2020. https://en.wikipedia.org/
wiki/Donald_E._Powell.

Wikipedia. "American Association of Universities." Accessed August 6, 2020.
https://en.wikipedia.org/wiki/Association_of_American_Universities.

American Association of Universities. "Texas A&M University." Accessed August 6,
2020. https://www.aau.edu/who-we-are/our-members/texas-am-university.

Texas A&M Rural and Community Health Initiative. "About ARCHI." Accessed
August 6, 2020. https://architexas.org/about/index.html.

Dickey, Nancy. Interview with the author, August 5, 2020.

Reed, Alan. "Nancy Dickey Resigns as Texas A&M Health Science Center President." *Eagle* (Bryan / College Station, TX), October 9, 2012. Accessed August 7, 2020. https://theeagle.com/news/a_m/nancy-dickey-resigns-as-texas-a-m-health-science-center-president/article_441009b3-ec98-5cb0-846c-773444319b90.html.

Sharp, John. Interview with the author, August 5, 2020.

Eagle (Bryan / College Station, TX). "Texas A&M System Chancellor John Sharp Proposes Transfer of Health Science Center." May 3, 2012. Accessed August 8, 2020. https://theeagle.com/news/a_m/texas-a-m-system-chancellor-john-sharp-proposes-transfer-of-health-science-center/article_30d74465-5311-5e93-9210-a23e9bb6b37f.html.

Cobler, Paul. "Trump's COVID-19 Testing Czar Spent Decades in Texas Preparing for a Pandemic." *Dallas Morning News*, March 27, 2020. Accessed August 8, 2020. https://www.dallasnews.com/news/politics/2020/03/27/trumps-covid-19-testing-czar-spent-decades-in-texas-preparing-for-a-pandemic/.

Hamilton, Steve. "Feds Approve New Vaccine Facility in Bryan-College Station." *Texas Tribune*, March 26, 2013. Accessed August 8, 2020. https://www.texastribune.org/2013/03/26/m-system-announces-partnership-glaxosmithkline/.

Watkins, Matthew. "A&M Health Science Center CEO 'Heartbroken' over Exit." *Texas Tribune*, June 1, 2015. Accessed August 8, 2020. https://www.texastribune.org/2015/06/01/biotech-leader-brett-giroir-leaving-texas-m/.

Peshek, Sam. "Health Science Center CEO Brett Giroir Leaving Aggieland after Being Asked to Resign." *Eagle* (Bryan / College Station, TX), June 2, 2015. Accessed August 8, 2020. https://theeagle.com/news/local/health-science-center-ceo-brett-giroir-leaving-aggieland-after-being-asked-to-resign/article_be674ccd-2a78-5833-b57e-a5ecd3d4f651.html.

Wiley, Kenny. "Byington Leaving Texas A&M Post for University of California System." *Eagle* (Bryan / College Station, TX), July 19, 2019. Accessed August 8, 2020. https://theeagle.com/news/local/byington-leaving-texas-a-m-post-for-university-of-california-system/article_a7fd28c4-a9dd-11e9-bf77-73f24a2a40fd.html.

University of California Office of the President. "Carrie L. Byington, MD." Accessed August 8, 2020. https://www.ucop.edu/uc-health/staff/bios/carrie_byington.html.

Reynolds, Kelli. "Greg Hartman Selected to Lead Texas A&M Health Science Center." Texas A&M Today, April 13, 2020. Accessed August 9, 2020. https://today.tamu.edu/2020/04/13/greg-hartman-selected-to-lead-texas-am-health-science-center/.

Hartman, Greg. Interview with the author, July 1 and August 7, 2020.

Fierke, Carol. Interview with the author, August 9, 2020.

Texas A&M Today. "Texas A&M System Invests Half-Billion Dollars in Texas Medical Center." February 20, 2020. Accessed August 9, 2020. https://today.tamu.edu/2020/02/20/texas-am-system-invests-half-billion-dollars-in-texas-medical-center/.

ENMED Engineering and Medicine. Home page. Accessed August 9, 2020. https://enmed.tamu.edu.

Pettigrew, Roderic. Interview with the author, July 21, 2020.

Wikipedia. "Roderic L. Pettigrew." Accessed August 9, 2020. https://en.wikipedia.org/wiki/Roderic_I._Pettigrew.

Rubin, Hannele. "Wanted: Invention-Minded Physicians." University of Miami Medicine, Spring 2020. Accessed August 9, 2020. https://magazine.med.miami.edu/wanted-invention-minded-physicians/.

Vital Record: News from Texas A&M Health. "Pettigrew Inducted into American Academy of Arts and Sciences." May 13, 2020. Accessed August 9, 2020. https://vitalrecord.tamhsc.edu/pettigrew-inducted-into-american-academy-of-arts-and-sciences/.

ENMED Engineering and Medicine. "Priya Arunachalam." Accessed August 9, 2020. https://enmed.tamu.edu/students-class-of-2023/priya-arunachalam/.

Sharp, John. Interview with the author, April 24, 2019.

Texas A&M University College of Agriculture and Life Sciences. "Patrick J. Stover, Ph.D." Accessed August 10, 2019. https://aglifesciences.tamu.edu/about/our-faculty/patrick-stover/.

CHAPTER 19

Gregg, Tim. *RELLIS Recollections*. College Station: Texas A&M University Press, 2019.

Britzky, Haley. "The Army Is Getting a New $130 Million Hypersonics Playground in Texas." Task & Purpose, August 14, 2019. Accessed May 15, 2020. https://taskandpurpose.com/news/army-futures-command-texas/.

Brading, Thomas. "Futures Command Forges Academia Partnerships, Breaks Ground on New Research Hub." US Army, October 17, 2019. Accessed May 15, 2020. https://www.army.mil/article/228589/futures_command_forges_academia_partnerships_breaks_ground_on_new_research_hub.

Texas A&M Engineer. "Bush Combat Development Center." Special edition. Accessed May 15, 17, 20, 2020. https://engineeringmagazine.tamu.edu.

Hardy, Michael. "Texas A&M Says Howdy to the Army Futures Command." *Texas Monthly*, November 29, 2018. Accessed May 15, 2020. https://www.texasmonthly.com/news/texas-says-howdy-army-futures-command/.

Wiley, Kenny. "Texas A&M System Plans $130 Million Facility at RELLIS Campus for Army Futures Command." *Eagle* (Bryan / College Station, TX), August 2, 2019. Accessed May 15, 2020. https://theeagle.com/news/a_m/texas-a-m-system-plans-130-million-facility-at-rellis-campus-for-army-futures-command/article_2d41d3e6-b554-11e9-a150-abd929454a02.html.

US Army. "Army Futures Command." March 28, 2018. Accessed May 15, 2020. https://www.army.mil/standto/archive/2018/03/28/.

University of Texas System. "University of Texas System to Serve as Home Base for U.S. Army Futures Command." July 13, 2018. Accessed May 15, 2020. https://www.utsystem.edu/news/2018/07/13/university-texas-system-serve -home-base-us-army-futures-command.

Livengood, Paul. "'Army Futures Command: Why Now? Why Texas?' Event Hosted at UT-Austin." KVUE-TV (Austin, TX), January 8, 2020. Accessed May 16, 2020. https://www.kvue.com/article/news/education/university-of -texas/ut-army-futures-command-austin-discussion/269-6a9ae61f-6f73-46de -9adc-aeb579890e9d.

Judson, Jen. "Army Futures Command Is Leading a Cultural Shift, Much to the Delight of Industry." *Defense News*, October 16, 2018. Accessed May 16, 2020. https://www.defensenews.com/digital-show-dailies/ausa/2019/10/16/army -futures-command-is-leading-a-cultural-shift-much-to-the-delight-of-industry/.

Texas McCombs News. "Modernizing U.S. Army Attracted to Austin." January 30, 2020. Accessed May 16, 2020. https://medium.com/texas-mccombs-news/ modernizing-u-s-army-moves-to-austin-489090de8f6c.

Texas A&M Today. "Texas A&M System Showcases Ways It Can Help Army Futures Command." November 20, 2018. Accessed May 16, 2020. https:// today.tamu.edu/2018/11/20/texas-am-system-showcases-ways-it-can-help -army-futures-command/.

Wiley, Kenny. "Army Futures Command Hosts Autonomous Vehicle Demonstrations at RELLIS." *Eagle* (Bryan / College Station, TX), May 17, 2019. Accessed May 16, 2020. https://theeagle.com/news/local/army-futures-command-hosts -autonomous-vehicle-demonstrations-at-rellis/article_1e200e04-7860-11e9 -8a5f-37e8bc729405.html.

Texas A&M Today. "Texas A&M System Regents Approve RELLIS to Be Army Futures Command Central Testing Hub." August 8, 2019. Accessed May 16, 2020. https://today.tamu.edu/2019/08/08/texas-am-system-regents-approve -rellis-to-be-army-futures-command-central-testing-hub/.

Kimmons, Sean. "In First Year, Futures Command Grows from 12 to 24,000 Personnel." US Army, July 22, 2019. Accessed May 16, 2020. https://www .army.mil/article/224744/in_first_year_futures_command_grows_from_12 _to_24000_personnel.

Bunja, Jack. "Soldiers and Scientists Share Perspective and Knowledge." US Army, March 4, 2020. Accessed May 16, 2020. https://www.army.mil/article/233399/ soldiers_and_scientists_share_perspective_and_knowledge.

Alexander, Moira. "Agile Project Management: 12 Key Principles, 4 Big Hurdles." IDG Communications, June 19, 2018. Accessed May 17, 2020. https://www .cio.com/article/3156998/agile-project-management-a-beginners-guide.html.

Currie-Gregg Observatory at Enid High School. "Dr. Nancy Currie-Gregg." Accessed May 17, 2020. http://wewillfindstars.space/nancy-currie-gregg.html.

Texas A&M Today. "Texas A&M System to Lead $100 Million Hypersonic Research Consortium." October 26, 2020. Accessed November 1, 2020. https://today

.tamu.edu/2020/10/26/texas-am-system-to-lead-consortium-on-advancing-hypersonic-flight-systems/.

Larter, David. "All US Navy Destroyers Will Get Hypersonic Missiles, Says Trump's National Security Adviser." *Defense News*, October 21, 2020. Accessed November 1, 2020. https://www.defensenews.com/naval/2020/10/21/all-us-navy-destroyers-will-get-hypersonic-missiles-trumps-national-security-advisor-says/.

Osborn, Kris. "How Fast Can the U.S. Military Build Hypersonic Weapons?" *National Interest* (blog), October 28, 2020. Accessed November 1, 2020. https://nationalinterest.org/blog/buzz/how-fast-can-us-military-build-hypersonic-weapons-171510.

Vergun, David. "DOD Awards Applied Hypersonics Contract to Texas A&M University." US Department of Defense, October 26, 2020. Accessed November 1, 2020. https://www.defense.gov/Explore/News/Article/Article/2394438/dod-awards-applied-hypersonics-contract-to-texas-am-university/.

University Consortium for Applied Hypersonics. "Hypersonics: Advancing Aerodynamics for Accuracy." October 23, 2020. Accessed November 2, 2020. https://hypersonics.tamu.edu/hypersonics-advancing-aerodynamics-for-accuracy/.

Texas A&M Today. "Construction on U.S. Army Hypersonic Test Center to Begin on RELLIS Campus This Fall." May 15, 2020. Accessed November 2, 2020. https://today.tamu.edu/2020/05/15/construction-on-u-s-army-hypersonic-test-center-to-begin-on-rellis-campus-this-fall/.

Hurtado, John. Email interview with the author, April 15, 2020.

Texas A&M University System. "U.S. Army Secretary Visits Texas A&M System Bush Combat Development Complex." September 30, 2020. Accessed November 4, 2020. https://www.tamus.edu/u-s-army-secretary-visits-texas-am-system-bush-combat-development-complex/.

Texas A&M Engineering Experiment Station. "Army Innovator to Lead Bush Combat Development Complex." July 1, 2020. Accessed November 5, 2020. https://tees.tamu.edu/news/2020/07/army-innovator-to-lead-bush-combat-development-complex.html.

CHAPTER 20

Physiopedia. "Disaster Management." Accessed October 17, 2020. https://www.physio-pedia.com/Disaster_Management.

National Aeronautics and Space Administration. NISAR: The NASA-ISRO SAR Mission. "Natural and Manmade Hazards in the State of Texas." Accessed October 17, 2020. https://nisar.jpl.nasa.gov/files/nisar/NISAR_Applications_Hazards_Texas.pdf.

Texas A&M University System. "Texas A&M System Adds Eighth State Agency, Takes on Greater Role in Disaster Management." August 28, 2019. Accessed

October 17, 2020. https://www.tamus.edu/texas-am-system-adds-eighth-state -agency-takes-on-greater-role-in-disaster-management/.

Wikipedia. "National Security Resources Board." Accessed October 17, 2020. https://en.wikipedia.org/wiki/National_Security_Resources_Board.

Marten, James. "Emergency Management." Texas State Historical Association, *Handbook of Texas*. Accessed October 17, 2020. https://www.tshaonline .org/handbook/entries/emergency-management.

Sharp, John. Interview with the author, October 21, 2020.

Governor's Commission to Rebuild Texas. *Eye of the Storm: Report of the Governor's Commission to Rebuild Texas.* November 2018. Accessed March 2020. https:// www.rebuildtexas.today/wp-content/uploads/sites/52/2018/12/12-11-18-EYE -OF-THE-STORM-digital.pdf.

Kidd, Nim. Interview with the author, October 11, 2020.

Gregg, Tim. *City Stories: College Station—a Recent History.* Independently published, 2019.

Texas A&M Task Force 1. "About Texas A&M Task Force 1." Accessed October 12, 2020. https://texastaskforce1.org/about-us/.

Vimeo. "TDEM and Texas A&M Executive Meeting, October 17th, 2019." Accessed October 14, 2020. https://vimeo.com/373169932.

Texas A&M Engineering Extension Service. "Disaster City." Accessed October 14, 2020. https://teex.org/about-us/disaster-city/.

EPILOGUE

Lee, Tai. Interview with the author, November 4, 2020.

Gregg, Tim. *City Stories: College Station—a Recent History.* Independently published, 2019.

Wikipedia. "Severe Acute Respiratory Syndrome." Accessed November 5, 2020. https://en.wikipedia.org/wiki/Severe_acute_respiratory_syndrome.

Worldometer. "South Korea." Accessed November 5, 2020. https://www .worldometers.info/coronavirus/country/south-korea/.

Centers for Disease Control and Prevention. "CDC, Washington State Report First COVID-19 Death." February 29, 2020. Accessed November 5, 2020. https://www.cdc.gov/media/releases/2020/s0229-COVID-19-first-death.html.

Falcon, Hannah. "Timeline of Coronavirus in Aggieland." *Battalion*, March 19, 2020. Accessed November 5, 2020. http://www.thebatt.com/news/timeline-of -coronavirus-in-aggieland/article_0cb61488-6a3b-11ea-904d-dfa8b855798e.html.

Costa, Chris. "Aug. 6 COVID-19 Case Count: 306 New Deaths in Texas, Single-Day High for Deaths in Houston with 23." KHOU-TV, August 6, 2020. Accessed November 5, 2020. https://www.khou.com/article/news/health/coronavirus/ coronavirus-numbers/august-6-covid-19-case-count-texas-306-new-deaths -houston-single-day-high-deaths-23/285-06eb1dcd-565f-42b9-95ce-7cf190e59eb6.

Ansaria, Talal, and Allison Prang. "U.S. Leads the Globe as Coronavirus Deaths Pass 150,000, Hospitalizations Rise." *Wall Street Journal*, July 30, 2020. Accessed November 5, 2020. https://www.wsj.com/articles/coronavirus-latest -news-07-29-2020-11596011647.

Centers for Disease Control and Prevention. "History of 1918 Flu Pandemic." Accessed November 5, 2020. https://www.cdc.gov/flu/pandemic-resources/ 1918-commemoration/1918-pandemic-history.htm.

Copelin, Laylan. Email interview with the author, November 6, 2020.

Texas A&M University System. "Texas A&M System Starts TV Series on COVID-19 Fight." April 6, 2020. Accessed November 6, 2020. https://www.tamus.edu/ texas-am-system-starts-tv-series-on-covid-19-fight/.

Texas A&M University. "The COVID-19 Fight: Episode 1 with Dr. Hotez." YouTube, April 9, 2020. Accessed November 6, 2020. https://www.youtube.com/watch ?v=-V2cMfj1ysc&list=PLn4ueEbqno_zXksAiX5gryVakZLFrpU6m&index=19.

Texas A&M University Texarkana. "Biology Faculty." Accessed November 6, 2020. https://tamut.edu/Academics/Colleges-and-Departments/CASE/ Undergraduate-Programs/Biology/Biology%20Faculty.html.

Eagle (Bryan / College Station, TX). "COVID-19: The Texas A&M System Responds—Ep.3." April 29, 2020, November 6, 2020. https://theeagle.com/ news/a_m/tamus/video_06c614a0-5104-5ae3-81d6-0b99e4dd31f0.html.

Neuman, Ben. Interview with the author, November 3, 2020.

Neuman, Ben. "Dr. Ben Neuman's Science Group." Facebook. Accessed November 6, 2020. https://www.facebook.com/groups/636035963633297/.

Texas A&M University System. "System Videos." Accessed November 7, 2020. https:// www.youtube.com/playlist?list=PLn4ueEbqno_zXksAiX5gryVakZLFrpU6m.

Henton, Lesley. "COVID-19 Testing Kiosks Debut This Week at Texas A&M." Texas A&M Today, October 12, 2020. Accessed November 7, 2020. https://today.tamu .edu/2020/10/12/covid-19-testing-kiosks-debut-this-week-at-texas-am/.

Mitchell, Rae Lynn. "What Is Contact Tracing, and How Will It Work in Texas?" Texas A&M Today, May 12, 2020. Accessed November 7, 2020. https://today .tamu.edu/2020/05/12/what-is-contact-tracing-and-how-will-it-work-in-texas/.

Texas A&M Today. "College Station Bio-Manufacturing Center to Produce COVID-19 Vaccines." July 27, 2020. Accessed November 8, 2020. https://today.tamu .edu/2020/07/27/college-station-bio-manufacturing-center-to-produce-covid -19-vaccines/.

Justin, Raga. "Texas A&M System Makes Plans for How to Handle In-Person Instruction This Fall." *Texas Tribune*, May 29, 2020. Accessed November 8, 2020. https://www.texastribune.org/2020/05/29/texas-am-reopening-fall -classes/.

Fierke, Carol. Interview with the author, November 8, 2020.

INDEX